The Logic of Internationalism

D1633498

Over the past few years the changes in the international political scene have been enormous. The end of the Cold War, the debates over the existence of a new world order and the arguments over a more united Europe have led to dramatic changes in the way in which we look at the international community. Kjell Goldmann's fresh look at internationalism is, therefore, timely.

A theory of internationalism is outlined and is shown to have two dimensions: one coercive (to enforce the rules and decisions of international institutions); and one accommodative (to avoid confrontation by means of mutal understanding and compromise). Three problematic features of the theory are then considered in detail: the assumption of an effective international opinion in support of international norms and institutions; the assumption that all international cooperation tends to inhibit war; and the tension inherent in the joint pursuit of coercion and accommodation.

The author seeks to examine the plausibility of internationalism under present day political conditions, to focus on unresolved problems and to establish a new agenda for research in the area.

Kjell Goldmann is Professor of Political Science and Dean of the Faculty of Social Sciences at Stockholm University. He has published extensively on the theory of international politics and foreign policy.

The New International Relations
Edited by Barry Buzan, University of Warwick and Gerald Segal, International Institute for Strategic Studies.

The New International Relations

Edited by Barry Buzan, University of Warwick, and Gerald Segal, International Institute for Strategic Studies, London.

The field of international relations has changed dramatically in recent years. This new series will cover the major issues that have emerged and reflect the latest academic thinking in this particularly dynamic area.

International law, rights and politics
Developments in Eastern Europe and the CIS
Rein Mullerson

The Logic of Internationalism

Coercion and accommodation

Kjell Goldmann

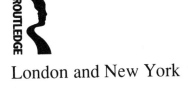

London and New York

First published 1994
by Routledge
11 New Fetter Lane, London EC4P 4EE

Simultaneously published in the USA and Canada
by Routledge
29 West 35th Street, New York, NY 10001

© 1994 Kjell Goldmann

Typeset in Times by
Ponting–Green Publishing Services, Chesham, Bucks

Printed and bound in Great Britain by
TJ Press (Padstow) Ltd, Padstow, Cornwall

Printed on acid free paper

British Library Cataloguing in Publication Data
A catalogue record for this book is available from the
British Library.

Library of Congress Cataloging in Publication Data
Goldmann, Kjell, 1937–
    The logic of internationalism: coercion and accommodation/
Kjell Goldmann.
        p.   cm. – (The New international relations)
    Includes bibliographical references and index.
    ISBN 0–415–09598–0: $59.95. –
    ISBN 0–415–09599–9 (pbk.): $16.95
    1. Internationalism.   2. International relations.   3. World
politics–1989–   I. Title.   II. Series.
JC362.G59   1994
327.1'01–dc20   93–46047
                            CIP

ISBN 0–415–09598–0 (hbk)
ISBN 0–415–09599–9 (pbk)

Contents

Figures

Tables

Series editor's preface

Part of the 'new international relations' since 1991 has been a wave of liberal triumphalism centred on the defeat of communism and 'the end of history'. This wave has already begun to break on the rocks of adversity in Bosnia, Somalia, Haiti, Iraq and North Korea, but it remains a powerful influence in both thinking about, and in policy-making for, the international system. Within this context, Kjell Goldmann has produced a valuable and timely challenge to the mainstream community of moderate liberal internationalists to put their intellectual house in order. His challenge is comprehensive, raising fundamental questions about the logical, empirical, philosophical and moral foundations of the liberal internationalist position. He mounts an impressive enquiry that exposes to rigorous scrutiny some of the major claims of rival positions about what can and should be done in the international system. Goldmann sets out very precisely what can and cannot be said with authority on this topic and why.

His method is a meticulous and systematic unpacking of the whole set of assumptions and ideas that underlie internationalism. He gives a clear-eyed and relentless assessment of both the details and the package as a whole, which is a welcome and long-overdue corrective to reams of both well-intentioned polemic and narrower empirical work. While doing this he retains a consistent position as a sympathetic, but detached observer, following the arguments wherever they go. He is, in effect, cross-examining a whole school of thought about its fundamentals, along the way nicely pointing out the methodological assumptions that it shares with its supposed realist rival. Goldmann has constructed a first-class intellectual challenge here, while at the same time organizing and clarifying much of the research agenda that is needed to strengthen (or challenge) internationalism as a policy agenda.

Barry Buzan
University of Warwick

Preface

This book is about a political programme, but the perspective is neither that of an advocate nor that of a critic; the object is neither to persuade the reader to adopt the programme, nor to demonstrate that the programme is flawed. The approach of this book is better described as that of a sympathetic sceptic. Here is a body of thought promising to make international relations less conflictual by such attractive means as international institution-building and cooperation. The aim of the book is to consider sceptically the sympathetic claim that the programme is compelling – to pursue a friendly critique of internationalism.

The idea of conducting this investigation dates back to the controversy over nuclear deterrence that raged throughout the Western world in the first half of the 1980s. This was a confrontation between impossibilities: the impossibility of staking everything on the hope that deterrence would work indefinitely, and the impossibility of resolving a fundamental political problem by removing some of its symptoms (intermediate-range missiles) or by wishing it away ('consciousness-raising', 'peace education').

There was a third strand in the debate, however. That the nuclear threat did not result merely from ignorance, oversight or evilness but from the independence of states was a *leitmotif* of one of the most influential peace publications of the period, Jonathan Schell's *The Fate of the Earth* (1982). The old idea of ameliorating the consequences of this fact with an increase in peaceful intercourse surfaced in various ways: in concern with renewing the *détente* of the 1970s with its Ostpolitik and Helsinki process, in the the slogan 'common security' coined by the Palme Commission, and in increasing talk of a need for '*détente* from below'. This notion, often called internationalism, is the object of the present book.

It was necessary to look 'beyond deterrence', as the slogan went in the early 1980s. Then came *glasnost* and *perestroika*. The end of the

Cold War did not make the plausibility of the internationalist programme an irrelevant issue. On the contrary, the ideas of internationalism moved from the domain of idealist hopes to the top of the agenda of international politics in the form of a debate over the feasibility of a 'new world order' and the shape of a new 'European architecture'. The issue was whether history could be prevented from repeating itself or whether traditional international politics would continue to prevail. Basically this was the issue of the validity of the internationalist programme.

Its topicality is very clear at the time of writing. Developments in the former Yugoslavia – both the ethnic cleansing and the pressure put on the weak to submit to the strong – have borne a tragic resemblance to what has happened before in Europe. This time, however, the international community has been heavily involved in efforts to rectify the situation. Major relief operations are being conducted. Three international organizations – the UN, the EC, and the CSCE – are trying to stop the fighting. A substantial international military force is present. The continuation of the tragedy despite such efforts is widely seen as a major failure on the part of the international community. Some argue that the tragedy could not have been prevented from the outside; others that foreign powers have intervened in various ways to encourage rather than to discourage the fighting and that this could have been avoided if there had been more international cooperation from the outset; still others argue that much would have been different had the international community intervened with decisive military force against the aggressors rather than with mediators and relief teams. It is not clear whether events in the Balkans have confirmed the futility of pursuing the internationalist programme in a world of competing nationalisms and diverging national interests, whether they have highlighted the role of avoidable diplomatic blunders in the pursuit of this programme, or whether they have demonstrated the need to pursue the programme with complete determination rather than hesitantly and inconsistently.

Take the ongoing debate about the role of the United Nations. The Gulf War has been widely thought to have heralded a new epoch. The UN is finally beginning to function as it was meant to, it has been argued. At the same time, however, the UN's dependence on a single major power has been demonstrated. UN peace-keeping operations have proliferated to an extent previously unknown: failure, controversy, and accusations of mismanagement have proliferated too. A revolutionary feature of these developments is the progressive undermining of a basic tenet of traditional international politics and of the UN itself: non-intervention in the affairs of others. What is the proper role and shape of the UN under these new conditions? What insight does traditional internationalism have to offer in this regard?

The further development of the European Community is a third item on the international political agenda of 1993 that is strongly related to the issue of the validity of the internationalist programme. Since 1989, European integration has been widely seen as an answer to German unification – as a way of ensuring that the worst aspects of European history will not repeat themselves in spite of the resurgence of a powerful Germany in the midst of Europe. This means putting advanced internationalism into practice. The issue is whether the idea of solving Europe's problems in this fashion is realistic or illusory, that is, whether the internationalist programme is valid or invalid.

What is called internationalism in this book is similar to, even if not identical with, what has been called the liberal tradition of international ethics (Smith 1992). The latter label is justified insofar as the founders of this approach to international relations were liberals (Kant and the British free traders) and some of its premises form part of what has historically been known as liberalism. It is misleading insofar as democratic socialists have been among the foremost supporters of the internationalist programme alongside liberals (McKinlay and Little 1986). The internationalist programme has, in fact, come to be taken for granted by people of many persuasions, and there is reason to avoid a partisan label for what has such broad support. What remains controversial is the degree to which the internationalist programme is likely to be effective in reinforcing peace and security. This is a debate to which the present book is meant to contribute – neither by advocacy nor by fundamental criticism but by sceptical and yet sympathetic enquiry.

A very reasonable objection at this point is that the validity of internationalism – of the liberal tradition, if you wish – has already been sufficiently considered in a vast scholarly literature. 'Political realism' *à la* Morgenthau's *Politics among Nations* and 'neo-realism' *à la* Waltz's *Theory of International Politics* may be read as major statements of the futility of internationalism, and some of the vast, indeed enormous, literature about Morgenthau's and Waltz's alleged shortcomings may be seen as an elaborate defence of the internationalist position.

The debate over 'political realism', the '*realpolitik* approach', or 'realist theory', as it is variously called, has obvious relevance for the assessment of the internationalist programme; many contributions will be cited in this book. However, the debate has more to offer those who seek consistent advocacy or fundamental criticism than sympathetic sceptics. This has been a confrontation of *Weltanschauungen* – of contending views of humanity, politics, and knowledge. The present book seeks to avoid such fundamentalism. It is based on the conviction that three issues treated as inseparable in the debate about 'realist theory' can be kept apart: (1) the explanatory power of international anarchy; (2) the immutability of the international system; and (3) the relevance of moral analysis for international politics. Critics of 'realist theory' are inclined to take it for granted that 'realist theory' assumes that the anarchy obtaining in a system of sovereign states explains much of what goes on in international politics, that this cannot be changed, and that this makes moral analysis irrelevant. In the present book, internationalism is presumed to share the first assumption with 'realist theory' but to reject the second; as to the third, the moral status of internationalism will be regarded as an open issue and not as decided by the assumption of the international system as anarchical. The perspective thus will not be one of a choice between two *Weltanschauungen* but one of evaluating a programme for resolving a problematic defined in the same way by both. I have argued elsewhere that the continuing controversy over 'realist theory' in academic discourse is a source of confusion (Goldmann 1988a), at least if the object is to establish the validity of theoretical propositions rather than to promote 'a more reflexive intellectual environment in which debate, criticism, and novelty can freely circulate' (Lapid 1989: 250).

The validity of the internationalist programme cannot be explored without going into the fundamentals of international politics. My focus, however, will be on three of the questions that need to be raised with regard to internationalist thinking: whether international opinion formation can be expected to play the leading part in world politics that internationalists expect it to play, whether the relationship between cooperation and conflict is as straightforward as the theory of internationalism presumes, and what internationalism is like when viewed from an ethical perspective. The theory of internationalism is considered in a general way in Chapter 2, but the core of the book consists of three studies with a more specific focus: one empirically-oriented about international opinions (Chapter 3), one essentially theoretical about international cooperation (Chapter 4), and one departing from familiar notions in moral philosophy (Chapter 5). Whether the bottom line is that the internationalist programme should be accepted or rejected, or whether it should remain an object of sceptical enquiry, will be for the reader to decide.

I owe a particular debt of gratitude to Alexa Robertson, my project associate, as well as to Jens Bartelson and Jan Hallenberg. Among those kind enough to comment on drafts, papers, and presentations, Hayward

Alker deserves special thanks for his very critical perusal of an early version of parts of Chapter 4. Kristina Boréus provided valuable assistance with regard to what has become Chapter 5. Thanks are also due to the editors of the present book series for suggesting important improvements.

This study has been supported by a grant from the Swedish Council for Research in the Humanities and Social Sciences. Parts of Chapter 3 have been published in *Political Studies*, parts of Chapter 4 in *Cooperation and Conflict*, and parts of Chapter 5 in *Statsvetenskaplig Tidskrift*.

Kjell Goldmann
Stockholm, 1993

1 Introduction

It is a widely held belief – a truism to some – that international peace and security benefit if international institutions are strengthened and cooperative ties multiply across borders. International law and organization as well as economic exchanges and other forms of communication will make war an increasingly unlikely occurrence, according to this belief. 'Internationalism' is a term that may be used to denote this conviction. The object of this book is to examine the plausibility of the case for internationalism as a programme for peace and security.[1]

What makes internationalism appealing is its promise to circumvent the contradiction between national independence and international security. The notion that there is such a contradiction is rooted in what is known as the Anarchy Model of international politics, that is, in the assumption that tensions, armaments, and war cannot be avoided in a system of independent states, since by definition such a system lacks the equivalent of a government maintaining order within each state and protecting its citizens from each other. The choice, in this view, is between insecurity and submission to world government. Internationalists venture to suggest that these are not the only alternatives and that the international system can be as orderly and peaceful as a well-functioning state and yet remain a system of independent states. Internationalism is thus a programme for combining national independence and international security.

The programme promises to do more than to safeguard peace and security. People may have many reasons for advocating internationalist views. One may be the belief that international exchange brings economic welfare. Another may be the feeling that even though national independence may be a fundamental human value, isolationism and self-sufficiency are not; openness enriches human life. A third may be the conviction that mankind cannot resolve its most pressing problems other than through international cooperation. The question posed in this

book, however, is whether internationalism is compelling as a programme for peace and security; other reasons for adopting internationalist views will not be considered. Thus the issue raised here
is the one of order in anarchy, an issue as fundamental to political
theory as it is to practical politics in the post-Cold War world.[2]

THE CONCEPT OF INTERNATIONALISM

'Internationalism' in this book thus denotes a set of beliefs to the effect
that if there is more law, organization, exchange, and communication
among states, this will reinforce peace and security. It is common to use
the term 'internationalism' in this sense in the scholarly literature.[3]
That, for example, is Hedley Bull's usage when he distinguishes
between the 'realism' of Hobbes, the 'universalism' of Kant, and the
'internationalism' of Grotius (Bull 1977: 24–7).[4] There are other ways
of using the term, however. Hitler had global ambitions and Lenin
advocated world revolution; both were internationalists, but not in the
sense of institution-building and cooperation for the sake of peace and
security. Furthermore, it is not unusual to regard concern with far-away
peoples in distress as more typical of an internationalist outlook than an
interest in international relations. In American terminology, moreover,
internationalism is the opposite of isolationism; this may, but also may
not, be the kind of internationalism considered in this book.

A way of mapping plausible but different usages of the term internationalism is shown in Figure 1.1. A political opinion, first of all, may

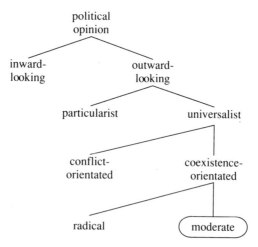

Figure 1.1 The concept of internationalism

be essentially inward-looking or essentially outward-looking in the sense of focusing primarily on the opinion-holder's own country or primarily on the rest of the world. In order for an opinion – a belief, a programme, an ideology – to be considered internationalist, it is obviously necessary that it is outward-looking in this sense.

An outward-looking opinion may in turn be essentially particularist or essentially universalist. The object in the former case is to further the interests of one's own country and in the latter case to realize values taken to be universally applicable. This is the essence of the difference between different forms of internationalism in the United States. Rosenau and Holsti, in their study of élite attitudes, thus distinguish between 'Cold War Internationalists' and 'Post-Cold War Internationalists'. The objective of the former type of internationalism is to:

> maintain alliance commitments; keep up with the Soviets militarily and respond to their efforts to extend their influence in the Third World

whereas the objective of the latter type of internationalism is to:

> promote a multiplicity of economic and political institutions to facilitate movement toward world order and away from confrontation.
> (Rosenau and Holsti 1983: 379)

A universalist outlook may in turn be of two kinds. The object may be to bring about the victory of one's own ideals over other ideals claiming universal applicability, or it may be to obtain peaceful coexistence between competing universal ideals. This is a watershed in the history of ideas (Parkinson 1977: 9–25). A distinction may thus be made between conflict-orientated and coexistence-orientated universalism. The difference has to do with the importance afforded to the ideal of peace and security. In the case of coexistence-orientated universalism, the overriding purpose is to solve the problem of international peace and security, whereas the overriding objective in the case of conflict-orientated universalism is to solve other problems relating, for example, to justice or equality.

It is important to note that whereas conflict-orientated universalism is straightforward, coexistence-orientated universalism entails a dualism epitomized by the making of war to end wars and by the accommodation of aggressors to preserve peace. When conflict-orientated internationalists meet with opposition, their problem is strategic: how do we gain the upper hand in this confrontation? When coexistence-orientated internationalists have to face up to an adversary who does not share their ideals, they face a dilemma that is a characteristic feature of their entire outlook.

The kind of internationalism considered in the present book is coexistence-orientated. Its theme is contact and cooperation between countries and peoples; its object is peace and security through community-building at the international level. The dualism of this view will remain our preoccupation throughout the book.

Coexistence-orientated internationalism can take different forms. In the *International Encyclopaedia of the Social Sciences*, the concept of internationalism is considered by Herz. He distinguishes between a mildly internationalist ideology and a more radical internationalism. Mild internationalism, he writes, aims at a world where states remain the primary units, where states are self-determining and democratic, and where disputes are settled by mediation, arbitration and the application of international law in the context of growing contact and cooperation. The object of radical internationalism is to replace the system of sovereign states with world government (Herz 1968: 72–3).

It is mild, or moderate, internationalism that forms the object of this book. That is what is meant when the term internationalism is used in what follows. Several of the views shown in Figure 1.1 may justly be called internationalism, but here we will limit ourselves to the notion of international peace and security without world government. Thus, law, organization, exchange, and communication for the sake of international peace and security are what will be taken to comprise the internationalist programme.[5]

What constitutes the problematic of internationalism in this sense – this cannot be emphasized too strongly – is the object of solving the problem of anarchy without replacing anarchy with hierarchy. The object, as it has been put, is 'governance without government' (Rosenau and Czempiel 1992); it is to build a 'half-way house. . . between systems of governance based on principles of anarchy and those based on hierarchy' (Holsti 1992: 55–6). The issue raised in the book is whether peace and security are likely to prevail in a half-way house.

Note, moreover, the twofold character of the internationalist programme for 'governance without government'. Internationalism seeks to strengthen international governance by the strengthening of international institutions, but it also seeks broader social change at the international level by means of, and in the form of, cooperative interaction. The issue is whether this combination is capable of solving the problem of order in anarchy.

Finally, in the terminology adopted here, internationalism is a programme for changing the international system rather than the internal features of states. This is logical from a semantic point of view but may seem to be at variance with common language in one respect: what is called internationalism in this book is similar to what is sometimes called the 'liberal' approach to international relations, and in this approach democracy within nations is generally a key element. I have thought it best, however, to avoid deciding *a priori* that international-systemic change must go hand in hand with domestic democracy. Rather than simply define internationalism so as to include domestic democracy, I prefer to consider this to be an issue in need of analysis. There will be much about this in what follows.

THE ROOTS OF INTERNATIONALISM

Two traditions form the roots of twentieth-century internationalism: the long history of proposals for international organization and classical liberalism with its belief in the benefits of free trade. A brief reminder of each may be useful. It has seemed sufficient for this limited purpose to rely mainly on two of the several surveys that have been published (Hemleben 1943, Silberner 1946; see also Hinsley 1963).[6]

Peace by international organization

To publish proposals for the setting up of new bodies to maintain peace is a genre with a long history. Some authors have gone into detail about membership, structure, and functions, others have been more summary. Some proposed bodies have been European or Christian, others have had a wider composition. The proposals have sometimes comprised supranational features such as majority voting and military enforce-ment. They have often made provision for the performance of both diplomatic and judicial functions. They have sometimes included specific measures such as disarmament and anti-aggression treaties. What is primarily important for our present purposes, however, is how the establishment of the proposed bodies have been thought to bring peace. Thus, the following discussion will focus on the compliance problem, as it is called in present-day writings.

It may be questioned whether a survey such as the one to follow is meaningful. A conventional account such as this is inadequate, it may be argued, since what was written long ago in political conditions different from those of today and on the basis of an epistemology different from today's must be interpreted in its own terms; to intimate that earlier thinkers were concerned with today's problems and conceived of them in today's terms is to commit what has been called the presentist fallacy (Bartelson 1993). Against this can be set the advantage of reminding ourselves, even if anecdotally and perhaps anachronistically, that some contemporary ideas have been expressed before.

Indeed, a point can be made of the fact that notions reminiscent of twentieth-century internationalism were put forward hundreds of years before a system of states in the modern sense even existed; some problems, and hence some proposed solutions, seem remarkably similar over the ages. Thus, *De recuperatione Terre Sancte* by Pierre Dubois dates back to the early fourteenth century; a council of nations and a court were proposed to decide quarrels by arbitration, and the kings and the council were urged to institute a boycott and to take concerted military action against offenders (Hemleben 1943: 1–4). Erasmus, in *Querela Pacis*, which was published *ca.* 1517, included what were to become two cornerstones of internationalist thinking. One was the notion that peace could be obtained if the peoples and not the rulers were to decide; wars should not be declared by heads of governments 'but by the full and unanimous consent of the whole people'. The other was an emphasis on arbitration; even unjust arbitration was preferable to war, according to Erasmus (pp. 18–19). Emeric Crucé, in *Le nouveau Cynée*, published in 1623, expressed the thought that commerce between nations would make wars less frequent by making nations dependent upon one another; therefore, the development of commerce and industry was essential in securing peace. He proposed a permanent assembly of ambassadors to settle differences between nations. Offending sovereigns were to be brought to reason by all the other princes; the princes were first to appease offenders by gentle means, but if necessary they would be 'pursue[d] with arms' (pp. 22–7).

Grotius, in *De jure belli ac pacis*, which was published in 1625, envisaged periodical 'Congresses of Christian Powers . . . in which the controversies which arise among some of them may be decided by others who are not interested; and in which measures may be taken to compel the parties to accept peace on equitable terms' (p. 45). William Penn, in *An Essay towards the Present and Future Peace of Europe* (published in 1693), proposed a 'Sovereign or Imperial Dyet, Parliament or State of Europe' to meet at least every two or three years. If any power refused to submit its case to it or to abide by its decision, all the other powers, 'united as one strength', were to compel submission by military force, if necessary (pp. 49–52).

Of great importance for subsequent thinking was a *Grand dessin* attributed to Henry IV of France but believed to have been authored by the duc de Sully and to have been worked out in the 1730s. This was a plan to destroy the House of Hapsburg. The Hapsburg empire was to be divided up, and then a council of Europe – a permanently assembled senate – was to be set up. Its decisions were to be regarded as final and irrevocable, since they were to be based on the united authority of all the sovereigns; the association was to be supported by armed forces contributed by the princes in proportion to their abilities (pp. 48–50).

One of the most detailed peace plans of earlier times was put forward by the Abbé de Saint-Pierre in a number of works, including *Projet pour rendre la paix perpétuelle en Europe*, which was published in 1713. War was to be renounced as an instrument of national policy, and arms were to be taken up only against an adversary declared to be an enemy of Europe. Disputes between the members of the confederation were to be reconciled by the mediating commissioners of the congress or senate and, if necessary, decided by majority in the senate itself. Strong sanctions were envisaged against members that violated their obligations, including forced disarmament, the imposition of indemnities, and the deprivation of territory (pp. 59–62).

Jean Jacques Rousseau also advocated a European federation with a court or parliament to arbitrate disputes. Its decisions were to be enforced by a federal army. However, enforcement was not a main issue in Rousseau's thinking, since he believed the formation of a federation to be in the self-interest of the sovereigns; it appears that he thought self-interest sufficient to uphold the federation once it had been formed. The main problem, he seems to have thought, was to persuade the rulers that this was what their self-interest dictated. If, but only if, this could be done, the federation could be set up, and this in turn would make Europe a community with a moral code, customs, and laws of its own 'which none of the component nations can renounce without causing a shock to the whole frame' (pp. 73–82).

Jeremy Bentham was the first of a series of eminent peace advocates to rely on public opinion to keep recalcitrant states in check. *A Plan for an Universal and Perpetual Peace* was written in the late 1780s but was published posthumously in 1843. Bentham proposed a world court or congress whose decrees were to be enforced mainly by public opinion, through the press and printed manifestos and, if necessary, by putting the offending state 'under the ban of Europe'. There might be no harm in having access as a last resort to 'the contingent to be furnished by the several States for enforcing the decrees of the Court' (pp. 83–6). But:

> the necessity for the employment of this resource would, in all human probability, be suspended for ever by having recourse to the much more simple and less burthensome expedient of introducing into the instrument by which such Court was instituted a clause guaranteeing the liberty of the Press in each State, in such sort that the Diet might find no obstacle to giving, in every State, to its decrees and to every

paper whatever, which it might think proper to sanction with its signature, the most extensive and unlimited circulation.

(Hemleben 1943: 86–7)

The most influential of the classical peace plans probably was Immanuel Kant's *Zum ewigen Frieden*, which was published in 1795. Kant had in mind a European confederation to form the nucleus of a State of Nations. A distinctive feature of this vision was the notion that the constituent states had to be 'republican' and not 'despotic'. It was not a world republic he envisaged but rather a 'negative substitute' – a federation to avert war and to stop the tendency of 'shrinking from the control of law'. The federation would not 'tend to any dominion over a state, but solely to the certain maintenance of the liberty of each particular state, partaking of this association, without being therefore obliged to submit, like men in a state of nature, to the legal constraint of public force'.

How did Kant believe that peace could be permanently maintained by this arrangement? Kant on this point proceeded from his theory of practical reason. Nature comes to the help of the general will by employing the selfish inclinations of man, he thought. Even if it wisely separates nations, it also brings together, through their mutual self-interest, peoples whom the idea of the cosmopolitan right alone would never have secured against violence and war. The spirit of commerce will take hold of every nation, and it is incompatible with war. Nature in this way can be relied upon to help bring about perpetual peace (pp. 90–4).

Thoughts similar to those that had long preoccupied philosophers were put into practice in the nineteenth century in the form of the Holy Alliance, the Quadruple (later Quintuple) Alliance, and the Concert of Europe. These in turn led on to the famous Hague conferences in the early twentieth century. In the nineteenth century, furthermore, peace associations began to be formed. In 1840 , the founder of the American Peace Society, William Ladd, published *An Essay on a Congress of Nations*, which has been characterized as 'one of the most celebrated and influential schemes for peace ever propounded'. Ladd proposed a congress of ambassadors from 'Christian and civilized' nations to decide on the principles of international law and to devise and promote plans for the preservation of peace on the basis of the consent of all nations. He also proposed a court composed of the most able civilians of the world to judge cases brought before it by the consent of contending nations.

The scheme depended on the force of public opinion – the 'queen of the world', in Ladd's words:

If an Alexander, a Caesar, a Napoleon, have bowed down to public opinion, what might we not expect of better men, when public opinion becomes more enlightened? . . . Already there is no civilized nation that can withstand the frown of public opinion. It is therefore necessary only to enlighten public opinion still farther, to insure the success of our plan.

(Ladd 1840)

Ladd was convinced that 'a revolution of public opinion' had begun, 'and revolutions do not go back' (pp. 105–11).

One of the most noteworthy plans proposed in the latter part of the nineteenth century was that of James Lorimer in *The Institutes of the Law of Nations*, which was published in 1884. Lorimer had in mind an international government with a separate, international executive, the latter perhaps an innovation. He thought that a spirit of mutual concession would be gradually evoked by the new reciprocal duties and the new international interests which would result from closer association. This spirit, together with the creation of an international profession of officials, would add to the stability of the institution. Lorimer's plan for a two-chamber legislative authority was detailed (he proposed, among other things, that the president of the authority be paid a salary of £10,000 per session). The decisions of the authority were to be implemented by military force if necessary. A small standing army would be set up, with each state supplying a contingent or the equivalent in money when called upon (pp. 118–24).

The final steps from vision to practical politics were taken during World War I. Most of the proposals that made an impact during this unfortunate but creative period were put forward by peace associations rather than individual thinkers, including the British League of Nations Society, the American League To Enforce Peace, the American League of Free Nations Association, the Fabian Society, the Union of Democratic Control, the ten-nation Central Organization for A Durable Peace, and the *Association de la Paix par le Droit*. A dominating thought was that international law needed to be strengthened; several of the proposed international organizations would have the function of codifying, clarifying, declaring, and amending international law (pp. 145, 150, 161, 163, 170–1, 177). Public opinion was to be relied upon to to promote peace; hence the demand that foreign policy be placed under democratic control and diplomacy be conducted in public (pp. 158, 165–8, 173–4, 176, 183). It was common to suggest that the proposed organization be backed up by military force, either in the form of collective measures to be taken by members against offenders (pp. 142, 145, 150–1, 158, 174) or by means of an international force placed at the disposal of the organization itself (pp. 162, 176).

All of this had been proposed many times before. A further thought experienced breakthrough at this time. This was the notion of taking economic sanctions against a recalcitrant state. Some proposed that measures of this kind should be taken jointly with military sanctions, others that they should be used to substitute for them (pp. 140, 142, 145, 150, 158, 161–2, 174, 176). Ideas such as these came to form the basis of the League of Nations.

To summarize, four reasons in particular were suggested in the early literature as to why international organization could be expected to bring peace: (1) because offenders would have to contend with military or economic sanctions, or with the condemnation of public opinion; (2) because organizations would be instrumental in strengthening international law; (3) because institutionalized procedures for conflict resolution – arbitration, adjudication, mediation, rational discussion – would be provided for; and (4) because once an organization had been set up, the members would have an interest in maintaining it. More will be said about these thoughts in what follows.

Peace by free trade

The key to the classical liberal analysis of war was the conviction that war was due to a false conception of the national interest. Free trade was immensely preferable to war, it was argued, contributing not only to the material prosperity of nations but also to the intellectual and moral progress of mankind. It would strengthen the peaceful ties that unite nations and the pacific spirit among men. Freedom of commerce would thus substantially reduce the risk of war or even eliminate it altogether (Silberner 1946: 280–3).

Richard Cobden was an energetic proponent of economic analysis to prevent international conflict. He was a pacifist agitator, and free trade was the core of his message. Linking all peoples by mutual exchanges, free trade was synonymous with universal concord. Free trade would make war between nations as unthinkable as war between counties in England. Each trading station, store, and factory would become the centre of a diplomatic system bent on peace (pp. 60–1). Cobden saw in the principle of free trade:

> that which shall act on the moral world as the principle of gravitation in the universe – drawing men together, thrusting aside antagonism of race, and creed, and language, and uniting us in the bonds of eternal peace.
>
> (Silberner 1946: 61)

John Stuart Mill found the economic advantages of trade to have become one of the greatest deterrents of war by the middle of the nineteenth century. However, its economic implications were surpassed by its moral and intellectual effects. Contact with foreigners was invaluable for peace, and trade offered the chief opportunity for such contact (pp. 65–6). Nations had to borrow not just technical procedures but also moral qualities from each other:

> [C]ommerce first taught nations to see with good will the wealth and prosperity of one another. Before, the patriot, unless sufficiently advanced in culture to feel the world his country, wished all countries weak, poor, and ill-governed, but his own; he now sees in their wealth and progress a direct source of wealth and progress to his own country. It is commerce which is rapidly rendering war obsolete, by strengthening and multiplying the personal interests which are in natural opposition to it. And it may be said without exaggeration that the great extent and rapid increase of international trade, in being the principal guarantee of the peace of the world, is the great permanent security for the uninterrupted progress of the ideas, the institutions, and the character of the human race.
>
> (Silberner 1946: 66)

The French nineteenth-century liberal, Jean-Baptiste Say, put forward an original variation on this theme. He considered the 'theory of markets' to be a landmark discovery of mankind that would 'change world politics'. The advancement of economic science would gradually lessen national rivalries, he thought: 'Ultimately one will come to understand that fighting is not in the interest of nations, that all the miseries of a lost war fall on them, and that the profits they reap from successful wars are absolutely *nil*.'

Awareness of the laws of economics, according to Say, would lead to international solidarity and to the peaceful cohabitation of nations. Progress in the field of political economy would enlighten public opinion, and this would make wars increasingly difficult to wage. Industrialization, Say believed, would make the peaceful attitudes of *les industrieux* – scholars, farmers, manufacturers, merchants, and workers – predominate over the attitudes of the military. The class of *les industrieux* would pursue a liberal policy inspired by the principle of international solidarity. Say thus envisioned peace as the result of industrialization and free trade, supported by a public opinion impressed by the advancement of the science of political economy (pp. 80–5).

Gustave de Molinari shared the assumption that peace would follow if the industrial classes gained power. This would not be easy, he thought, since the ruling class would not voluntarily consent to placing the national interest before their own particular interest. Ultimately, however, the classes interested in peace would put an end to protectionism, étatism, and socialism ('substitutes of militarism', according to Molinari) and establish a regime of free trade. Molinari, in contrast to other liberals, thought international organization to be essential to this end and contributed a detailed plan to the literature surveyed in the previous section. The main purpose of his proposed League of Neutrals was evidently to make it easier for the classes interested in peace – the industrial classes – to exploit their *puissance d'opinion* (pp. 120–5).

These glimpses may suffice as a reminder of the key ideas in classical liberal-economic pacifism. Uninhibited international commerce, to the minds of many liberals, was associated with (1) the growing realization that, in each nation, free trade was to the advantage of everybody but a small minority; (2) the growing realization that nations had a common interest in peaceful relations with one another and in each others' welfare; and (3) the growth of those forces or classes in society with especial interest in peaceful international intercourse, and the decline of elements less interested in the maintenance of peace (the state apparatus, particularly the military). It is not always clear whether all of this was supposed to follow from free trade itself or from an understanding of the theory of political economy. Twentieth-century internationalists may have borrowed both from nineteenth-century liberalism: both the idea that if people realize the advantages of free trade, the world will be peaceful, and the idea that the actual pursuit of free trade will give this insight to everybody.

It was common for eighteenth- and nineteenth-century liberals to be uninterested in international organization; Molinari was an exception. Twentieth-century internationalists, on the other hand, have often believed that economic relations and international organization have to go hand in hand to make for peaceful international relations. An example will be cited in the next few paragraphs.

Internationalism in 1919

In 1919 the Norwegian Nobel Foundation began to publish a major work called *Histoire de l'internationalisme*. Part One was written by Christian Lange, whose work was later completed by August Schou. In the first chapter, Lange outlined his conception of internationalism (Lange 1919: 1–16). This may be taken to articulate what internationalist thinking was like seventy-five years ago.

Lange departed from the concept of the division of labour. Feudalism had been undermined by division of labour in ever widening circles. Peace had benefited from this development insofar as conflicts between smaller groups had been replaced by solidarity with a wider community. Thus, economic change had paved the way for pacification: the consolidation of sovereign states had been substituted for the feudal wars of the Middle Ages.

Now, however, the division of labour had widened even more and had led to an 'interdependence comprising all civilized states'. The political institutions had not been adapted to the new economic conditions, however. The nation-state, a form of organization suitable for the technology and economy of a previous age, had exploited technical progress for its own purposes. Increasing trade 'should logically reduce the significance of borders between states', but instead the 'new technology of communications, armaments, and administration' had 'made the state an absolute ruler of its subjects to an extent previously unknown'.

World War I had proved that the opposition between war and modern civilization was absolute. Everybody realized this, including those who defended war. They no longer argued that war promotes human development. They had resorted instead to idolizing the nation-state and to justifying war by reference to this idolized state.

Lange eloquently set down the implications of what he called the 'militarist thesis'. The state is an object in itself and therefore sovereign. It has no moral obligations and is obliged merely to take its own interests into account. Its relation to other states is inimical; other states are its enemies 'in their essence and as a matter of principle'. Strategic and military considerations dominate the politics of states, and since war is an ever-present possibility, the economic autonomy of the state is a major consideration.

He contrasted the 'militarist thesis' with the 'pacifist thesis', on the one hand, and the 'internationalist thesis', on the other. The 'pacifist thesis', Lange wrote, lacked a constructive element: 'a sociological theory remains sterile unless it can show the way to the future'. This, he thought, was the strength of internationalism.

Internationalism, according to Lange, departs from the assumption that war is inevitable as long as relations between human societies are unorganized and there is no other way of resolving conflict. Lange emphasized, however, that internationalism does not propose to eliminate the existence of separate societies; to do this would be 'childish and harmful'. Internationalism opposes cosmopolitanism by definition. It is based on the existence of nations; it recognizes the principle of national self-determination; it is convinced that 'the development of the nationalities can only favour international interests as a whole by guaranteeing variation and richness'. True internationalism is impossible without nations.

Internationalism provisionally accepts the existing states as representatives of the nations, Lange continued. Thus most internationalists consider defensive warfare to be legitimate; they accept it as a necessary consequence of the acceptance of the state itself. The right to self-defence must be narrowly defined, however, and there must be guarantees against its misuse. Force should not be abolished, but it should be put in the service of international law.

Economic interdependence is regarded by internationalism as a fundamental fact, Lange continued, and political organization should correspond to this 'economic and intellectual reality'. Internationalism, in fact, wants the relations between peoples to be as developed as possible and is therefore a determined supporter of free trade and opponent of protectionism. It opposes not just the parasitic interests that make gains from armaments but also those class and industrial interests that benefit from protectionism. Internationalism fights war alongside pacifism, but on a different basis: it combines pacifist theory with a 'constructive sociological conception'.

INTERNATIONALISM TODAY

Classical internationalism remains remarkably up to date almost a century later. The main addition since the 1920s would seem to be functionalism. The core of traditional liberal thinking, especially in Great Britain, had been that state and economy ought to be disconnected; thus the fatal link between economic wealth and military potential would be cut and the balance of power would shift in the direction of those with a vested interest in peace. Scepticism toward the state had weakened by the end of the nineteenth century, and in the 1930s David Mitrany launched the theory of peace by the transfer of practical state functions to institutions at the international level. International divisions were to be overlaid with a web of inter-state agencies. An international welfare system would emerge, resulting in a transfer of attachment from the national to the international level (Parkinson 1977: 95, 99). Not just peace organizations but international organization for any purpose would contribute to solving the problem of peace and security.[7]

The failure of the League of Nations did not discredit the ideas of internationalism more than temporarily. To be sure, political 'realism', with its explanation of why efforts to reform the system of states along internationalist lines were bound to fail, gained ground in the 1930s. Nevertheless, a new internationalist effort was being planned while World War II was still in progress, and the UN system was launched as soon as the war was over. The Cold War was a new setback and contributed to placing 'realist theory' at the centre of research and teaching in the field of international relations. At the same time, however, an innovative effort to establish lasting peace by what can only be described as advanced internationalism went on in Western Europe. In the East–West *détente* of the 1970s, furthermore, classical internationalist thought played a part, including the belief in peace and security by law and organization (viz. the Helsinki Final Act of 1975) and the idea that economic relations create ties that inhibit governments from going to war.[8] By the same token, when the Cold War had ended, it was widely taken for granted that the UN could now be vitalized to serve the cause of peace and security more effectively, and there was much concern with how to devise an institutional 'architecture' capable of preserving peace in Europe.

Herz points out that 'mild' in contrast to 'radical' internationalism came to be adopted by a variety of progressive forces in the Western world during the nineteenth century: the labour movement, parts of the trade and industrial elite, churches, and the peace movement (Herz 1968: 72–3). A ten-nation survey study conducted in the late 1960s confirmed the retention of very broad public support for this programme for peace and security. Respondents in ten countries were asked about their views on twenty-five peace proposals. The most popular of these proved to be the proposition that in order to obtain peace, 'hunger and poverty should be abolished all over the world', a thought that is not part of the internationalist programme as defined here. However, the next most popular proposal was that peace be obtained through 'increased trade, exchange and cooperation between countries that are not on friendly terms', immediately followed by the proposal to 'improve the United Nations so as to make it more efficient than it is today'. Large majorities at the same time rejected both radical internationalism ('to obtain peace we should have a world state with disappearance of national borders and with an efficient world government') and non-internationalism ('to obtain peace countries should have less to do with each other and become more self-sufficient') (Ornauer *et al.* 1976: 98–9, 665–71). A study of the West European peace debate in the early 1980s found internationalist ideas to be advocated only in broad terms and only by liberals, social democrats, and some churches; however, so far as East–West relations in Europe were concerned, change of the internationalist type was urged by a wide variety of political parties, churches, and peace groups (Goldmann and Robertson 1988). The internationalist programme, it should be added, has remained a prominent feature in the foreign policy of several states (for an example, Sweden, see Goldmann 1991).

By the end of the twentieth century, then, the basic ideas of internationalism were widely taken for granted in Western politics at both the élite and popular levels. They could not be identified with a specific ideology or party and even less with specific individuals. Few outside the seminar rooms of academia seemed to doubt that peace and security benefit from international institution-building and cooperation.

The transformation of internationalism from controversial policy to what amounts to Western political folklore is remarkable against the background of the fact that nations have continued to arm themselves and to make war against one another as before, in spite of international organization having increased exponentially and international economic exchanges having multiplied. Internationalists may argue in reply that history is a poor guide to the future in this case, since the context of international relations is changing. Four radically new features of world politics are making the internationalist programme increasingly promising, according to this way of thinking: nuclear weapons, advances in communication, the dissemination of democracy, and institutional innovation. Nuclear weapons, together with other modern means of mass destruction, have made war unacceptable as never before in history.[9] The communications revolution is bringing about a qualitative jump in the exchange of goods, services, people, and especially ideas. The democratic form of government is gaining ground. Furthermore, whereas the UN and the CSCE represent a traditional inter-governmental approach to the maintenance of peace and security, the European Community represents something new. There is reason to expect international relations to become different in the future from what they have been in the past (Rosenau 1990), and if not globally, then at least so far as relations between industrialized countries are concerned (Holsti 1991). Internationalist change may prove to be effective tomorrow, even if it has not been effective yesterday, it may be maintained.

We thus are dealing with a set of widely held beliefs that promise to gain an increased relevance in world politics. This is why an effort to reconsider the case for internationalism is worthwhile. To facilitate an evaluation of its strengths and weaknesses, an overarching theory of internationalism is outlined in the next chapter – a theory purporting to explain in a general way why law, organization, exchange, and communication may be expected to protect international peace and security. This is done for the purpose of identifying the problematic issues – those that need to be looked into more closely when it comes to evaluating the case for the internationalist programme. The main part of the book is devoted to a detailed consideration of three such questions. Then, in the final chapter, conclusions are drawn about: (1) the features of internationalism when seen as theory of international politics; (2) post-Cold War international relations when assessed in the light of this theory; and (3) the extent to which the case for pursuing the internationalist programme is compelling.

2 A theory of internationalism

A theory of internationalism will be outlined in this chapter. The internationalists' problem is to show that peace and security can be obtained by law, organization, exchange, and communication in spite of the fact that the international system is presumed to remain one of independent states. The object of this chapter is to outline an argument that plausibly justifies the belief that this will work, that is, a plausible theory linking means to ends as causes to effects.

One way of explicating the theory of internationalism would be to go deeper into the texts of classical authors like Cobden and Kant or to cite the publications of modern social scientists with an internationalist orientation such as Karl Deutsch and Robert Keohane. What has prompted this study, however, is not an interest in recapitulating a tradition in political philosophy that has already been the object of a large literature. Nor has it seemed worthwhile to review current scholarship about matters such as international regimes and institutions in yet another work. Instead I shall proceed directly to the task of outlining the assumptions needed to circumvent the stability problem presumed by internationalists as well as by others to be inherent in anarchy so as to be able to identify weak points in need of more thorough analysis. It is worth emphasizing that the object of study in this book is neither a philosophical tradition nor a theory of social science but a widely held common-sense belief – a piece of political folklore, to repeat a term already used. It is such a belief that this chapter seeks to justify.

A weakness in what follows is the impossibility of proving that the theory about to be outlined is necessary to justify the internationalist programme. Those who think that I have misconstrued the theoretical basis of internationalism and hence perhaps underestimated its potential are urged to demonstrate that there is another, more plausible way of justifying the assumption that the internationalist programme will be effective in inhibiting war.[1]

THE THEORY OF INTERNATIONALISM: GENERAL FEATURES

Internationalism and the dual causation of war

What internationalism tries to do is to ameliorate rather than solve the problem of stability presumed to be inherent in a system of independent states. A concept that may be used to characterize this problem is what I propose to call inherent conflict. Organizations may confront each other in conflicts of interest resulting from the functions they perform in the system to which they belong rather than from matters of their own choice; their very existence implies that there cannot be a harmony of interest. Such conflicts of interest can be abolished only if the system is changed or the organizations are dissolved. This is the case, for example, with associations of employers and employees and with political parties in a multiparty system. It is also the case with states in the international system, according to the line of thought pursued here. Interest organizations, political parties, and states share the fact of being inherent adversaries; their opposition is inherent in the fact of their being interest organizations, parties, and states. The nature of the adversity is obvious in the case of interest organizations and parties; so far as states are concerned it is supposed to result from the anarchic features of a system without central authority. The issue is whether major behavioural conflict – strikes, political confrontations, wars – can be permanently avoided in spite of the fact that the underlying conflict of interest cannot be fully resolved. Internationalists need to show that this can be done at the international level.

The internationalists' problem may be specified by setting internationalism against its alternatives. Hedley Bull distinguishes internationalism from 'realism' and 'universalism', as we have seen, and this is a useful point of departure (Bull 1977: 24–7).

There is, at one extreme, the 'realist' belief that the conflictive features of a system of independent states are inescapable. It is an illusion, according to this line of thought, that law, organization, exchange, and communication can change this fact. States are anxious to preserve their independence, and therefore the measures that can be taken in a system of states are necessarily insufficient to resolve its built-in stability problem. States will remain inherent adversaries, and this will continue to produce major behavioural conflict among them – not between all states and not at all times, but most of the time most states will run a significant risk of having to wage war against at least one other state.

There is, at the other extreme, the 'universalist' belief in the essential unity of mankind. Since mankind is one, it is a myth that states are inherent adversaries; the Anarchy Model of international politics is a mere discourse, as it may be put.[2] If the true community of interest that obtains among men were permitted to prevail, the conflictiveness of international relations would diminish; indeed, the very system of states would begin to fade away.

The disagreement between 'realism' and 'universalism' is thus one about human motivation. This is how Morgenthau explains in *Politics among Nations* why it is impossible to set up a world state:

> [T]he overwhelming majority would put what they regard as the welfare of their own nation above everything else, the interests of a world state included. . . . [T]heir overriding loyalty to the nation erects an insurmountable obstacle to its establishment. . . . [T]he peoples of the world are not prepared to . . . force the nation from its throne and put the political organization of humanity on it. They are willing and able to sacrifice and die so that national governments may be kept standing.
>
> (Morgenthau 1961: 511)

One can say, perhaps, that according to 'realism' national independence is, and is generally considered to be, a fundamental human value. Man's attachment to national independence is not a superficial attitude and does not result from false consciousness. The states system is thus both desirable and unavoidable. There is inevitably a degree of tension between national independence and international order, but since men afford priority to national independence, the system of nations is inevitably characterized by a measure of disorder.[3]

'Universalism' may be taken to disagree on two accounts: since mankind forms a true community, national independence and international order need not be opposed to each other, and the continuous striving for national independence need not be taken for granted. What matters are individuals and perhaps social classes but not nations; what is important from the point of view of individuals and classes does not presuppose a political system of the kind that 'realism' takes for granted.

'Internationalism' differs from both by regarding an international system of independent states as inevitable and perhaps desirable,[4] on the one hand, but denying that national independence and international order are incompatible, on the other. It is possible, according to internationalism, to solve or significantly ameliorate the instability problem of the states system. The inclination of people to 'put what they regard as the welfare of their own nation above everything else' need not prevent very significant legal regulation, organization, exchange, and communication from taking place and from producing order even in the absence of central authority. It is both necessary and possible to constrain the independence of states for the sake of peace and security, but it is neither possible nor necessary to replace anarchy with hierarchy. Even though the inherent conflict obtaining in a system of independent states cannot be fully resolved, it can be reduced and contained. To demonstrate this is the task of the theory about to be sketched.

The starting-point is the conception of a dual causation of war illustrated in Figure 2.1. Internationalism is concerned with reducing incompatibilities of interest that might lead to war as well as with inhibiting the escalation of disputes to dangerous levels. It is difficult to explain why law, organization, exchange, and communication may facilitate the attainment of this twin objective without explicitly distinguishing between them. Therefore a distinction will be made between two ways of explaining why wars occur: by reference to a basic incompatibility of interest between the parties, and in terms of the interaction between them.

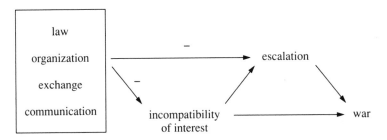

Figure 2.1 The theory of internationalism: overview

In the former perspective, war results from the fact that the long-term interests of the parties are incompatible. In the latter perspective, it results from the dynamics of conflict. The very process of escalation, according to this line of thought, creates pressure for further escalation and ultimately for war, for example, by raising the stakes, making emotions more conflictive, and reducing the ability of the parties to keep developments under control. This second type of war causation may be called autonomous; the term comes from Snyder and Diesing and is useful in conveying the notion of a chain of events that, even though it can be traced back to an underlying incompatibility of interests, has a logic of its own that is divorced from this incompatibility and may result in a war that neither party would have considered sensible before the process of escalation began (Snyder and Diesing 1977: 234–43). Among classical writers on peace and war, Carl von Clausewitz's rationalism may be taken to illustrate the former approach and Leo Tolstoy's view of war as beyond the control of any leader to exemplify the latter (Gallie 1978). The former explanation of war may be termed structural, since it refers to the structure of the relationship between contenders defined in terms of their long-term interests. The latter explanation may be termed processual, since it refers to the dynamics of the process of interaction between them.

The two types of explanation of war are not mutually exclusive. On the contrary, both types of causation are probably present in most cases. Furthermore, they are difficult to keep apart, since process can have an impact on structure: the dynamics of the Cold War must have reinforced the underlying East–West incompatibilities. Still, peace proposals often address a single type of causation: when reducing the gap between rich and poor countries is proposed for the sake of peace, the presumption is that war results in part from this underlying incompatibility, whereas proposals for stopping arms races are concerned with arresting the autonomous dynamics of escalation. The internationalist programme, however, may be taken to aim at changing both structures and processes, thus both reducing incompatibilities of interest and inhibiting escalation.

This presumption, which is illustrated in Figure 2.1, is difficult to reconcile with 'realism' and 'universalism' alike. 'Realism' would seem to presuppose that the incompatibility of interest inherent in the anarchic structure of the international system is a fundamental condition of international politics, inevitably compelling states to engage in a 'security struggle' and maybe in a 'power struggle' (this distinction is made in Buzan 1983: 157). Incompatibility of interest with regard to security and power cannot be avoided in an anarchic system, according to 'realism', and anarchy in turn is inevitable, since peoples put such a high premium on national independence. This fact explains the conflictiveness of international politics and cannot be changed by law, organization, exchange, and communication.

'Universalism', on the other hand, considers anarchy-related incompatibilities of interest to be superficial if not mythical. This need not mean that there is no conflict, but the real incompatibilities of interest are rooted in economic inequality, political oppression, or the like rather than in an unnecessary security struggle. The task is to solve the underlying conflicts rather than to embed them in a network of institutions and patterns of cooperation, and there is no built-in reason why this should be impossible. The internationalist programme, from this point of view, is irrelevant rather than ineffective.

Internationalism occupies the middle ground in assuming that security and maybe power are unavoidably important concerns of government but that even anarchy-related incompatibilities of interest can be reduced. Furthermore, it may be taken to differ from both 'realism' and 'universalism' in regarding escalation-related causation of war as a fundamental problem. Internationalists are more prone than either 'realists' or 'universalists' to think of war as unintentional and accidental, that is, as the result of autonomous conflict processes rather than of underlying incompatibilities of interest. The relevance of measures such as law, organization, exchange, and communication is increased on this assumption.[5]

Internationalism is thus here taken to assume: (1) that anarchy-related concerns are the source of some of the incompatibilities of interest leading to war; (2) that even anarchy-related incompatibilities of interest can be significantly reduced without replacing national independence with world authority; (3) that war results to a large extent from escalation rather than directly from underlying incompatibilities; and (4) that the components of the internationalist programme – law, organization, exchange, and communication – contribute to reducing both the scope of the incompatibilities of interest and the probability of escalation.

I shall argue that they may be thought to do this in two ways. Internationalism will be taken to comprise two dimensions, one coercive and the other accommodative. The object from a coercive point of view is to set up, maintain and reinforce international standards of behaviour designed to prevent incompatibilities of interest between states and peoples from leading to escalation and war. The object from an accommodative point of view is to bring states and peoples closer to each other, thus reducing the incompatibilities of interest between them. To ostracize law-breakers and to empathize with adversaries are the two basic obligations of internationalists. Both are needed, in the internationalists' view, to make the international system approach the orderliness of domestic society. In a well-functioning national society there is rule of law as well as social cohesion; internationalism aims to promote both at the international level, thus relying on what has been called the domestic analogy in international politics (Suganami 1989). The task is to show that this can be done in spite of the presumption that states will remain independent and hence inherent adversaries.

Internationalism as problem-solving theory

The theory about to be outlined has two features that are widely denounced by critics of mainstream international relations theory. First, it is general in the sense of purporting to be valid in a variety of contexts; it is generally the case, according to this theory, that law, organization, exchange, and communication affect peace and security in a specific way, and not just at a particular time and place or with regard to a particular issue.[6] Second, the theory is structural in the sense of accounting for the actions of states in terms of social arrangements produced by lawmaking, organization, exchange, and communication, rather than in terms of the thinking of statesmen. These are typical features of theories known as problem-solving rather than explanatory or critical.

It is not necessary to review the criticisms that have been levelled against this approach to the study of international relations (see, e.g. Ashley and Walker 1990). Suffice it to recall that critics have been prone to argue that international politics is strongly context-dependent and that therefore generalization often is not meaningful. International political action, it has been added, is often determined by thinking that is independent of structure and therefore structuralism in the above sense is mistaken (on the latter point see Carlsnaes 1993). The ideal of a general, structural theory of international relations, applicable to the task of assessing and controlling the future, is based on a false analogy with the natural sciences, as has been put many times. Much time has elapsed since it was considered self-evident that such a theory is the meaningful object of international relations research.

It may seem debatable against this background to insist on writing a book in which internationalism is presumed to be based on such theory. A more meaningful explication of internationalism arguably would be concerned with ideas rather than structures and linked to the immediate historical situation rather than conceived as general.

There is, however, no getting away from the fact that internationalism, like many other programmes for social reform, assumes social problems to have structural causes and to be solvable by structural change, and takes it for granted that scientific theory can be used to diagnose the problem and identify the solution. Internationalism departs from a diagnosis which relates the international problematic to the independence of states, the weakness of international institutions, and the limited extent of cooperative international interaction. Hence its programme is one of structural change. The presumption is that structure is a significant determinant of action. Furthermore, the presumption is that institutions and interaction are related to peace and security in a law-like fashion that can be identified by social-scientific research. It is difficult to do justice to this body of thought other than by treating it as problem-solving theory in the above sense.

Note that the concept of structure is used here in a broad sense to encompass what is often meant by culture. The distinction between structure and culture is not easy to make. Structure carries overtones of social relations whereas culture refers to norms and values, but the concept of institution, which is very central in the theory of internationalism, occupies a grey area between the two. What is important for this study is what institutions have in common with social structures in a more narrow sense: they are exogenous to each individual actor and yet result from action. The contrast made here is thus not one between culture and social relations, both of which can be accommodated within a problem-solving theory of international relations, but one between culture and social relations, on the one hand, and the autonomous thinking of individuals, on the other. Therefore the concept of structure is used in this book in a sense broad enough to encompass institutions.

It may be useful at this point to compare the theory of internationalism about to be outlined with another view of the factors sustaining international order. According to Rosenau, the 'basic patterns that sustain global order can be conceived as unfolding at three levels of activity': (1) the 'ideational or intersubjective' level, which involves 'attitudinal and perceptual screens'; (2) the 'behavioral or objective' level, which consists in regular and patterned behaviour; and (3) the 'aggregate or political' level, which 'involves the more formal and organized dimension of the prevailing order'. Rosenau emphasizes that the three levels are interactive and that 'each dimension is a necessary but not a sufficient determinant of the prevailing order' (1992: 14–16). Law and organization, two basic components of the internationalist programme, would seem to be the essence of Rosenau's third level; exchange and cooperation, the other two components of the internationalist programme, appear to be what Rosenau has in mind with his second level. Attitudinal and perceptual variables, furthermore, also play a part in the theory of internationalism, as the reader will soon discover. The difference between this theory, as it will be interpreted here, and Rosenau's argument is that attitudes and perceptions are regarded as secondary in the former case but not in the latter. According to the theory of internationalism, structural features like behaviour patterns and institutions can be trusted to create appropriate attitudes and perceptions, whereas attitudes and perceptions cannot be relied upon to inhibit conflictive action in an enduring way unless backed up by structures.

It should be emphasized that some of the criticism that has been levelled against the problem-solving approach to the study of international relations is beside the point when it is a matter of evaluating a political programme. Critics of general and structural theory have focused on the explanatory and interpretative and perhaps on the critical use of knowledge; their argument is that such theory is a poor aid in explaining and interpreting international politics. Explanation and interpretation are not the main objectives of the theory of internationalism, however. If the main object is not to understand what has been and what is but to anticipate what may be, it is difficult to avoid making assumptions of the kind here seen as typical of the problem-solving approach. However important context and autonomous thinking are for a proper understanding of action, the predictions that may be made on the basis of such factors are more limited in time and space than those needed to pursue a programme for large-scale social reform such as internationalism. Internationalism and problem-solving theory hang together. If the problem-solving approach is invalid in principle, as some argue, so is internationalism.

This book does not reflect an irrevocable commitment to the problem-solving approach to the study of international relations, but it does reflect an assumption to the effect that a demonstration of its weaknesses does not suffice to invalidate internationalism. The assumption made here is that general and structural theory is not inherently useless and that internationalism cannot be dismissed in this simple way. The theory of internationalism will be examined on the assumption that its lack of validity cannot be taken for granted in advance.

Internationalism is thus regarded here as a set of general beliefs about international relations and not as a feature of specific policies, policy proposals, or actions. In the terminology adopted here, it is not meaningful to characterize a position taken with regard to a particular situation – removing Iraq from Kuwait, convening a peace conference about the Middle East, mediating between Serbs and Croats, trading with particular adversaries, strengthening an international organization – as more or less internationalist. Specific measures such as these may be advocated in internationalist terms, but they may also be advocated in other ways. Internationalism as defined here is nothing more and nothing less than the belief that there is a general tendency for international law, organization, exchange, and communication to inhibit war.

It is implied by this phraseology that the beliefs of internationalists are not taken to be deterministic in a strong sense. Internationalism is not defined here as the view that international law, organization, exchange, and communication will categorically prevent war; it would not be necessary to write a book to show that this is a questionable thought. Internationalists are presumed to believe that there is a *tendency* for international law, organization, exchange, and communication to inhibit war. When such developments take place between adversaries, there is *generally reason to expect* the *likelihood* of war to diminish – this is the core of internationalism as defined here. There is no certainty but there is considerable ground for optimism, so to speak.

The theory of internationalism is thus taken to be deterministic only in the weak sense of suggesting likely incentives and constraints. It shares with other structural theories of international relations the claim to explain some but not all of the variance.[7] Such theories cannot provide strong predictions. What they can do is provide plausible ideas of what the future may be like; they may indicate opportunities and constraints; and they may suggest what to do in order to influence opportunities and constraints. Just as internationalism presumes state action to result in part, but only in part, from the anarchic structure of the international system, it takes it for granted that structural modification will affect state action but not always, everywhere, and in a fully predictable fashion.

In what follows, the coercive and accommodative dimensions of the theory of internationalism will first be outlined. Then some of the main question-marks in this theory will be highlighted.

COERCIVE INTERNATIONALISM

Concern with institutions is what makes coercion a dimension of internationalism. The essential feature of an institution, in the words of one author, is that it comprises rules for what are allowable alternatives and eligible participants (Shepsle 1989: 135). International relations, in the words of another, are institutionalized in the sense that 'much behaviour is recognized by participants as reflecting established rules, norms, and conventions' (Keohane 1989: 1). Interest has traditionally been focused on two types of international institution: law and organization. Internationalism aims at strengthening both, even if this may mean coercing unwilling governments into compliance.

Thus, in order for legal rules to affect international politics it is necessary that governments comply with them. In order for international organizations to have an impact, governments must comply with their rules of procedure as well as with their substantive decisions. A main task of a theory of internationalism is to demonstrate that international institutions are likely to be effective in the sense that governments will generally abide by them even when this goes against what they consider to be their vital interests. A further task is to show why it is reasonable to expect effective institutions to be set up in a system of states that are, and are presumed to want to remain, independent and hence intent on retaining control of matters they consider vital.

In what follows we will consider how compliance with international institutions may safeguard international peace and security; how compliance may be brought about; and what may make governments set up effective international institutions in spite of the fact that they are intent on retaining the independence of states. Each of the four parts of the internationalist programme – law, organization, exchange, and communication – will be discussed in turn to assess its contribution to the programme's coercive dimension.

Law

International norms

The internationalist ideal is an international society in which conflictive behaviour is effectively constrained by the rule of law. Norms do not necessarily have to be strictly legal in order to be relevant for internationalists, however. There is a grey area between law and non-law that is occupied, for example, by the resolutions of the UN General Assembly and by major international documents such as the Helsinki Final Act of 1975.[8] Internationalists are concerned with strengthening law that is 'soft' in this sense just as much as 'hard' law, even though they may have reason to be particularly concerned with hard law, since hard law may be more effective in influencing governmental behaviour than rules of a more ambiguous status. There are, furthermore, non-legal ethical standards – principles of fairness, justice, and humanitarianism – to which internationalists are prone to refer. However, even though internationalists are eager to increase the impact of such standards on international politics, they have reason to be more concerned with legal (hard) or quasi-legal (soft) rules than with ethical norms, since law is an instrument of policy rather than a fact of social life and policy is what internationalists are out to influence. A traditional concern of internationalists is to translate non-legal standards into law in the hope of increasing their impact.

No clear distinction will be made in what follows between international law and other international rules and conventions. Expressions like international law, international rules, and international norms will be used as synonyms unless otherwise indicated. It will thus be assumed that even though internationalists tend to single out the strengthening of international law as a special concern, they are also interested in increasing the impact of other types of international norms that promise to inhibit war.

Some international norms are directly concerned with the regulation of conflict behaviour between states, namely, prescriptions of non-conflictive action, such as the obligation to settle conflicts peacefully (UN Charter, Articles 2:3 and 33) and proscriptions of conflictive action, such as the prohibition of war except in self-defence (Articles 2:4 and 51). Internationalists obviously want such rules to be strengthened in various senses; see below.

A second type comprises the myriad of international rules regulating politics in other ways: by prohibiting customs duties, setting environmental standards, defining rights and duties in the oceans, and allocating radio frequencies, for example. If a legal instrument is set up to resolve a conflict of interest, this conflict will be less likely to lead to war. It appears that laws can create new conflicts as well as resolving old ones, however; treaties about human rights, for example, have made a legitimate international issue out of what was formerly within each state's exclusive jurisdiction.[9] A further consideration is that legal regulations, if repeatedly violated, may undermine law-abidingness in general, including the propensity to abide by rules directly designed to inhibit conflictive behaviour. It has appeared reasonable not to consider the internationalist programme to include the strengthening of the normative framework of international politics *in toto*. Internationalists will be assumed to focus on the normative regulation of the use of force.

There is a third type of rule, however, comprising criteria for membership in the system of states. This is a crucial issue for internationalists, since internationalism is a programme for modifying relations between states rather than conditions within them, a programme for creating a community of states rather than a world society of individuals. The rules that internationalists set out to strengthen are those relating to inter-state action; the regulation of intra-state conflict is not part of the internationalist programme, except insofar as escalation to the international level is concerned. However, one type of conflict contains elements of both, and that is conflict over state formation. This is historically an important source of war (Holsti 1991) and a major issue in present-day Europe. The internationalist programme may be taken to encompass a concern with subjecting such conflicts to the same normative constraints on the use of force as conflicts between established states.

So much for the substance of the rules that internationalists want to strengthen. The strengthening would seem to have three aspects: the making of new international rules; the codification or definition of existing rules; and an increase in the extent to which the rules are obeyed. Internationalists urge governments to minimize the lawful use of force and threat of force, to codify customary norms so as to make their existence unquestionable and their meaning precise, to adhere scrupulously to existing rules, and to take action against states that do not. Internationalists believe that all of this will strengthen the normative framework of international politics in such a way as to make war less likely.

Compliance

How can we assume that governments of independent states will comply with rules constraining their freedom of action even when they consider supremely important interests to be at stake?

Oran Young's essay *Compliance and Public Authority* (1979), although general in approach, is mainly concerned with the particular problem of compliance in international politics. Young identifies six bases of compliance, namely: (1) self-interest in the sense of behaviour based on utilitarian calculation in which sanctions or social pressures are not taken into account; (2) enforcement; (3) inducement; (4) social pressure; (5) obligation; and (6) habit or practice (pp. 18–25). His thesis is that it is wrong to assume compliance in what he calls decentralized social systems to be weak, an assumption that rests on 'a tendency to single out certain extreme cases' and to equate all problems of compliance with them (p. 30).

Hierarchy, Young asserts, is not a condition for compliance. Members of decentralized systems have more reason to be concerned with the social consequences of their behaviour than members of centralized systems and have a stronger self-interest in compliance so as not to damage the social fabric of the system (p. 33). Sanctions may be more difficult to organize in a decentralized than in a centralized setting, but it would be a mistake to exclude the possibility of enforced compliance altogether (pp. 34–6). Furthermore, 'the international equivalent of social pressure can be expected to be an important basis of compliance in [the international] system, even in the absence of organized agencies dealing with enforcement and inducement' (p. 38). Indeed, 'all those actors which are likely to experience collateral damage from the noncompliant behaviour of others can ordinarily be counted upon to exert considerable pressure for compliance in specific situations'. The international system thus possesses 'a well-informed public, which can be counted on to express concern about the occurrence of violations and which can be expected to exert pressures for compliance on potential violators' (p. 44).

Young emphasizes the limited extent to which compliance has been the object of study in political science as well as in the field of international relations (pp. 148–53). Compliance has been an issue in recent writings about so-called international regimes, however. There is no agreement in this literature about what is an international regime (Haggard and Simmons 1987: 493), but Krasner's definition has been influential. An international regime, according to this definition, consists in 'implicit or explicit principles, norms, rules, and decision-making procedures around which actors' expectations converge in a given area of international relations' (Krasner 1982: 186). International regimes differ from international institutions in the above sense of 'rules for what are allowable alternatives and eligible participants' only by being 'more specialized arrangements that pertain to well-defined activities, resources, or geographical areas' (Young 1989: 13). Thus the problem of regime compliance is similar to, if not identical with, the problem of compliance in the theory of internationalism.

A distinction has been proposed between a structural and a cognitive approach to the problem of regime compliance, that is, between two different ways of answering the question of why regimes matter (Haggard and Simmons 1987: 419–517). In a structural perspective, action is determined by the situation in which the actor finds itself; decisions result from decision situations. In a cognitive perspective, action results from knowledge and purpose. This distinction runs parallel to the one Keohane has proposed between the rationalistic and the reflective approaches to the study of international institutions (Keohane 1989, ch. 7). As it has also been put: institutions affect both what we do and whom we are, both our behaviour and our identity.[10]

From a structural point of view, the way to produce compliance is to see to it that defection from regime rules is more costly than compliance. From a cognitive point of view, compliance results from socialization and information, that is from processes inducing decision-makers to internalize regime rules. Among the various bases of compliance identified by Young, (2), (3) and maybe (1) would seem to be essentially structural in this sense, whereas (5) and maybe (6) are essentially cognitive. Young's category (4), which is of particular interest for a theory of internationalism and to which much attention will be devoted in this study, may be seen as structural in part and cognitive in part.

There is no question that compliance with international norms is common in international politics, that structural as well as cognitive factors contribute to this result, and thus that institutions can be effective in spite of anarchy. This does not suffice to justify the expectation that the internationalist programme will work. Young's 'extreme' cases are the ones that are crucial for internationalism. The issue raised by the internationalist programme is not whether international norms tend on the whole to be effective but whether they can be relied upon at the crucial moments when governments choose between peace and war. This is why there is so much wrestling with the problem of compliance in traditional internationalist writings.

The structural approach

The oldest suggestion in this literature about how to bring about compliance would seem to be military force. Pierre Dubois, as we have seen, proposed as early as in the fourteenth century the establishment of a council of nations to resolve conflicts by arbitration; nevertheless if war broke out, concerted military action should be taken against the offender (Hemleben 1943: 3: Hinsley 1963: 15). This thought has persisted over the centuries. It has come in two forms: supranational armies and collective security.

Internationalists have two reasons not to rest content with this idea, two reasons to seek to demonstrate that military force is not the only basis of compliance with international norms at decisive moments.

One is limited credibility. The assumption that compliance is induced by the threat of military sanctions is an instance of rational deterrence theory (Achen and Snidal 1989). Credibility is a core variable in this theory. Collective sanctions against international rule-breakers have hardly been common enough and substantial enough in the past to provide the basis for a credible threat. States have received the assistance of allies, but collective self-defence in this sense (the sense of the UN Charter) has often reflected a traditional struggle over power and security rather than the common reaction of the international community against violations of the law. This, from the point of view of internationalism, is part of the problem and not of the solution.

The credibility problem of internationalism appears as a natural result of the fact that the potential sanctioners, the governments of the rest of the world, are apt to have weak or opposing interests in international conflicts, or differing views about what constitutes a violation of the rules. It is an old thought that collective sanctions against international rule-breakers are implausible under the conditions that obtain in international politics (for a recent formulation see Suganami 1989: 178–81). In this perspective, the UN-sponsored action against Iraq in 1990–91 is unlikely to have heralded a new era in world politics. It rather reflected a combination of national interests unlikely to be repeated more than occasionally. After the end of the Cold War, it has been suggested, we are not faced with a revitalized UN but with reluctance to get involved (Freedman 1992). The limited credibility of collective military measures remains a problem from the point of view of the coercive dimension of internationalism.

The other reason internationalists have to search for non-military solutions to the compliance problem is the fact that internationalism is meant to be a programme for peace. Internationalism is not pacifism; still, credibly to threaten to kill people is not an ideal way of protecting lives.

Economic sanctions promise to solve or at least to ameliorate the latter problem; if they kill, they are apt to do it to a lesser extent than military force. Whether they solve the problem of the limited credibility of collective military measures is more debatable. Judging from experience, what has been termed economic statecraft is often successful (Baldwin 1985). However, what is at stake for internationalists is the impact of the threat of economic sanctions on the most fateful decisions that governments may make. The issue is whether the imposition of decisive economic sanctions will be sufficiently credible to deter governments from the use of force, and not just occasionally but in most cases where deterrence is needed. There is reason to question whether collective security by economic means is easier to uphold in a system of independent states than collective security by military means.

Internationalists may argue at this point that even if scepticism about the effectiveness of economic deterrence may have been justified in earlier times, matters are becoming different. Not only is the degree of international economic interdependence increasing, but the public is becoming increasingly active and influential. The fact that an international public opinion can now be mobilized against rule-breakers will make substantial economic punishment more likely and hence more credible. Internationalists may contend that the international campaign against apartheid is suggestive of this possibility: political and economic élites were initially opposed to sanctions against South Africa, but public opinion was mobilized, strong sanctions were put into effect as a result, and this was essential in ending apartheid. The case of apartheid may thus be taken to illustrate the plausibility of what stands out as a cornerstone of present-day internationalism, namely, that public opinion is less prone to think in terms of short-term national interests than national élites, that international public opinion is increasingly capable of influencing world politics, and that this makes the internationalist programme more plausible than previously. There will be more about this below.

The cognitive approach

Internationalist speculation has traditionally been more concerned with the structural than with the cognitive approach to compliance. However, several compliance-producing factors of an essentially cognitive kind are mentioned in the regime literature. One is fear of getting a reputation that may prove to be costly in future situations. Another is the propensity if not necessity of using a rule of thumb in lieu of a full calculation of costs and benefits. A third is what has been called empathetic interdependence. A fourth is a tendency for regime rules to be internalized by decision-makers and thus to be considered morally obliging (Keohane 1984: 105–16, 115–16, 123–6). Factors such as these undoubtedly help to account for compliance with the rules of international regimes and with international norms generally. Here, however, we are not concerned with regime compliance on day-to-day matters but with the ability of international norms to preserve peace and security when war is imminent over matters that the contenders consider to be supremely important. Possibly central features of the international political economy may be peripheral so far as war-avoidance is concerned.[11]

US decision-making during the Cuban Missile Crisis of 1962 may serve as a reminder of the possibility that *pacta sunt servanda* and other fundamental norms may have an impact even in an extreme crisis, because decision-makers are anxious to behave morally (Schlesinger 1965: 689). The incident does not suffice to prove that international norms are generally internalized and influential at critical moments, however. Optimism in this regard presumably needs to rely on the belief that public opinion is more likely than national leaders to internalize international norms, that public opinion is becoming increasingly important in world politics, and that for this reason, if for no other, internalization is an increasingly important source of compliance.

One can have doubts about the plausibility of the argument that peoples, and hence governments, are increasingly inclined to set common ideals before the national interest. This is what makes Kant's argument in *Zum ewigen Frieden* important. Kant purported to show, as we have seen, how the selfish implications of man were put in the service of the general will. The argument basically was one about reciprocity, which many have assumed to be a major reason for compliance with international norms.

That bilateral agreements may be upheld by fear of destroying them is a truism. That governments are reluctant to increase the freedom of action of an adversary in this fashion can be taken for granted. This obvious mechanism may be called direct reciprocity.

A more interesting possibility from the point of view of internationalism is indirect reciprocity, that is, the possibility that not only bilateral agreements but also multilateral norms risk being undermined by single violations. The idea that reciprocity makes subjects abide by norms presumes that actors take into account how a violation on their part might affect the future behaviour of others. In the case of direct reciprocity, actors are thought to be deterred by the negative consequences of increasing the freedom of action of a particular adversary. In the case of indirect reciprocity, they are thought to be deterred by the risk of increasing everybody's freedom of action. Considerations of indirect reciprocity, furthermore, need to be made not just by the original contenders but also by third parties; one reason to take action against an aggressor is that if this is not done, future aggression from whatever source may be more likely. Indirect reciprocity is a basis of Kant's peace proposal in *Zum ewigen Frieden*: the proposed federation would be kept together by its members' interest in preserving it (Gallie 1978: 27–9). According to this line of thought, the members of an institution set up to preserve peace and security will become increasingly convinced of their interest in maintaining it, and this long-term interest will increasingly take precedence over any short-term interest they may have in violating its tenets.

This thought would seem to be essential for a theory of internationalism. It implies: (a) that whether a norm is obeyed or disobeyed in a particular instance affects its future effectiveness as well as the effectiveness of other norms; and (b) that governments find it more important to keep the freedom of action of others constrained than to do what is most advantageous to themselves in the immediate situation. The latter is Kant's assumption. The former adds a new element. The reciprocity argument is that rules are effective because their future effectiveness would be impaired if they were violated. Internationalist reasoning may be taken to include the notion that the rules of international politics are integrated with each other in the sense that if one is violated, others are undermined, just as if one is obeyed others are strengthened.

A reason to consider this a realistic assumption is given by Young, as mentioned above: norms are likely to be more vulnerable in an anarchy than in a hierarchy, and this may make indirect reciprocity a more important factor at the international level than inside states. Paradoxically, the very vulnerability of international norms may help to uphold them. Of course, the more successful public opinion is in making leaders internalize international norms, the less credible the threat of undermining the system of norms by single violations; the main cognitive bases of compliance in the theory of internationalism tend to work at cross-purposes.

International opinion

Collective sanctions, internalization, and reciprocity are obvious components of an internationalist theory of compliance. An addition made in this attempt to explicate the theory of internationalism is the assumption that public opinion can be counted on to make sanctions credible and internalization plausible. Whether this suffices to make the internationalist programme convincing may be debatable. This is why it is important for internationalists to follow in the footsteps of Richard Cobden, William Ladd and many others and make world opinion a major basis of compliance in its own right. As such it is both structural and cognitive, as it were. From a structural point of view, world opinion is a sanctioner; to be ostracized is less than to be made the object of military or economic punishment, but the threat is likely to be more credible. From a cognitive point of view, world opinion is a participant in a debate over what to do in difficult situations. It is difficult to make a convincing case for internationalism without an assumption to the effect that international opinion formation is an important feature of world politics in this dual sense.

The argument owes a debt to traditional sociological theorizing about social control (Goldmann 1971). The significance of social pressure at the international level, as we have seen, is emphasized by Young in his study of compliance. In a later study, Young is concerned with variables that may be critical in order for an international institution to be effective. One such variable, he writes, is transparency, that is, the ease of monitoring or verifying compliance. The role of enforcement as a basis of compliance is regularly exaggerated, Young argues. Therefore, '[t]he realization that the prospect of exposure . . . is a key determinant of compliance in international society is . . . a matter of considerable importance'. Its significance in fact has 'increased markedly in recent years' because of technological factors (Young 1992; 176–8).

Sceptics may insist that experience proves this to be idealistic nonsense. Internationalists may respond that this is the point where international relations are being profoundly transformed; even if it may have been naive to rely on world public opinion to uphold international peace and security in earlier times, this is now becoming a realistic thought since the nature of world politics is changing (Rosenau 1990, ch. 13; 1992). The validity of the assumption of opinion formation on an international scale as an increasingly significant phenomenon is so important a question for the validity of the theory of internationalism that a large part of this book will be devoted to this matter (Chapter 3).

Rule-making

If international norms are often complied with even in extreme cases, which it must be assumed that internationalists believe, how can governments be expected to participate in the strengthening of what will deprive them of their freedom of action at what they consider to be their decisive moments?

Internationalists may take a clue from Hedley Bull's *The Anarchical Society*. Bull argues in effect that to preserve their independence, states have an interest in maintaining 'rules of coexistence'. They have an interest, in other words, in maintaining rules designed to support the system of independent states even at the price of reducing the freedom of action of their own. Indeed, rules to protect the independence of every state are integral to protecting the independence of one's own state (Bull 1977: 16–18, 69–70).

The objection to this is that since states are cross-pressured on this score, there is no reason to take it for granted that governments will always set the former (protecting everybody) before the latter (preserving their own freedom of action). There is no better illustration, the sceptic may argue, than Article 51 of the UN Charter. This Article, which permits the use of force in self-defence, including so-called collective self-defence, is a necessary feature of a system of independent states, the sceptic may suggest; its generous flexibility reflects the difficulty of gaining the acceptance of norms decisively constraining the use of force in a system of actors striving to maintain their independence. A commensurate flexibility was a feature of the documents formalizing the East-West *détente* of the 1970s, including the Helsinki Final Act and the US-Soviet Basic Principles Agreement (Goldmann 1988: 91–7). The difficulty of decisively proscribing conflictive action while retaining a right of individual and collective self-defence reflects the limit of what can be obtained in a system of independent states, in the sceptic's view.

But then internationalists may try a different thought: the strengthening of international norms need not be the product of deliberate decisions but may result from an evolving custom, that is, from decisions made about specific situations rather than about general norms. Normative constraints on the freedom of action of states need not be deliberate but may emerge inadvertently.

The sceptic's comment to this is that since governments are aware of the fact that their actions may serve as precedents, they take this into account in all their considerations and avoid setting precedents that they do not want to set. Customary norms are thus unlikely to be different from those that have been created deliberately, the sceptic may argue.

At this point, internationalists may resort to playing their trump card: world opinion. Even if governments remain convinced of the necessity of preserving the freedom of action of states, public opinion in many countries may increasingly see things differently and may be increasingly influential. And even if single governments were to remain committed to traditional conceptions, the pressure of world opinion might prove too strong even for them. What formerly may have made the strengthening of the legal constraints on escalation and war appear overly difficult may be less formidable in present-day conditions. Indeed, to organize opinions urging governments to reinforce normative constraints on conflictive action at the international level as well as condemning the violators of rules is a prime task of anybody setting out to influence world politics along the lines of the internationalist programme.

We began with the notion that internationalism has two dimensions: one coercive and the other accommodative. The core of the coercive dimension is the strengthening of international law and other norms constraining escalatory action at the international level. The 'strengthening' includes rule-making and codification as well as the punishment of offenders; all of these are taken to reinforce normative inhibitions against escalation and war. Compliance has never been negligible because of the threat of sanctions, the occurrence of internalization, and the principle of reciprocity, and it is an increasingly realistic expectation because of the increasing role of international opinion-formation. By the same token, the strengthening of the normative framework of world politics is becoming an increasingly realistic objective in view of the increasing role that world opinion is playing. This, in brief, is how the theory of internationalism may be taken to explain why the strengthening of international law is an integral part of a realistic programme for peace and security.

Organization

International organization is the second cornerstone of the internationalist programme. There is no agreement in the literature about how to typologize what international organizations do. Harold Jacobson, in his standard work *Networks of Interdependence*, groups their functions into five categories: informational, normative, rule-creating, rule-supervisory, and operational (Jacobson 1984: 83). Karns and Mingst prefer to distinguish between agenda-setting, norm-setting, and dispute settlement (Karns and Mingst 1987: 460–4) and this is more useful for explicating the theory of internationalism. Internationalists trust international organization to provide the three last-mentioned services and add a fourth: to substitute for nation-states as objects of allegiance.

The distinction between the coercive and the accommodative dimensions of internationalism is not precise. So far as the functions of international organizations are concerned, however, norm-setting and agenda-setting are related mainly to the normative regulation of international politics and will therefore be considered in this section. Dispute settlement and allegiance have a closer relation to the accommodative dimension and will be considered later on.

Norm-setting

The codification, clarification, and extension of international law has long been considered a main task of international organizations. The idea has not only been that an international institution can provide a practical solution to the problem of organizing multilateral negotiations about complex matters. It has also been that the very existence of an organization set up to codify, clarify, and extend international law provides an impetus to such efforts and that the strengthening of international law benefits from the exposure of recalcitrant minorities to the collective pressure of an international majority in a world assembly.

Historical experience would seem to have proven this to be a realistic expectation (Jones 1992). The validity of this tenet of the theory of internationalism need not be seriously questioned. If norm-setting at the international level is essential for international peace and security, then international organization is a useful part of an internationalist peace programme for this reason if for no other.

The question is whether the argument applies at the regional level and not merely globally. Regional organization may facilitate regional norm-setting; what is not self-evident is that global peace and security benefit from the strengthening of regional norms.

Regional organization poses a problem for internationalism. On the one hand, the internationalist programme is unquestionably easier to implement on a regional than on a global scale. On the other hand, the build-up of regional organizations can conceivably increase inter-regional tensions in some circumstances – between Europe and the Third World, for example, or between Europe and its economic rivals in Asia and North America. There was controversy from the outset over whether the European Community represented a step forward or backward from the point of view of internationalism; this reflects a general problem in the theory of internationalism.

It seems, however, that the problem is modest so far as the coercive dimension of internationalism is concerned. The existence of norms prohibiting escalation and war within a region is unlikely to conflict with global efforts to the same end. Indeed, if world peace is indivisible in the sense that horizontal escalation of wars may occur, the regional prohibition of war should contribute positively to global peace and security. Matters may be different with regard to the accommodative dimension, as will be argued later on.

Agenda-setting and implementation

Internationalism, as we have seen, invests considerably in the assumption of well-functioning social control at the international level. Compliance with international norms is taken to presuppose a credible threat that violations will be placed on the agenda of world politics and that some kind of collective punishment be meted out as a result. Since mere criticism of the offender is considered to be a significant sanction in the theory of internationalism, there is no clear borderline between placing an offence on that agenda and meting out punishment; this is why agenda-setting and implementation are seen as indistinguishable here.

The facilitation of social control at the international level is a major purpose of international organization, in the internationalist view. The utility of international organizations, from the point of view of coercive internationalism, is primarily that they make it easier to confront offending states with world opinion. The mere conduct of an international debate about an international offence is likely to have an impact, internationalists believe, and an international organization is a useful device for organizing the debate. Furthermore, the resolution of an international organization expresses an international opinion in a clear and concise fashion, more clearly and concisely than if it were pieced together from the statements of individual opinion-holders made at different times and places. Even more importantly, the existence of international organizations makes it difficult for governments to side-step difficult issues: as members of an organization they are expected to put forward their views and cannot avoid taking a stand. The very machinery of international organization thus places the crucial issues on the agenda of every member, which is a necessary condition for the formation and expression of a strong international opinion, internationalists may argue. They may add that more substantial sanctions – economic and military – are easier to bring about if a collective machinery exists in the form of an international organization.

What is being described here, of course, is a main function of the UN with its General Assembly, Security Council, and Secretary-General – a key institution from the point of view of internationalism. The way in which the international community responded when Iraq invaded, occupied, and then annexed Kuwait in 1990 stands out as a textbook example of the way in which an international organization may serve the purposes of coercive internationalism.

Exchange

The third cornerstone of the internationalist programme, the exchange of goods and services, also has a long tradition, dating back as it does to the classical free traders. According to the theory of internationalism as interpreted here, international exchange reduces the likelihood of war: (1) by making states increasingly dependent on one another; and (2) by making international relations increasingly complex.

This thought can be interpreted in two ways: at the level of the dyad and at the level of the actor. The suggestion at the dyadic level is that exchanges between two contenders has a pacifying impact on their mutual relationship. The suggestion at the actor level is a bolder one: the more a state engages in international exchange, the less likely it is to become involved in conflictive behaviour generally (Domke 1988: 118–19). The internationalist programme may be taken to encompass both perspectives and thus to be a programme for transforming both bilateral relationships and international relations generally. The tension that may obtain between bilateral or regional *détente*, on the one hand, and global peace and security, on the other, will be considered later on.

The rationale for assuming exchange-induced interdependence to contribute to peace and security mainly belongs to the coercive dimension of internationalism, as will be shown in a moment. Exchange-induced complexity fits better in the accommodative dimension, referring as it does to the presumed difficulty of determining what national interests are like. The former will be considered here; the latter will be discussed in due course.

The theory of internationalism is here taken to include the assumption that the exchange of goods and services makes the participants increasingly dependent on the continuation of the exchange and hence increasingly vulnerable to economic sanctions. Put differently, exchange increases the power of upholders of peace and security to compel recalcitrant states to comply with international norms. If a state violates a proscription of conflictive action, then others – the immediate adversary in the first place and maybe also the community of states – will cut off economic relations, and since exchange increases the costs that can be inflicted on the offender by cutting it off, it reduces the inclination to undertake conflictive action in the first place. This is the essence of the thought.

The idea may be developed in unitary actor terms: escalation and war result from a weighing of costs and benefits, and dependence serves to increase costs. Or it may be developed by reference to domestic power-balances: like the classical liberals we may assume exchange to strengthen the position of those who have an interest in avoiding action that will provoke retaliation. Commerce, as John Stuart Mill put it, renders war obsolete by strengthening and multiplying the interests of those who are opposed to it (Chapter 1).

There are three links in this chain of argument: (1) exchange leads to dependence on continued exchange; (2) exchange is endangered by conflictive action; and (3) the risk that exchange may come to an end deters conflictive action. None of these assumptions is a self-evident truth.

The rationale for expecting exchange to create a need for its own continuation may be explicated with the help of the concept of structural adaptation, which I have elaborated upon elsewhere (Goldmann 1988: 31–3). The idea is that states engaging in the exchange of goods and services adapt structurally to their continuation: they change their own structure so that it becomes more costly for them to do without the exchange than would have been the case if the exchange had never come about. Obviously, structural adaptation is not inevitable; some exchanges are more difficult to do without than others. Thus the import of energy leads to more dependence than the import of home electronics. Internationalists may be taken to presume the former to be typical and to assume that the international exchange of goods and services leads on the whole to a commensurate dependence on its maintenance.

The assumption that exchange is endangered by conflictive action is not self-evident even in the case of war: a war may be won so easily and rapidly that an exchange is easily restored. In the case of lesser conflict, it is even more uncertain whether an ongoing exchange needs to be interrupted. This is due to the mutuality of mutual dependence. Everybody, and not just the offensive party, has an interest in maintaining an ongoing exchange. Just as with regard to nuclear deterrence, the deterrers are deterred to such an extent that the credibility of their deterrence is undermined. Internationalists may reply that when it is a matter of an outright violation of an international norm proscribing conflictive action, public opinion may be counted on to enforce the interruption of economic relations.

There remains the question of whether the risk of economic deprivation suffices to deter from war and escalation. That it does not when fundamental ₍national interests are thought to be at stake is a longstanding objection to internationalism. That it may must be presumed to be an internationalist assumption.

Communication

There remains the fourth cornerstone of internationalism: the thought that communication across national borders makes international war unlikely. This is the most diffuse aspect of the internationalist programme. However, those who advocate law, organization, and exchange for the sake of peace commonly seem to assume that international contacts have independent positive effects that add to those of other measures. The mere coming together of statesmen and students, businessmen and scholars from different countries, and the mere sharing of ideas across borders are widely seen as contributions to peace and security. This may be a more recent idea than those of international organization and exchange – quite naturally, since the contemporary technology of transportation and electronics has revolutionized international communication.

The theory of internationalism is here taken to include the belief that all international communication supports international peace and security: transnational communication as well as intergovernmental, and meetings as well as the transmission of information. The presumed effect mostly relates to the accommodative dimension of internationalism, as we shall see. One thought is related to the coercive dimension, however: the idea that international communication contributes to making world opinion an essential feature of world politics.

It is a truism that international communication facilitates international opinion formation. There is also an indirect relationship, however: the formation and impact of international opinions may be taken to benefit from openness to people and ideas from abroad, and national openness in turn may be taken to benefit from international communication. Thus there may be a mutually reinforcing relationship between two conditions for effective opinion formation at the international level: international communication and national openness.

That societal openness is a condition for broad international communication is more or less self-evident. The reverse assumption may be less obvious, namely, that the more people from different countries meet and the more they are exposed to each others' ideas, the more open their societies will become. International communication, according to this assumption, helps to open up closed societies, thus improving the conditions for successful internationalism. Contacts between Soviet academics and Western scholars helped to pave the way for *perestroika* and *glasnost*, and watching West German television helped to undermine the DDR – such impressions of recent history suggest how internationalists may relate domestic-political change to international communication.

We meet here the thought of a relation between the internationalist programme and the democratic form of government. That there is a link between international peace and domestic-political system has been taken for granted by internationalists, at least since Cobden and Kant. Nowadays internationalism and democracy appear to be widely regarded as inseparable. The issue of the relationship between the two is of great importance, but since it is equally relevant for the coercive and accommodative dimensions it will be considered in a later context.

Coercive internationalism: summary

The essence of coercive internationalism as interpreted here is outlined in Figure 2.2. Causal assumptions such as those indicated in the figure would seem to be essential features of a theory of internationalism.

Note, first of all, that coercive internationalism takes the incompatibilities between states for granted. The object of coercive

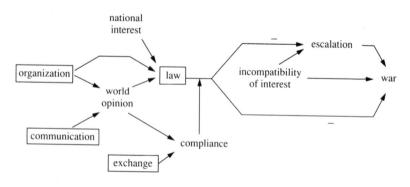

Figure 2.2 Coercive internationalism

internationalism is to make governments abstain from escalation and war regardless of the extent to which their interests collide.

The main method is to strengthen the impact of law and law-like rules in international politics: to set up rules circumscribing lawful conflictive action, to codify customary norms to this effect, and to increase the propensity of governments to comply with the rules even when compliance goes against their self-interest.

National self-interest, as a matter of fact, is a factor promoting the strengthening of international law in the theory of coercive internationalism outlined here: states have an interest in reducing the freedom of action of other states and are willing to pay the cost of reducing their own. Fear of undermining existing norms, by the same token, is a reason for compliance in specific situations. Still it is not convincing to suggest that national interest suffices to bring about the strict and effective normative regulation of conflictive action among independent states. This is why the theory of internationalism must be taken to include two further thoughts about the strengthening of international law. One is the belief in world opinion as a pressure group for effective constraints. The other is the assumption that international organization facilitates the strengthening of international law and other international norms. World opinion, furthermore, is taken to be a key factor in bringing about compliance, aided in this instance by exchange-induced dependencies. International communication is supposed to reinforce world opinion in both of its roles as pressure group and sanctioner.

A theory of internationalism must indicate a solution to the problem of devising the effective normative prohibition of the use of force in a system remaining one of independent states. The institutions presumed to maintain law and order inside states cannot be copied. The solution that has been suggested here is in essence an attempt to practise small-group social control at the inter-state level in lieu of a traditional model of political authority. A main purpose of the internationalist programme is taken to be to make informal social control effective in inter-state relations even in situations in which decision-makers believe everything to be at stake. Whether the assumptions illustrated in Figure 2.2 represent a plausible theory of international relations is one of the questions raised in this book.

ACCOMMODATIVE INTERNATIONALISM

The coercive dimension of internationalism takes for granted the incompatibility of interest between states. The accommodative dimension aims at reducing it. If the strengthening of international institutions

– law and organization – is the heart of the former, communication and exchange are the key features of the latter.

There is another difference between the two dimensions. Whereas the implementation of coercive internationalism mainly consists in taking measures that cannot be justified other than in terms of peace and security, the basis of accommodative internationalism is the conviction that developments that take place mainly for other reasons may strengthen peace and security as a byproduct. Communication and exchange should be encouraged for the sake of peace and security but they help to inhibit escalation and war regardless of why they occur, in the view of internationalists.

Communication

Communication across borders is apt to make interests less incompatible in two ways, according to the theory of internationalism as interpreted here. One is to diminish misperception; the other is to increase empathy.

Reduced misperception

A distinction between real and perceived conflict is implicit in internationalist reasoning. Perceived conflicts are taken to be unreal in large measure. Governments as well as peoples are apt to have unfounded fears of other countries and to hate other countries for imaginary reasons, according to an internationalist line of thought. Thus international relations are propelled by the devilish images that governments as well as peoples have of one another just as much as by real conflicts of interest. It is the task of those who are out to strengthen international peace and security to see to it that people become aware of their misperceptions and of their real interests. This is a reason why communication is a central feature of a theory of internationalism.

Sceptics may question the argument on two grounds. First, it remains to be proven that conflicts of interest between states are in fact imaginary to a large extent. If they are not, personal contact and the exchange of information are unlikely to make much difference. Second, it is not clear that international communication is more likely to lead to information than to disinformation and hence it cannot be excluded that it does harm just as much as good. Internationalists reject both objections; according to the theory of internationalism, communication across borders does make governments and peoples better informed about other countries, and this does reduce the perceived incompatibility between their interests.

Increased empathy

A related thought is that it is good for peace and security if peoples and governments empathize with one another – if they endeavour to put themselves in the shoes of others, to see things from the point of view of others, to comprehend the needs and feelings that others have. If there were more mutual understanding in this sense between peoples and between governments, conflicts would be less likely to escalate and easier to solve, and war would be a less likely outcome, according to this view. If large numbers of people were to empathize with their fellow human beings in other countries, it would not be easy for their governments to mobilize them in international conflicts. Furthermore, if there was more mutual understanding between governments, they would find it easier to reduce or to solve their conflicts by mutual accommodation. Empathy across borders, furthermore, is apt to facilitate the formation of international opinions, and this is important for internationalism.

Communication between intellectuals and professionals plays an especially interesting part, internationalists may add. If intellectuals and professionals in opposing countries come to analyse the situation in similar terms, thus forming an 'epistemic community' (Haas 1992), this will pave the way for *détente* if not reconciliation, according to this notion. Thus the Western contacts of Soviet academics have been credited with having helped to end the Cold War (Risse-Kappen 1991).

The questions here run parallel with those concerning misperception: can it really be taken for granted that empathy matters, and can it really be assumed that communication increases empathy? Internationalists answer in the affirmative: international communication, on the whole, does make people in different countries empathize with one another, and this does make international relations less conflictful.

Exchange

One reason for internationalists to favour economic exchange is their assumption that exchange produces dependencies that are essential from the point of view of coercive internationalism. They also have other reasons, however. Richard Cobden regarded trading stations, stores, and factories as parts of a diplomatic system bent on peace; men would be drawn together, 'thrusting aside antagonism of race, and creed, and language, and uniting us in the bonds of eternal peace'. John Stuart Mill believed that commerce made the patriot see in the wealth and progress of others a 'direct source of wealth and progress to his own

country' and argued that commerce rendered war obsolete 'by strengthening and multiplying the personal interests which are in natural
opposition to it' (Chapter 1). The belief that exchange substitutes
common for conflictive interests has remained as widely held in the
twentieth century as in earlier times. A genuinely twentieth-century
notion may be added: the observation that as exchange multiplies the
relations between the parties become increasingly complex, a complexity from which peace and security might benefit.

Communality of interest

A long-standing view about the way in which economics affects politics
is that economic exchange creates common interests superseding those
that divide. Everybody – the 'patriot', as Mill put it – will realize this.
What is more, those to whom peace is a personal interest – businessmen
– will gain in political influence as exchange proceeds.

There is an affinity between this thought and a tenet in traditional
small-group theory: interaction increases positive effect (Homans
1950). The peaceful exchange of goods and services is thought to create
cooperative bonds between nations that are based not only on the
deterrent effect of dependence but also on a growing communality of
interest. Economic exchange is believed to bring about what the Palme
Commission had in mind when it launched the concept of 'common
security' two hundred years after Cobden wrote about the uniting of
men: a realization on the part of everybody that his welfare is
contingent on the welfare of the adversary (SIPRI 1985).

No presumption in the theory of internationalism has been more
criticized than this. There has always been scepticism among scholars:
the liberal criticism of mercantilism as a source of war has certainly not
been generally accepted (Buzan 1984), nor the view that trade creates
bonds that importantly influence decisions about war and peace (Blainey
1973). Not to mention the wave of anti-capitalistic writings about
international relations in the 1960s and 1970s: economic exchanges had
done a lot to North–South relations, it was argued, but they had not
exactly promoted a communality of interest.

Internationalists need not deny the validity of some of the observations made by their critics on the right and the left. They may argue that
even if exchanges help to create a communality of interest only in some
circumstances, this is important enough for international peace and
security. Granted that North–South colonialism complicates the matter,
the argument still holds for North–North as well as South–South
relations, internationalists may contend. It holds in particular for great

power relations, which is the main issue so far as peace and security is concerned. Great power relations are special because great powers can do more damage than small states and because their involvement is the main vehicle of horizontal escalation. Everybody, including small countries in the South, is dependent on the avoidance of great power war. Exchange does seem likely to promote the emergence of a communality of interest between great powers, and if not always at least in most cases. Thus, granted that the assumption that exchange creates common interests does not hold for each and every international relation, there is still reason to believe that it tends to be valid with regard to those international relations that matter most from the point of view of the internationalist programme, on the line of thought pursued here.

Complexity

A more recent addition to internationalist thinking is the concept of complex interdependence (Keohane and Nye 1977), that is, the notion of a network of exchanges so complex that governments are unable to conduct the foreign relations of their countries in a consistent and coordinated fashion. In a condition of complex interdependence, a radical increase in the amount and variety of transgovernmental and transnational relations has taken place. An increasing variety of agencies, organizations, and individuals pursue international exchanges of an increasingly varied kind independently of one another.

It is an obvious thought that such a network of crisscrossing international exchanges reduces the incompatibility between national interests by making these interests more difficult to define. A variety of sub-and transnational interests are substituted for a single national interest. The notion of states waging war against each other in a single-minded pursuit of their conflicting interests is becoming obsolete as a consequence.

Organization

Two functions of international organizations are seen here as essentially belonging to the accommodative dimension of internationalism: to settle disputes and to serve as objects of allegiance. They will now be discussed.

Dispute settlement

Conciliation and mediation are traditional diplomatic pursuits; supervision and peace-keeping are additional services third parties may provide in the interests of peace and security. Internationalists may be assumed to expect international organizations to be useful for purposes such as these and thus to provide effective dispute settlement, including the resolution of long-standing conflicts.

Terms like conciliation and mediation indicate that this is a matter of accommodation rather than of coercion. Conciliating, mediating, or engaging in peace-keeping is different from taking sides against international offenders. The objective of dispute settlement may in fact prove to be incompatible with the objective of maintaining peace by strengthening international law. This is the essence of what will be called the Internationalists' Dilemma, to which attention will be devoted later in the book.

There are three ways in which international organizations may participate in the settlement of disputes. First, organizations may be used to put pressure on the parties to settle their dispute peacefully. Internationalism may be taken to include a norm to the effect that peaceful settlement should be sought regardless of rights and wrongs, a norm that may be more effectively implemented if the power of world opinion is brought to bear on the parties; to assist in the formation and expression of world opinion is one of the functions of international organizations, as pointed out previously. Second, organizations provide a setting for negotiations between the parties and may themselves function as conciliators or mediators. Third, their machinery may be essential in providing services ranging from the supervision of truces and elections to large-scale peace-keeping operations.

This is familiar stuff. The issue is not whether international organizations perform functions such as these but whether they are indispensable. Internationalists may be taken to believe that international organizations cannot easily be replaced when it comes to pressurizing and at the same time helping adversaries to settle their disputes peacefully.

Allegiance

The thought that international organizations may reduce the affection people feel for their own state comes from functionalism *à la* Mitrany (see Chapter 1). According to this idea, if international organizations are set up to perform welfare functions, the attachment of people will begin to shift from the national to the international level. It may be seen as part of the theory of internationalism that if this occurs – if people begin to identify less with their own state and more with international agencies – it will be more difficult for governments to mobilize support for conflictive action. The existence and activity of international organizations, according to this way of thinking, help to reduce incompatibilities between national interests in a way reminiscent of the complexity of interdependence: by making national interests more difficult to define.

An international allegiance may imply a commitment to the enforcement of one's ideals, but that is not the outlook of internationalism as defined in the present book. In the theory of 'mild' internationalism, to take an international rather than a national point of view implies a commitment to mutual adaptation, compromise, and coexistence between opposing ideals and thus to pursue accommodative rather than coercive internationalism. The aggressive pursuit of universalist ideals that are not universally accepted is not what internationalists have in mind when they think that international organizations may be substituted for nation-states as objects of attachment and that this is good for peace and security. International organization represents the ideal of accommodating opposing views in internationalist thinking.

But also the ideal of the rule of law. Hence the Internationalists' Dilemma.

Accommodative internationalism: summary

Accommodative internationalism as outlined here is summarized in Figure 2.3. Causal assumptions to this effect would seem to be essential parts of a theory of internationalism. One feature of the model shown in the figure is the assumption that escalation is inhibited by the availability of organizations suitable for settling disputes. Apart from this, the figure summarizes a number of assumptions about the way in which

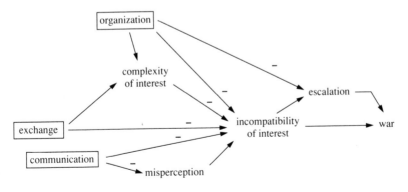

Figure 2.3 Accommodative internationalism

incompatibilities between national interests are reduced by the components of the internationalist programme.

Communication is thus presumed to reduce misperception in international politics, that is, to make both governments and peoples aware of the extent to which their perceived conflicts of interest are unreal and their perceptions of threat unjustified. Since international conflict is thought to result from misperception to a very large extent, communication at all levels is seen as an important contribution to peace and security in the theory of internationalism.

Redefinition of real interests is another presumed result, if the internationalist programme is put into effect. Communication leads to empathy. Exchanges make states and peoples dependent on each others' welfare. They also make national interests so difficult to define that differences between national interests are increasingly blurred. Organizations serve as objects of allegiance, and this further confounds the differences between national interests.

I have likened the theory of coercive internationalism with the theory of social control. Such reasoning is based on a Hobbesian view of man as conflictual: he or she must be kept in check by some social mechanism or arrangement in order for peaceful social life to be possible. Accommodative internationalism is based on a different assumption: just as man may be seen as intent on peaceful social life, accommodative internationalism is rooted in a vision of how states, nations, and peoples get to know each other and learn to do things together, thereby realizing how much they have in common. There are reminiscences not only of *gesellschaft* but also of *gemeinschaft* in the theory of internationalism. Hence the Internationalists' Dilemma, to which we will return.

The relationship between regional accommodation and global peace is another problematic issue. A case can be made, and often has been, to the effect that regional organization together with a regional build-up of exchange and communication may harm rather than help peace and security at the global level, however beneficial its regional impact. Internationalists are faced with the fact that whereas their objective is global, the historical cases of successful internationalism are regional, the European Community in the first instance. What if regional cohesion promotes global polarization?

It is not necessary to ascribe to the theory of internationalism the presumption that there is no tension between the global and the regional. Instead internationalists may be assumed to take the more reasonable position that the relationship between regional change and global effect may vary. Internationalists, when faced with the problem of deciding whether to support or oppose a particular instance of regional change, may be taken to make two considerations. One is whether this instance of regional change is likely to be perceived by others as an example to be followed or as a threat to be met; it may have been justified at times to make such a distinction between the EC and NATO. The other consideration concerns the regional threat to peace and security that may be averted by regional change along internationalist lines; reconciliation between Germany and France may be such an important gain for world peace that the disintegrative impact of European integration, if any, may have been a fair price.

ADDITIONAL FEATURES: DEMOCRACY AND DYNAMICS

The essential features of a theory of internationalism have now been outlined. It remains to consider two notions that may be regarded as part of this theory. One is democracy: what is the role of democratic principles in internationalist thinking? The other is dynamics: do internationalists have a theory of the dynamics of international systemic change and not merely one about the implications of such change for international peace and security?

Internationalism and democracy

There is an affinity between internationalism and democracy. The internationalist' vision of what the international system ought to be like is rooted in an analogy presumed to obtain between democratic and international politics. Just as opinions are freely formed and expressed within democracies, and just as democratic leaders are expected to be influenced by them, opinions can be formed at the international level and ought to influence international politics – an assumption to this effect is implicit in internationalist reasoning, as we have seen. Just as democratic decisions are made by representative parliaments after rational deliberation, international political decisions ought to be made in international organizations modelled on democratic parliaments. And just as democracy presumes pluralistic diversity within a consensual framework, cooperative links ought to multiply across national borders so as to promote both transnational diversity and consensus on fundamentals.

What makes the parallel between domestic democracy and international politics problematic is the fact that internationalism does not aim at setting up a world state. The object of internationalism is to make the inter-state system peaceful but not to replace it with something else.

There is a tension between applying principles of democracy at the international level and yet retaining the independence of the separate states, a tension illustrated by the difficulty of reducing the 'democratic deficit' in the European Community by increasing the power of the European parliament without diminishing the power of national governments and hence the independence of the member states. Therefore, even if the object of internationalism may be said to be to make international relations more 'democratic' in a loose sense, democracy in a strict sense at the international level – a democratic world state – is not part of the internationalist programme as defined in this book.

Democracy may come into internationalist thinking in another way, however. That there is a link between domestic-political system, on the one hand, and international peace and security, on the other, has been widely assumed, at least since the publication of Immanuel Kant's *Zum ewigen Frieden*. In Kant's view, the success of his proposed federation was contingent on participating states being 'republican' so that the consent of the subjects would be needed before war could be embarked upon. The demands for internationalist change at the international level and democratic change at the domestic level have continued to go hand in hand. For a leading internationalist such as Woodrow Wilson, internationalism and democracy were inseparable. It accords with the tradition of internationalist thinking to consider law, organization, exchange, and communication to be more likely to lead to peace and security if states are democratic than if they are authoritarian.

What is less clear is whether internationalism assumes democracy inside states to be a necessary condition for international peace and security. Do internationalists consider internationalist change – the establishment of international institutions, increases in peaceful exchanges – incapable of safeguarding peace and security unless all states concerned are democratic? It seems best to consider the theory of internationalism to be undecided on this point.

More will be said in subsequent chapters about the role of domestic democracy for international peace and security.

The dynamics of internationalism

The theory of internationalism as outlined above is static. It purports to show what will happen to international peace and security if international institutions get stronger and cooperative international interaction gets more intense. There is no consideration of what may strengthen institutions and increase interaction.

The theory is easily made dynamic, however. The dynamics of

internationalism are partly endogenous and partly exogenous, as it were. What the endogenous dynamics may be like are outlined in Figure 2.4. Organization and exchange are suggested to be basic variables. The analogy with domestic society is clear: the exchange of goods and services is essential for social life, and political institutions are needed to give it an organized framework. Internationalists want to replicate this at the international level, but only to a degree; the international system remains one of independent states in the internationalist vision.

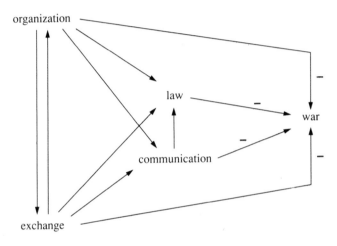

Figure 2.4 The endogenous dynamics of internationalism

Organization and exchange are presumed not only to be the driving forces of the process but also to reinforce each other. A distinction has been made in the literature between a 'federalist' and a 'functionalist' view of integration. If organization is taken to represent a 'federalist' approach and exchange a 'functionalist' approach, the model outlined in Figure 2.4 implies that both are essential. Communication is suggested to be an effect rather than a cause of organization and exchange, and the strengthening of international law is seen as essentially a result of the other three processes.

The exogenous dynamics of internationalism are not indicated in the figure. However, the theory of internationalism may be taken to include the assumption that a process such as the one outlined in Figure 2.4 is propelled by a combination of technological imperative and political will. Technological change is presumed to increase exchange and communication in international relations to the benefit of peace and security; technological optimism historically is a feature of internationalist thinking with its roots in the enlightenment. However, technology-induced change is thought insufficient to avert war. Internationalism is not an analysis of the predetermined consequences of technological progress but a programme for political action. There is a need for deliberate political action to encourage and facilitate technology-induced change and to supplement it with institutions aimed at inhibiting war.

It is not necessary for the purposes of the present study to consider the dynamics of internationalism in more detail. Two assumptions about dynamics seem necessary in order for the validity of the internationalist programme to be worthy of consideration. One is that internationalist change depends in part on political will. The other is that the four pieces of the programme are mutually supportive. Both of these assumptions seem plausible. The critical issues are different. Will internationalist change avert war? And will there be sufficient political will to bring it about? That is what the rest of the book is about.

THREE QUESTIONS

Nobody rejects or accepts internationalism categorically. Sceptics admit that measures such as those advocated by internationalists may contribute to peace and security in some circumstances. Enthusiasts accept for a fact that they do not always succeed. The issue is whether, on the whole, the internationalist programme is likely or unlikely to work, that is, whether in most cases, in most circumstances, and in the long term, peace and security will benefit significantly from the strengthening of international law and organization and from increases in international exchange and communication.

That it will is a truism to some; that it will not is trivially obvious to others. The fact that intuitions collide justifies further consideration.

The debate over so-called realist theory has not exhausted the issue. This debate, as pointed out previously, has limited relevance for a consideration of the validity of the internationalist programme. Internationalism as defined here does not obviate the realist diagnosis of the human problematic. It sets out, on the contrary, to devise a solution on realist premises. The difference pertains to a relatively limited issue: whether, given the fact of international anarchy, the structure of the international system can be modified so as to reduce significantly the conflictiveness of international relations. To assert that this can be done is not to adopt an 'idealist' antithesis of 'realism'.

Some issues raised by internationalism have long been debated in the international relations literature, including for example the premises of collective security and the relation between trade and security. There is, furthermore, a literature in which the correlation between individual components of the internationalist programme and the incidence of war is examined empirically, such as Nye's work on regional organization (Nye 1971) and Domke's work on the impact of foreign trade and international institutions (Domke 1988). The contribution I hope to make in the present book is to focus attention on three problems that: (1) relate to the internationalist edifice as a whole rather than to its constituent parts; (2) go beyond what can be directly determined by empirical observation; and (3) have not been exhausted in the theoretical literature. They represent three fundamental questions with regard to the theory of internationalism outlined in this chapter. Together they form what may pretentiously be called an internationalist research programme. The first part of this programme is mainly empirical and is concerned with the role of world opinion; the second part is essentially theoretical and concerns the relationship between cooperation and conflict; the third deals with the problem of combining coercion with accommodation and will bring us into the field of normative political philosophy.

Opinion and politics at the international level

World opinion is a *sine qua non* of internationalism. It is difficult to see how a plausible theory of internationalism could be set up without an assumption to the effect that broad opinions can be formed at the international level in support of peace and security and that such opinions can have an impact on governmental action. Internationalist thinking is permeated by the thought that public opinion matters in questions of peace and war, that world opinion is essential for bringing about internationalist change, that such change in turn will make opinions more internationally oriented and therefore less conflictive, and that world opinion stands ready to support international institutions against offenders. Opinion formation on an international scale is a strategy for pursuing internationalist causes. World opinion is a major resource of internationalists.

In order to evaluate the current validity of the internationalist programme this assumption must be examined. It turns out that this is easier said than done. International opinion formation is almost virgin territory for social scientists, not to mention the study of the political effects of international opinions. The problem is ultimately empirical: what factors facilitate and inhibit the formation of international opinions, and what is the impact of such opinions on governmental action? Conceptual groundwork must be carried out before answering these questions, however. There is confusion about the phenomenon to be researched: terms like world opinion, international opinion, and public opinion have deliberately been used interchangeably in this chapter to reflect a confusion in internationalist thinking about whom to influence and whose influence to rely on. There is, furthermore, a need for the systematic consideration of factors that may stand in the way of opinion formation at the international level as well as of factors that may prevent international opinions from having political impact. There is a need, in other words, for a theory about what may make the relationship between public opinion and governmental action different at the international level from what it is at the national one.

Some of this groundwork is carried out in Chapter 3. An attempt is made to explicate the concept of international opinion and to specify what may be problematic about the assumption of a vast, peace-oriented, and influential opinion of this kind. An empirical case study will also be reported. The validity of this aspect of the theory of internationalism will be discussed, but it will be emphasized that more empirical research is needed in order for a well-founded assessment to be possible.

Cooperation and conflict in international relations

Internationalism aims at inhibiting war by means of cooperative international interaction of all kinds: rule-making, organization, exchange, and communication. There is implicit in internationalism an assumption to the effect that cooperation inhibits conflict. The assumption goes beyond the truism that if specific conflicts are resolved by specific actions, these conflicts will not lead to war. Internationalists do not merely believe that if a particular treaty is ratified and implemented by those concerned, one source of conflictive action is eliminated. They do not merely believe that if two nations begin to exchange goods and services, their interest in continuing this particular exchange will prevent them from going to war with each other. Nor do they merely believe that if an organization is set up to manage an issue area, these issues will be less likely to cause war. Internationalists believe all of this, but more: that any kind of cooperative interaction across borders tends to reduce the likelihood of war over any issue. All steps toward law and organization as well as exchange and communication contribute to making international relations generally less conflictive, on this view.

This is not a tautology or a truism. The proposition that any kind of cooperative behaviour tends to reduce the inclination for any kind of conflictive behaviour between the same actors, or even in the system as a whole, is non-trivial if not audacious. Is it really a plausible suggestion that cooperation with regard to one issue inhibits conflict over other issues? The validity of the assumption of a general negative relationship between cooperation and conflict is one of the questions that needs to be addressed in an attempt to assess the internationalist programme.

Chapter 4 is devoted to this issue. A relatively detailed theory will be sketched about the various ways in which cooperation may reduce the inclination to escalate and to wage war. The theory will then be exposed to a critical analysis in an attempt to specify its strengths and weaknesses.

Ostracism and empathy in international ethics

World opinion is crucial for coercive internationalism, and cooperation is the core of accommodative internationalism. It remains to consider the tension between coercion and accommodation. This tension becomes acute when an international norm is violated and the ensuing situation cannot be rectified except by the use or threat of force. What do internationalists do in such a situation? On the one hand, action must be taken against the offender so as to uphold the rule of law, which is a main objective of the internationalist programme. On the other hand, since conflicts should be solved by mutual understanding and compromise, since this is also a norm that should be upheld, since future cooperation must not be impaired, and since the overriding objective is to avoid war, uncompromising and escalatory action must not be taken. Internationalists are supposed to ostracize norm-breakers as well as to empathize with everybody. The tension between the two is what is called the Internationalists' Dilemma in this book.

The opposition between the demands of coercion and those of accommodation is a concomitant of social life. It is problematic especially if a division of functions is lacking between those caring for single individuals and those responsible for the maintenance of systemic order – between social workers and the police, as it were. There is no such division of functions in a system of independent states; as argued by Waltz, the lack of functional differentiation is a characteristic feature of the international system (Waltz 1979: 93–7).

The validity of the internationalist programme hinges in part on whether a solution in principle can be found to the Internationalists' Dilemma in the form of a rule for when to ostracize and when to empathize. This matter is examined in Chapter 5 in the context of a more general consideration of the ethics of internationalism.

If it is a plausible assumption that international opinion formation is becoming a significant feature of world politics, if the assumption of a general negative relationship between cooperation and war can be upheld, and if a solution in principle can be found to the Internationalists' Dilemma, then this may justify the conclusion that the internationalist programme is worth pursuing or even that there is an obligation to pursue it. If the result is negative on all three accounts, there may be reason not to take internationalism seriously. What we are about to find in this book, however, is that the situation is not clear-cut and that a sort of limited and conditional internationalism may be the appropriate position to take.

3 International opinion and world politics

To many of those who set out to construct the peace to follow World War I, public opinion was 'the great weapon [to] rely upon'.[1] The League of Nations, Woodrow Wilson explained at Mount Vernon in 1918, would safeguard peace and security by 'affording a definite tribunal of opinion to which all must submit and by which every international readjustment that cannot be amicably agreed upon by the people directly concerned shall be sanctioned' (Ambrosius 1987: 43). The dictatorships of the 1930s, World War II in the 1940s, and the Cold War in the 1950s convinced many that this had been an illusion. Power politics or imperialist expansionism seemed more likely to be fuelled by popular sentiments than to be kept in check by international opinion. 'Modern history', Morgenthau wrote in *Politics among Nations*, 'has not recorded an instance of a government having been deterred from some foreign policy by the spontaneous reaction of a supranational public opinion' (Morgenthau 1961: 261).

The internationalist programme cannot be evaluated without a consideration of this issue, as we have seen. World opinion plays a crucial role in this body of thinking, both as a pressure for internationalist reform and as a sanctioner upholding international norms. Now a case can be made for the view that several changes affecting world politics are making views such as Morgenthau's less and less justified. The communications revolution has facilitated the dissemination of information and ideas around the world, it may be argued; in particular, the mass media are becoming internationalized in terms of both coverage and audience, as illustrated by newspapers such as *The International Herald Tribune* and *The European*, magazines such as *Newsweek* and *The Economist*, and television networks such as Sky and CNN. Economic growth and the expansion of education, furthermore, have made it possible for more than just a small élite to devote time to, and to comprehend the implications of, international issues. The ideals of

Western democracy, moreover, are gaining ground around the world, and hence the idea that widespread opinions ought to be taken into account (Rosenau 1990: 333–87; see also Flynn and Rattinger 1985: 387). It is an important question whether changes such as these are making opinion formation an increasingly significant phenomenon at the international level, and whether the internationalist programme is becoming increasingly plausible as a consequence.

Views about the relationship between opinions and politics often imply a model such as the one outlined in Figure 3.1. An opinion is formed in this model under the influence of some situation or event. If sufficiently strong, the opinion leads on to a political decision that, in turn, feeds back on the situation having given rise to it, thus making the opinion more favourable toward the decision-makers. However, an

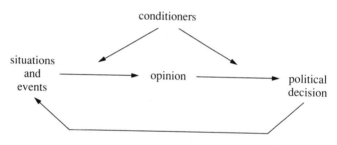

Figure 3.1 Opinions and politics

essential feature of the model is the conditioners, that is, the factors explaining why opinions cannot always be predicted from situations or events and why they do not always influence politics as expected. The internationalist programme would seem to comprise three assumptions about what these relationships are like at the international level:

1 In the face of a situation or an event that poses a threat to peace and security, an international opinion will be formed in opposition to the threat and in favour of measures to protect peace and security. If adversaries refuse to negotiate, an opinion will be formed against the deadlock. If an arms race threatens to get out of hand, there will be an opinion demanding disarmament. If an aggression is committed, the aggressor will be condemned. No conditioners will interfere to inhibit significantly the formation of an unbiased opinion on an international scale.

2 International opinions have a significant impact on governmental decisions. Governments are impressed by international opinions and

are anxious to anticipate them. Where a relevant international opinion is in evidence, governments will make efforts to break deadlocks and make concessions on disarmament; the risk of being condemned by an international opinion inhibits them from going to war. No conditioners will interfere to prevent international opinions from producing significant political effects.

3 Peace and security will in fact benefit from governmental actions taken in response to international opinions.

The third assumption, which is obviously crucial to internationalist theory, will not be considered in this chapter. It is not always self-evident whether the kind of measures world opinion is presumed to advocate would help or hurt peace and security if they were implemented. For example, it is not always easy to determine whether peace and security benefit from appeasement or from firmness, from *détente* or from deterrence, from empathy or from ostracism. This is essentially what is called the Internationalists' Dilemma in the present book; it is considered in Chapter 5.

The present chapter is concerned with the first two issues: whether it is plausible to expect, as internationalists do, that international opinions will be formed when needed and that such opinions, if formed, will have a significant impact on governmental action. The focus will be on the 'conditioners'. There are constraints on opinion formation even in well-functioning democracies, just as governmental policies do not always reflect prevailing opinions in such countries; these familiar matters will not be considered here. The issue raised in this study is whether additional constraints obtain at the international level. Internationalism assumes that this is not the case; the object of this chapter is to consider the validity of that assumption.

Whereas statesmen are in the habit of expressing themselves as if world opinion were of great importance while academic specialists on international relations have tended to profess the opposite view, little research has been done about the matter. The only major study known to the author is a Harvard thesis presented in 1985 by Mark Hunter Madsen, to which we shall return. Essentially we must start from scratch. A framework of analysis will be outlined and applied to one of the few instances in which a vast public opinion has been mobilized in large parts of the world over a major issue of international peace and security. This is meant to pave the way for more extensive and intensive empirical research about a potentially important phenomenon in world politics and one that is decisive for the plausibility of the internationalist programme for peace and security. Even in its present shape the framework provides an improved basis for evaluating a main assumption of this programme.

The case to which the framework will be applied is the anti-nuclear protest that exploded in the early 1980s. The interaction between the mobilization of what was known as the peace movement and ongoing US-Soviet bargaining about intermediate-range nuclear missiles provided a test of the notion that world opinion can be relied upon to give effective support to international peace and security. Much of what follows aims to examine what can be learnt from this test case about the plausibility of the theory of internationalism.

THE CONCEPT OF INTERNATIONAL OPINION[2]

World opinion means different things to different people. Madsen based his thesis on interviews with about 180 diplomats from about 80 countries. It proved to be common among these professionals to conceive of a world opinion that 'speak[s] for the world, not just for part of it' (Madsen 1985: 39). This opinion was thought to be expressed, in the first instance, by the UN and especially by the governments of small, democratic, and nonaligned states. However, world opinion was also taken to be expressed in other ways: by political, financial, religious, and ideological élites, by the 'world' press, by cultural personalities and scientists, by polls, demonstrations, and taxi-drivers. To some it was revealed by intuition, introspection, or God.

Distinctions are in order. Opinions, in the terminology to be adopted here, can be formed at three levels: the governmental, the organizational, and the individual. The terms *official* opinion, *organized* opinion, and *popular* opinion will be used to denote each of these. Organized opinion will be further subdivided into *established* opinion, which is expressed by permanent or quasi-permanent organizations such as political parties, interest organizations, and churches; *media* opinion, which consists in the views expressed by the mass media; and *ad hoc* opinion, which is expressed by temporary, single-issue groups or movements (Figure 3.2). It is common to distinguish between élite opinion, on the one hand, and popular or mass opinion, on the other; élite opinion, in the present terminology, can be of the official, established, media, and even ad hoc types. It is also common – even though terminology varies – to distinguish between opinion as behaviour and as a mental state; in this book, official and organized opinions are presumed to be behavioural, whereas popular opinions are presumed to be mental but possibly revealed by behavioural indicators.

Distinctions such as these have not always been made by those

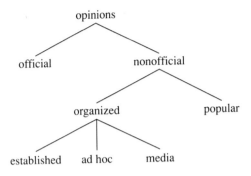

Figure 3.2 Five types of opinion

professing to believe in the impact of world opinion. On the contrary, a content analysis of two leading newspapers, the *International Herald Tribune* and the *Frankfurter Allgemeine Zeitung*, suggests references to 'world opinion' to be obscure in this regard (South Africa has incurred 'world attention and opprobrium', 'the entire world was able to observe' as Benigno Aquino was being shot, the Afghans have been given the feeling that 'the outside world has not completely forgotten them'; Rusciano and Fiske-Rusciano 1990). There is in fact a tendency, strongly suggested by Madsen's findings, to take it for granted that the five types of opinion go together or even that they are one and the same.

The source of this confusion seems to be clear. The very notion of a world opinion that ought to have an impact on world politics is rooted in an analogy presumed to obtain between international politics and democracy, an assumption to the effect that just as democratic leaders are expected to be influenced by the majority view in their country, governments ought to follow the dictates of the majority view at the world level. Believers in world opinion seem prone to take it for granted that what they perceive as world opinion represents the wishes of a majority of mankind and that its various manifestations – UN resolutions, élites, media, taxi-drivers – are worthy of attention because they are valid indicators of the majority view.

A serious student of the role of opinion in international politics must be on guard against such mythology. Hence the need for distinctions such as those proposed here. Opinions of the various types – official, established, media, ad hoc, and popular – are different phenomena; this is the crucial point. Whether they are similar or dissimilar is an empirical question, and whether there are causal links between them and what the links are like if they exist is an object of study for those concerned with opinion formation and not a matter to be determined *a priori*.

The five types have in common that they are manifestations of 'public' opinion in some sense. What makes an opinion 'public' in day-to-day language is both that it is concerned with public affairs and that it is widely held – a combination of substance and acceptance, in other words. This can be taken as a point of departure for defining the concept of 'international' opinion. In order for an opinion of any of the five types to be considered 'international' in what follows it is necessary: (a) that its object (that which the opinion is an opinion about) is foreign, inter-state, or transnational; and (b) that it is held in several countries. It is not considered necessary that it has been formed by an international process; the nature of the process of opinion formation is here kept apart from the nature of the resulting opinion.

Thus a common feature of international opinions is that they are concerned with foreign countries, or with international relations, or with problems that several nations have in common. International opinions are concerned with matters that are decided abroad or in an international relations context and not by the opinion-holder's country alone. The term 'international issue' will be used to denote such matters. An opinion is not international unless concerned with an international issue.

The point is to exclude opinions that, even if held in many countries, are about matters that are domestic for each country. It is conceivable that large numbers of people in several countries identify street crime as a growing problem in their respective country. This would not qualify as an international opinion in the terms outlined here, in contrast for example to a widespread concern over conditions in Sub-Saharan Africa or over the shape of the UN.

It is sometimes difficult to determine whether an issue is international in this sense. Defence policy is located in a grey area: if a demand is voiced by opinion-holders in many countries that their respective countries stop exporting arms, this demand is national in the sense that it calls for a unilateral national decision, but it is international by virtue of being justified in terms of international rather than national security. Whether an issue is international or not should be seen as a matter of degree.

In order for an opinion to be considered international in what follows it is also necessary that it is widely held internationally. This is even more clearly a matter of degree: the more widespread an opinion is internationally, the more 'international' it is. A unanimous resolution of the UN General Assembly is maximally international in terms of this criterion. An opinion held in the Scandinavian countries about, say, Russian activities in the Baltic republics, which is not widely shared elsewhere, is only weakly international in this regard. The peace movement of the early 1980s was quite international on both accounts, as will be shown later on.

The degree to which an opinion is international should be kept apart from the question of its strength. The two coincide only with regard to official international opinions, where the number of opinion-holders by definition is a measure of the degree to which the opinion is international. So far as a non-official opinion is concerned, the number of opinion-holders and the number of nations in which it is held are different variables. An opinion may be held by many people in few countries or by few people in many countries and thus may be strong but weakly international or weak but strongly international. The anti-nuclear movement of the 1980s was obviously quite international, but its precise strength was more difficult to determine. These are different matters.

A note on terminology: even if the international character of an opinion is a matter of degree, the expression 'international opinion' will be used for the sake of simplicity as if the difference between international and non-international opinions were qualitative. It will denote an opinion that is above some unspecified but reasonably high threshold with regard to the 'internationalness' of the issue and the opinion-holders.

A further comment on phraseology: the term 'international opinion' – indeed, 'opinion' generally – tends to be used in two different ways. We often express ourselves as if International Opinion were an agency monitoring world politics on a continuing basis and sometimes coming out against particular aggressors or in favour of particular policies: the International Opinion is said by some to have condemned Israel for occupying foreign territory and to be requesting an end to international arms trade. At other times, our choice of words implies that international opinions exist merely with regard to particular objects: an international opinion has been formed about Israeli but not about, say, Indonesian occupation of foreign territory. In what follows, the term 'international opinion' is used in the second sense. When a term is needed for International Opinion, 'world opinion' will continue to be used.

So much for the distinction between domestic and international opinions. It has been pointed out that the way in which an opinion has been formed is irrelevant for this distinction. The process of opinion formation may also be domestic or international, however. In the former case, its dynamics are internal to the country or countries involved; in the latter case, opinion formation in one country is affected by opinions abroad. An opinion that is international in the sense outlined above need not have been formed by an international process but may have resulted from the fact that opinion-holders in various countries have responded in the same way to the same stimulus independently of one another, just as an opinion that is domestic in the present sense may have resulted from an international diffusion of ideas (Karvonen 1981). The formation of international opinions thus does not presuppose international opinion formation.

When internationalist ideas are put forward, 'world opinion' sometimes refers to the positions governments have taken in the UN and elsewhere, sometimes to the views of non-official professionals such as political leaders, churchmen, and columnists, and sometimes to the attitudes of people in general. However, internationalist theory need not be taken to depend on the questionable assumption that official, organized, and popular opinions go together.

Internationalists welcome the formation of strong international opinions at the official level in support of peace and security and put much of their faith in this feature of inter-state politics. They may be taken to realize that such opinions are not always formed when needed and are not always effective, however, especially not when the target is a great power. This is why non-official opinion – 'international public opinion' – is such an essential feature of internationalist thinking. Internationalists may accept for a fact that popular majorities are unlikely to rise around the world in support of internationalist causes. Therefore they mainly pin their hope on organized opinion. This kind of international opinion is easier to mobilize than either official or popular international opinion, they may be taken to believe. Once mobilized, however, it may have an impact on both official and popular opinion, which will make it even more effective against the target government or governments.

The anti-nuclear opinion of the 1980s was mainly of this intermediate, organized type, comprising as it did peace organizations of various kinds in conjunction with churches, unions, and political parties. The extent to which it succeeded in influencing governments and popular majorities will be considered later on.

That there is an affinity but also a tension between internationalism and democracy was pointed out in the previous chapter. An additional complication should now be evident. The notion of various élites – leaders of churches, unions, and political parties, advocates of special interests, perhaps newspaper editors and columnists – imposing their views on elected governments may well be considered problematic from a democratic point of view. Democracy presumes leadership, internationalists may reply, relying as they may on a variety of élites to exercise leadership on an international scale in a way conducive to peace and security when governments let them down.

THE FORMATION OF INTERNATIONAL OPINIONS

It is part of the democratic ethos that opinion formation is a rational process and that people know best what is best for them. If there is freedom of expression and organization, competition between views will make it possible for people to form opinions about what should and should not be done that are unbiased in the sense that they accord with their interests. No 'conditioners' will interfere with the formation of opinions that are unbiased in this sense (Figure 3.1).

Internationalism assumes this to be reasonably true at the international as well as the national level. Just as the citizens of a democracy are capable of determining for themselves what is in their interest, governments as well as organizations and individuals all over the world can form rational opinions about international issues. Conditioners generally will not prevent unbiased international opinions from being formed – this will here be called Proposition I.

The proposition is not that every situation and event will call forth an appropriate international response. Internationalism need not be taken to rest on such an absurdity. It is obvious that many situations and events fail to catch international attention; internationalism need not be taken to deny this fact. The proposition is that relevant situations and events *may* cause international opinions to be formed at the organized as well as the official and popular levels, that this is a *plausible* development rather than one that is unlikely a priori, and that the likelihood is *sufficient* to influence political decisions.

The proposition may be criticized on two grounds that reflect different assumptions about the conditioners of international opinions. A distinction may be made between conditioners that are general and those that are nation-specific. A general conditioner of opinion formation, such as a general tendency for international news to be unsatisfactorily reported in the media, may facilitate the formation of international opinions but may cause them to be systematically biased. Israelis are prone to complain that this has happened to them; spokesmen of developing countries have argued for many years that international media are structurally biased to the detriment of Third World interests. Nation-specific conditioners, on the other hand, tend to produce nation-specific opinions; the larger their impact, the smaller the lowest common denominator and the less specific the resulting international opinion, if one is formed at all. Proposition II is thus that opinion formation on international issues tends to be systematically biased, and Proposition III is that opinions on international issues tend to be nation-specific. Either proposition is an alternative to the internationalists' view.

A plausible case can be made for each of the three propositions, as will now be shown.

Proposition I: There is a significant probability that unbiased international opinions will be formed

Opinion formation must be taken to include the making of autonomous assessments of the situation or event in question, but is essentially an interactive process whereby people are influenced by the assessments of others. Proposition I may be explicated with the help of a simple theory of this interactive process. It appears that there are mainly three reasons for adopting a political opinion espoused by others.

First, the factual argument in support of an opinion may make an impression. The prototype is what has been termed rational political discourse (Vedung 1977), the idea being that governments, organizations, and individuals wrestle with the substance of the issue, strive to form a position on it in a considered manner, and are assisted in this effort by the views of others. Just as scholars strive to draw conclusions on the basis of data, so governments, organizations, and individuals forming an opinion seek and are influenced by factual information and analysis provided by others. Just as moral philosophers set out to clarify the implications of ethical principles, governments, organizations, individuals strive to relate unfolding situations and events to their values and are influenced in this regard by the views of others. Opinion formation in this perspective is not unlike an academic seminar.

Second, those advocating a particular stance may wield authority in the eyes of the the government, organization, or individual forming an opinion. The prototype here is leadership. It is not the factual argument that matters in this case but the fact that the stance has been adopted by someone whom one holds in respect or in whom one has confidence (an international organization, a government, a church, a trade union, even a professor, maybe public opinion itself). Time and other constraints make it impossible to form an independent opinion on every issue, whether it is a matter of an individual, an organization, or even a government. Regardless of this, it is not always easy to come to a definite conclusion on complex matters. To rely on authority may be unavoidable.

Third, the government, organization, or individual forming an opinion may have reasons unrelated to the specific matter at issue for aligning their views to those promoting a given position. The prototype in this case is strategic adaptation. The principle working behind this aspect of opinion formation is adjustment to the stances of those one wants to support or with whom one wants to be identified. What is important is neither content nor authority but the company one keeps.

Opinion formation, then, has a content, an authority, and a strategic aspect. This is a well-established trichotomy in opinion research, as evidenced by the very title of Kelman's early article 'Compliance, Identification, and Internalization: Three Processes of Attitude Change' (Kelman 1958). Influencees are presumed to take the substantive views of the influencer into account when analysing a situation or an event; they are presumed to ponder whether the influencer has special authority; and they are presumed to consider whether it is advantageous or disadvantageous to be seen to join forces with the influencer.

The essence of this view of opinion formation is thus this. A situation or an event occurs. Opinions are formed about it by means of a discussion about the implications of the situation or the event in relation to values and objectives. The arguments put forward in this discussion make an impression, especially the views of those whom there is reason to regard as authoritative. Strategic considerations reinforce the momentum of the process. If many have similar values and objectives, compatible authorities, and converging strategic interests, a strong opinion will be formed.

Opinion formation often differs from this rationalistic ideal type: facts are not always assessed and related to basic values; those whose views are taken into account should not always have qualified as authorities; considerations of suitable company may be emotional rather than strategic. However, one should not go to the other extreme and assume political opinion formation to be entirely irrational. We are not dealing here with opinions in general but with opinions about major political issues, and we are concerned with organized rather than popular opinions in the first instance. Furthermore, even in the case of popular opinions on international issues, findings suggest it to be wrong to consider them to be the superficial result of political manipulation and media disinformation.[3]

The issue in the present context is rather whether opinion formation at the international level is subject to complications that make the rationalistic model less, perhaps one should say even less, plausible than otherwise. Proposition I is that this is not the case. Propositions II and III are about possible complications at the international level.

Proposition II: Opinion formation on international issues tends to be systematically biased

The rationale of Proposition II has to do with the mass media. The point of departure is the observation that opinion formation can be taken to be even more dependent on the mass media when it is a matter of international issues than otherwise. For organizations and individuals to take a stance on a case of apparent aggression, a new development with regard to nuclear armaments, or a foreign government's violations of human rights, it is the media which must relay the relevant information. For pressure groups seeking to increase their support and win others over to their cause, it is essential that their campaigns and messages be favourably reported. It is difficult to see how a broad opinion could be formed on an international issue without media participation.

There is dependence on the media even at the official level. While governments have at their disposal worldwide systems for the collection and analysis of information through their foreign ministries, many embassy reports are based on newspaper reading (Sjöstedt 1986: 144). According to one study, personal contacts comprise diplomats' most important source of information pertaining to what they call world opinion, but the mass media do not lag far behind (Madsen 1985: 301–2).

The media, then, are particularly vital for forging the link indicated in Figure 3.1 between situations and events, on the one hand, and opinions, on the other, with regard to international issues. There are two reasons why they may fail to forge this link, two reasons for their disturbing rather than promoting the process of opinion formation: the necessary information may not be accessible to the media, and the media may fail to report accessible information or may report it in an unsatisfactory way.

Both problems may be particularly serious with regard to matters of peace and security. Whether a war has broken out or disarmament is being negotiated, actors often have an interest in keeping the media under- or misinformed; in war truth is the first casualty. To this can be added several much-discussed features of the reporting of international news, such as a tendency to overemphasize the dramatic, a tendency towards superficiality and misunderstandings on the part of ill-informed reporters coming from abroad, and dependence on a small number of

Western news organizations and indeed on a single television network, the US-based CNN. There is, it has been argued, a homogeneity in the international reporting of foreign news that is due to factors such as these (Van Dijk 1988). The formation of international opinions is facilitated by uniformity in media reporting, we may surmise, but the opinions that are formed risk being systematically biased. Hence Proposition II.

Proposition III: Opinions on international issues tend to be nation-specific

Proposition II is familiar since it was put on the agenda of UNESCO in the form of a demand for a new international information order. It is difficult to test, since it presumes that there is an objective truth with which news reporting can be compared; it is not easy to determine objectively whether Palestine is more important than Sudan, what exactly is the truth about Serbian activities in former Yugoslavia, or whether Soviet nuclear rearmament in the 1970s implied an increased threat to the West in the 1980s. Proposition III, which introduces the question of nation-specific conditioners of international opinion formation, differs on both accounts: less attention has been devoted to it, but it is more easily testable. Note, furthermore, that Proposition III implies a more fundamental criticism of internationalist theory than Proposition II. A biased opinion may fail to strengthen international peace and security in the way internationalists envisage, but if no opinion is formed, the question of its effects does not even arise. The more that conditions for opinion formation differ between countries, the less likely is it that internationally widespread opinions will be formed at all. There is reason to devote more attention to Proposition III than to Proposition II in the present context.

Three nation-specific obstacles to the formation of international opinions will be considered here: differences in external orientation, in domestic politics, and in mass media system. The idea is that factors such as these work as national filters sorting international impulses, and as hammers shaping the resulting opinion into a form peculiar to each country. The stronger the impact of such factors, the less likely an international opinion is to be formed, and the more likely that an apparent international opinion will rather be a case of several nations responding simultaneously but differently to the same stimulus. Put differently, the stronger the impact of nation-specific factors, the weaker the lowest common denominator, and the less specific the substantive content of a resulting international opinion. Internationalism presumes that opinions respond similarly to given situations and events regardless of nationality and that the resulting opinions are highly international and yet reasonably specific. The essence of Proposition III is that this assumption does not hold.

External orientation

The scepticism of a Morgenthau is rooted in the conviction that the heterogeneity of national interests inhibits the formation of international opinions. States differ in their geopolitical situation, in their power, and in their historical experience. They therefore differ in their international orientation as evidenced, for example, in their varying adversities and alignments and their different policies with regard to international institutions and international cooperation. This will colour the way in which international issues are perceived and the way in which the media report on them, and that in turn will condition the formation of broad opinions. Differences in external orientation – the heterogeneity of national interests – thus inhibit the formation of non-official as well as official international opinions.

It is worth noting that this has been the view not just of an arch-realist like Morgenthau but also of Norman Angell, a Nestor in the pacifist literature. Angell regarded the irrational nationalism of 'the public mind' as the main obstacle to peace (Miller 1986: 55–63, 124–32). The difference, of course, is that what Angell considered irrational Morgenthau found inevitable, given what he saw as the realities of international politics.

Anecdotal examples are not difficult to find. Calls for nuclear disarmament seem to have had more credence in strategically exposed, non-nuclear countries (West Germany, Canada, Sweden) than in those which have invested in a national deterrent (France, the UK, the USA). There is little question that essential features of German and Japanese views on international affairs can be traced back to their experiences of World War II. Opinions in Britain regarding the apartheid regime have tended to differ from those in other countries, in a way reflecting the degree to which British investment in and historical ties with South Africa differ from the extent of other countries' involvement. And so on.

The notion of a heterogeneity of national interests is not exactly new, nor is the thought that there is a tendency for people to see things in a national perspective. How important an objection this is to the internationalist programme is difficult to determine, however. Systematic research is lacking. A study comparing British and Swedish media coverage of the Israeli invasion of Lebanon in 1982 is suggestive of what needs to be done. Reporting proved to differ between British and Swedish media, and especially between the newscasts of British and Swedish television, in a way running parallel to differences between British and Swedish foreign policy (Riegert 1991). This finding supports the hypothesis that media reporting may reinforce a tendency for opinion formation on international issues to vary between countries as a function of their external orientation, and perhaps that mass-orientated media like television and tabloids are particularly likely to see the world in a national perspective; these media may thus serve as crucial links between external orientation and opinion formation. However, this remains hypothetical, and more research is needed. The issue is whether foreign policy orientation determines opinions about the world rather than the reverse.

Domestic politics

Just as domestic-political factors may affect the foreign policy of a country, they may have an impact on the formation of opinions about international issues. The domestic politics of foreign policy remains underresearched and little attention has been devoted to the impact on opinion formation. What can be done here is to sort out the main ideas.

A distinction may be made between political culture, political system, and political situation. 'Political culture' is used here to refer to norms and beliefs about politics that prevail in a country; differences in such norms and beliefs may affect the formation of opinions about international issues. Such differences may obtain even between countries that are otherwise similar, such as the UK and Sweden, resulting perhaps in a tendency to see, say, the Israeli invasion of Lebanon in different ways. (British media tended to picture the conflict as a military confrontation and Swedish media as an onslaught on civilians; Riegert 1991.) More fundamentally, in order for people in two countries to respond similarly to an event or situation and to influence one another's responses, they must have similar views on whether actions should be judged in terms of their consequences or in terms of their intrinsic qualities, and, in the former case, similar theories about causes and effects. It goes without saying that if opinion formation is affected by the differences in political culture that obtain between countries as similar as the UK and Sweden, political culture represents a serious problem for internationalist theory.

Whether an international issue, or opinions abroad, can penetrate into a political system may also depend on what may be called its political opportunity structure, that is, the ease with which new ideas can gain a foothold (cf. Kitschelt 1986). The more constrained the political opportunity structure of a country, the more the formation of opinions on international issues is contingent on its government; it may be taken for granted that the formation of international opinions at the non-official level is facilitated by open opportunity structures. A basic requirement is obviously freedom of information and expression; this is one of several reasons why the feasibility of the internationalist programme is related to the spread of democracy. There is variation in openness between democracies, however, related for example to electoral systems, party systems, and systems of interest representation. Germany may have a more open political opportunity structure than the UK because of having proportional representation and a multiparty system; the USA may have a more open political opportunity structure than the UK and Germany thanks to weak political parties and the ease with which new interest organizations can be set up and gain influence.

It seems obvious, furthermore, that the ability of issues and views from abroad to penetrate into the politics of a country is also affected by the current domestic-political situation. It may matter who is in power and who is in opposition. It may matter what the political agenda is like at the critical moment; sometimes a new issue may fill a political vacuum and sometimes it must compete for attention. It may matter, furthermore, whether the political climate prescribes a conciliatory or an aggressive stance on the world stage (cf. the second Nixon and the first Reagan administrations). And it may matter whether there is a current leader seeking to project an image of proselytizing internationalism (Trudeau, Palme) or rather one of ardent nationalism (Thatcher).

This is scraping the surface. The object has been limited to indicating a number of ways in which domestic-political factors may inhibit the formation of international opinions. What has been said may be useful as a starting-point for empirical research to establish the extent to which such factors in fact condition the formation of opinions on international issues.

The mass media

The importance of the mass media for the formation of international opinions, according to Proposition II, makes international opinions subject to universal features of media reporting. According to Proposition III, national variation in this regard is more important: national media – overwhelmingly more important for opinion formation than internationalized media such as *The International Herald Tribune* and CNN – tend to report the same events in different ways.

News reporting is often discussed under the heading of 'agenda-setting', the term used by Bachrach and Baratz in their conception of the way in which those in power limit the scope of the political process to issues that do not threaten them (Bachrach and Baratz 1963). The role of the media as political agenda-setters is well established (Bäck 1979; Iyengar and Kinder 1987). It is obvious that the media may set the agenda to serve the interests or objectives of groups other than the current power-holders, such as the left in the late 1960s. They may also do it on the basis of their own ideas of what is important. Regardless of this, there may be national variation in what the media picture as the pressing issues – unemployment, sex scandals, international tensions – and this, according to Proposition III, may produce differences between countries in the propensity to react to international events or situations.

Another way in which the media may affect opinion formation is by indicating the terms in which an event or a situation should be interpreted. It matters whether participants in an armed conflict in a foreign country are depicted as terrorists or as freedom fighters, whether an on-going war is described as an unfolding series of military events or as a military onslaught on civilians, whether an arms race is presented as the result of an international political conflict or of the machinations of military-industrial interests, and whether the failure of adversaries to reach a settlement is suggested to be due to the intractability of the issue or to the intransigence of one of the contenders. That this aspect of media reporting may influence opinion formation hardly merits discussion. That it may vary between countries is part of Proposition III.

What has been said relates not merely to the reporting of events and situations but also to the reporting of what people think about them. British media have been accused of selective and misleading reporting of opinions about issues of peace and war (Glasgow University Media Group 1985: 136–43); West German media are said to have reported a wave of anti-Americanism in the early 1980s that allegedly did not exist but was taken seriously in the USA, thus acquiring international political weight (Noelle-Neumann 1983). It goes without saying that the reporting of opinions is crucial to opinion formation and that national variation on this score may complicate the formation of international opinions. If a particular position is represented on television in one country by emotional women in the street and in another by detached university professors in the studio, one should not be surprised to find public opinion going in different directions.

What are the causes of differences in reporting between countries?

Speculation on this matter may begin with the pattern of ownership and control, such as the degree of market dependence and state supervision. Regardless of this, the media system of a country may be uniform, polarized, or pluralistic, depending on whether it basically represents a single point of view (as in most non-democracies), or the views of two competing camps (as the British press, long polarized between conservative and centre-left newspapers) or a wider range of political viewpoints.

A related question concerns the implications of variation in the range of viewpoints offered by each individual medium. In media systems that are not uniform, a distinction may be made between polarized and pluralistic reporting. In the former case, each medium takes a consistent stand in the service of a particular ideology, party, or interest; in the latter case, each medium strives for balance in its reporting. Differences such as these may also affect opinion formation on international issues.

A further factor that may vary from country to country is reporting style. The balance between 'quality' and 'downmarket' press is significant, but also the extent to which and the way in which foreign news are reported in 'quality' and 'downmarket' newspapers, respectively, and whether television and radio reporting tends to be of the 'quality' or of the 'downmarket' type. This too may help to produce differences between countries in the formation of opinions about international issues. It need not be pointed out that most of this is hypothetical and in need of testing; it is not a matter of established facts.

Summary

The internationalist programme is based, among other things, on a theory of opinion formation which has been outlined here as Proposition I. Internationalism need not be taken to presume that a strong international opinion will arise in the interest of peace and security whenever necessary, but it does presume this to be a credible possibility. An argument justifying this assumption has been outlined.

The issue in the present context is whether there are special constraints on opinion formation at the international level. Two arguments to this effect have been outlined. One is that the mass media play a uniquely important part when it is a matter of opinion formation about international issues and that they are likely to make such opinions systematically biased; this is what has been called Proposition II. The other argument is based on the assumption that politics in a system of separate countries is different from politics in a single country: Proposition III is that a number of factors, summarized under the headings external orientation, domestic politics, and media system, act to make peoples and countries respond in different ways to the same situations and events. The more important the influence of nation-specific conditioners of opinion formation, the less persuasive the internationalist programme for peace and security.

THE IMPACT OF INTERNATIONAL OPINIONS

Suppose that an international opinion has in fact been formed. How will this fact affect world politics? Internationalism assumes the impact to be substantial. Is this a realistic assumption?

A distinction must be made at this point between impact on thinking and impact on action. Consciousness-raising was a main objective of the European peace movement in the 1980s (Robertson 1992: 58), and consciousness about the problem of nuclear deterrence was undoubtedly raised in Europe. The conventional wisdom about the anti-nuclear protest, as a matter of fact, is that regardless of its 'direct effect on policy', it had an 'enormous [indirect] effect on politics' by attracting the attention of political élites and demonstrating that an alternative existed to nuclear deterrence (Rochon 1988: 208). This, however, simply means that the process of opinion formation affected the thinking of important people. The key question is different: how was governmental action – the production and deployment of nuclear weapons in this case – affected by the fact that a strong international opinion had been formed? Internationalism is concerned with impact on action rather than merely on thinking.

This is a question about power. World opinion may be thought of as a constraint on the exercise of power by governments; the issue is whether this constraint is significant. Or international opinion formation may itself be seen as an attempt to exercise power; the issue then is whether opinion formation is an effective means of statecraft. In internationalist reasoning a third perspective may be found, by which world opinion is conceptualized as a transnational actor; the issue from that point of view is whether this actor is powerful.

The most obvious remark that can be made about this matter is that international opinions are likely to have a greater impact if they are strong than if they are weak. International opinions, furthermore, are obviously more likely to have an impact if they are backed up by economic or military sanctions than if they are not. Going beyond truisms, internationalism would seem to presume that such international opinions as can realistically be expected to arise may be effective in themselves. Sceptics object that international opinions are likely to be inconsequential because other concerns dominate the considerations of decision-makers. They may even contend that international opinions may be counter-productive, since they are apt to complicate inter-governmental bargaining about the issues and thus make it more rather than less difficult to avoid escalation and war. Accordingly, three propositions may be set against each other: international opinions may be effective, irrelevant, or counter-productive. The case for each will now be outlined.

Proposition Ia: International opinions are effective

An opinion is effective if it succeeds in producing the outcome it is intended to produce. Opinion formation can be seen as an attempt to exercise power, as suggested already.[4] To see how power is exercised in this way it is useful to consider three reasons a government may have for taking an existing opinion into account: the strategic implications of the fact that many share a particular view, the legitimate authority of a widely shared view, and the substantive content of this view. This runs parallel to the three aspects of opinion formation considered in the foregoing section.

The strategic reason to do what an opinion tells you to do is obvious: it may be essential to your power and influence. Going against others on one issue may diminish your overall support and hence your ability to exert influence on other matters. Conversely, adapting your decisions to the views of others may be a way of increasing your overall power.

What may give an opinion legitimate authority is the fact that it is a common assumption that politics ought to reflect prevailing views. The fact that many share a particular view, even when not strategic-ally crucial, may suffice to justify taking decisions in accordance with this view.

The substantive aspect may be less obvious. How can a viewpoint gain substantive weight from the fact that many people share it? The answer may be that many issues are ambiguous and that many decisions necessitate painful trade-offs. It may be comforting to know that your judgment corresponds with that of others in such cases.

Do these considerations apply at the international level? Reference has been made to Madsen's interview study of some 180 diplomats from about 80 countries. Madsen reports several examples of the way in which what is perceived as world opinion has affected governmental considerations according to those he has interviewed.

Its strategic impact is illustrated by a 'European minister to the United Nations [who] asserted that considerations of world opinion played heavily in his country's reaction to a Soviet submarine's violation of it's [sic] territorial waters; indeed, the exposed violation was characterized, above all, as an international public relations problem'. It was important, this diplomat told Madsen:

> that we gave the image of [our country] to the world as a country which handled this in an evenhanded way, where we could see to it that our sovereignty was respected and we would not be bullied by our neighbor, and that we would handle it in accordance with international law. . . . There was obviously the risk that the world – in this case particularly the West – would feel that we yielded too easily and that would have unfortunate consequences. . . . At the same time we did not want to present ourselves to the world as being unreasonable and riding on formalities.
>
> (Madsen 1985: 658)

The special legitimacy of what is perceived as world opinion is indicated in this statement by another European ambassador:

> Of course, in an internal democracy we take democratic decisions seriously, even if we don't happen to agree with [them]. . . . Well, of course, we all somehow feel that the world has an opinion that is not yet expressed in a vote democratically. . . . [T]here is a sort of world opinion process parallel to democratic voting and opinions forming, which history will take into consideration whether we like it or not.
>
> (Madsen 1985: 618)

That world opinion may have a substantive impact transpires from the following statement by an Arab diplomat with a Palestinian background:

> [O]ut of practical reasons and out of what world public opinion tends to think about this issue, I have revised some of my views on the subject. I am now much closer to accepting a compromise on the issues, and I'm much more susceptible to certain ideas than I was before. . . . When I was exposed more to foreign public opinion on the subject, that change came about. I mean opinion mainly at the U.N., mainly at some special session at the U.N., and some sessions with Western media people. And this is one of the interesting things about world public opinion: when you have a problem you tend always to neglect the viewpoint of the other fellow. . . . But with world public opinion you tend to get at least an indirect way of getting that counter point of view.
>
> (Madsen 1985: 607)

Judging from Madsen's interviews, what is perceived as world opinion is seen as fair, intelligent, impartial, and lacking in ulterior motives (Madsen 1985: 608–10). Still, when Madsen asked the diplomats why they themselves attached significance to world opinion and why they thought others did, the result was very clear: in spite of the common perception of world opinion as fair and intelligent, what is here called the strategic aspect dominated completely (pp. 622–31).[5]

Madsen's findings support the view that Proposition Ia represents a realistic possibility. It is however necessary to take the further step of asking whether this is the case with regard to the type of opinion and the type of contingency with which internationalism is primarily concerned.

One possibility is that different types of international opinion (official, organized, and popular) influence decision-making in different ways (strategically, authoritatively, or substantively). It may appear that the influence of official opinions is most likely to be strategic, that organized opinions are most likely to have a substantive effect, and that popular opinions are most likely to carry authority by virtue of their democratic legitimacy. Then, if we generalize from Madsen's finding that diplomats consider the effect of world opinion to be mainly strategic, this would suggest that the kind of international opinion most likely to have an impact is the official one – resolutions in the UN General Assembly rather than newspaper editorials and mass demonstrations. This may pose a problem for internationalism, since the plausibility of the internationalist programme depends in part on the effectiveness of non-official international opinions.

There remains the question whether international opinions are likely to be effective in the type of situation that is critical in terms of the internationalist programme. Opinions may play two different parts in a political process, as we have seen: they may act as sanctioners and as pressure groups. Their role in the former case is to reward or punish after the fact by reacting to what has already occurred. Their role in the latter case is to demand action in advance. Opinions, furthermore, may be concerned with actors, on the one hand, or with conditions – situations, developments, problems – on the other. Thus there are four contingencies to consider; see Table 3.1.

Table 3.1 Opinions and politics: four contingencies

	Opinions about actors	Opinions about conditions
reactions	I	II
demands	III	IV

Criticism of aggression that has already occurred is an instance of case I. Despair over an arms race is an instance of case II. A demand for the withdrawal of an occupying force is an instance of case III. The call for international action to reduce the gap between rich and poor is an instance of case IV.

It goes without saying that opinions may be difficult to classify unambiguously in these terms. The distinctions in the table are nevertheless useful in that they focus attention on two factors that may help determine the impact of an international opinion. The difference between reactions and demands is that the former, but not the latter, can influence decisions only if anticipated by the decision-maker; in this sense demands are real and reactions merely potential. The impact of an existing opinion can be taken to be greater than that of an opinion that may or may not be formed. Therefore, world opinion can be taken to be a more important factor in cases III and IV than in cases I and II, other things being equal.

The difference between opinions about actors and opinions about conditions is that the targets are specified in the former case but not in the latter. An opinion directed to a particular actor can be taken to be more effective than one concerned with, say, the outcome of an action-reaction sequence. Therefore, world opinion can be taken to be a more important factor in cases I and III than in cases II and IV, other things being equal.

On these assumptions, the impact of international opinions is largest in case III and smallest in case II – largest in the case of demands directed to specific governments and smallest in the case of the expression of views about existing conditions. In case I, the critical variable is the probability that a particular opinion will be formed. The greater this probability – the larger, that is, the credibility of reactions – the closer case I is to case III. Internationalists putting their faith in the ability of world opinion to uphold international norms assume not merely that international opinions tend to be effective if formed but that their formation tends to be sufficiently credible to deter from violations. Whether they are correct is essential for evaluating their approach to peace and security.

There remains case IV, the case of an opinion's demanding that a particular change take place in an international condition – that a conflict be resolved, that negotiations begin, that an ongoing negotiation produce a particular result, etc. The question raised here is how bargaining is affected by outside opinions requesting a particular outcome. This neglected topic is essential for the study of the links between opinion formation and politics at the international level, and hence for the evaluation of the internationalist programme. Whereas the question of the credibility of reactions is straightforward and has been the object of comment since the functioning of international law began to be debated centuries ago, the issue of third party opinion formation as an aspect of bargaining is more intriguing, even though equally crucial for internationalism. What could make bargainers heed such an opinion?

A conception of bargaining, which may be used to explicate the idea, is to see it as taking place in a two-dimensional space defined by the utilities of the contenders, as shown in Figure 3.3 (Snyder and Diesing 1977: 33–7). Each point in this space represents a possible bid. Eastward movement represents an increase in utility for *B* and northward movement an increase in utility for *A*; movement to the northeast represents an increase in utility for both parties. The diagonal is called the conflict line, defined as the empirically possible limit of northeast movement. The bargaining range stretches between *A*'s minimum and *B*'s minimum. Bids may first fall outside the bargaining range but the agreement, if there is one, will fall within it.

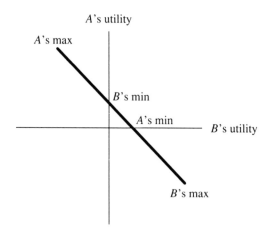

Figure 3.3 The bargaining space between two actors, *A* and *B*

A demand put forward by a third party, such as an international opinion, may be symmetrical or asymmetrical, depending upon whether it is directed to both contenders or to one of them. A symmetrical demand typically is that both *A* and *B* should revise their positions so that a compromise can be reached; this can be conceived as an effort to move the conflict line toward the northeast. An asymmetrical demand typically is that only one party should revise its position; this can be conceived of as an effort to change the inclination of the conflict line. Proposition Ia is in essence that such efforts will succeed.

The argument presumes the impact of opinions on bargainers to be strategic. A supplementary argument can be made in other terms. An outside opinion may change a bargaining situation in the same way as a mediator does: by giving a particular option special legitimacy since it comes from a disinterested third party. Such an option may serve as a 'focal point' in Schelling's sense: as an aid for the parties to coordinate their expectations of what the adversary will accept (Schelling 1960). Furthermore, one should perhaps avoid ruling out the possibility that bargainers may be influenced by the substantive persuasiveness of outside opinions.

Thus, there is a parallel between the internationalists' rationalistic view of the formation of international opinions and their thoughts about the political impact of such opinions. The political impact appears as the culmination of the process of opinion formation: even decision-makers become convinced by the substantive arguments, the authority of those putting them forward, and the strategic advantages of accepting them – convinced to the point of actually making the decisions the opinion-holders want them to make. The very possibility that a particular action will unleash an opinion may suffice to deter decision-makers, according to this line of thought. Even when the object is to bring a process of interaction to a particular conclusion and not simply to influence a single actor, international opinions tend to be effective.

Proposition IIa: International opinions are irrelevant

Proposition IIa is that opinion formation is an ineffective way of exercising power in international politics because neither publics nor governments care. The assumption that opinion formation is inconsequential at the international level may be defended on two grounds: the special features of international issues, and the 'foreignness' of views from abroad.

It is an old idea that the demands of democracy are incompatible with those of international politics and that the latter tend to take precedence over the former (Goldmann, Berglund, and Sjöstedt 1986). Questions of foreign and defence policy, according to this line of thought, touch upon interests too vital for domestic controversy to be acceptable and hence for public opinion to be a significant consideration even when it is a matter of democracies. Furthermore, they require information that is not available to the public and skills that are available only to the professionals; hence not only the strategic but also the substantive import of public opinion is necessarily weak on such issues.

The strategic and substantive weaknesses of public opinion should be even more pronounced in the matter of views that come from abroad. Foreign opinions are even less likely than domestic ones to be found interesting from a substantive point of view, since foreigners are apt to be considered incapable of understanding the situation and the responsibilities of those they are meant to influence (Stenelo 1984: 50–78, 138–43). Foreign views, furthermore, are even less likely than domestic ones to carry strategic weight in the minds of national political leaders. On top of this, whereas public opinion at home may be considered to have a certain authority in view of its democratic legitimacy, opinions from abroad risk being pictured as illegitimate intervention. Hence the proposition that the impact of international opinions on foreign policymaking is marginal. Neither the location nor the slope of the conflict line in Figure 3.3 is likely to be much affected by a manifestation of international concern.

According to this argument, then, non-official international opinions are unlikely to be taken into account by those to whom they are directed. Even official international opinions are unlikely to carry substantive weight or legitimate authority in the minds of the prospective influencees. There remains the possibility that an official international opinion may have influence by virtue of its strategic implications. Internationalism cannot rely on official international opinions alone, however.

Proposition IIIa: International opinions are counter-productive

One problem with utility models of bargaining, such as the one in Figure 3.3, is that they do not take into account the dynamics of bargaining processes. These dynamics are likely to make international opinion formation counter-productive, according to the third proposition to be outlined here. Opinion formation, even if effective when the object is to influence a single actor, may produce a result that is contrary to what has been intended when it is a matter of influencing a process of interaction.

Bargaining, following Snyder and Diesing, may be taken to comprise a coercive phase and an accommodative phase (Snyder and Diesing 1977, espec. p. 249). The function of the former is to make the parties agree about their relative bargaining power. The function of the latter is to work out an agreement on the substantive issue that reflects the distribution of bargaining power. The latter presumes the former: unless both parties consider the distribution of bargaining power to be settled, they will continue to make moves designed to change the situation to their advantage and to impress the adversary with their superior determination, thus inhibiting a common search for agreement.

How may opinion formation interfere with this process?

One possibility is that it adds to the uncertainty about and the perceived manipulability of the distribution of bargaining power, thus inhibiting accommodation. The precise way in which the parties respond to this situation may be taken to depend on the kind of demand put forward by the emerging third party, that is, the international opinion that is being formed. A distinction has been made above between symmetrical and asymmetrical demands. It is useful to distinguish in addition between genuine and spurious asymmetry. Genuine asymmetry obtains when one party is asked to accept the demand of the other. Spurious asymmetry obtains when one party is asked to make a unilateral concession which the other party is expected to reciprocate, thus paving the way for compromise rather than one-sided capitulation; spurious asymmetry shares the goal of symmetry but differs in method.

When it comes to the effect on an ongoing process of bargaining, genuine asymmetry is the easy case: the third party – an international opinion, in our case – indicates that one contender, say A, will be punished unless he accepts the position taken by B. The third party simply adds his weight to that of B, thereby changing the balance of bargaining power to the disadvantage of A. Still there is a complication. Third-party pressure may compel A to consider how his bargaining power in future situations would be affected by his bowing to the third party in the immediate situation. Specifically, a government exposed to an adversary international opinion has reason to demonstrate that opinion formation does not work against it. A is compelled in effect to bargain with the third party as well as with the original adversary, and the need to engage in coercive bargaining with the former may interfere with accommodation in relation to the latter.

In the case of spurious asymmetry, A is faced with a third party who professes to believe that a unilateral concession by A is necessary and sufficient to produce a compromise between A and B. This, just as the preceding case, puts A in the position of bargaining with both B and the third party, with the significant difference that now the unilateralism of the third party is merely tactical. This opens a possibility for A to change the position of the third party by devising offers that may seem reasonable to the third party but will be rejected by B, thus attempting to convince the third party that unilateralism does not work. At the same time, B has an interest in remaining intransigent as long as A may be pressured by the third party to make further concessions. It will likely be difficult for *A* and *B* to arrive at a common and stable estimate of the distribution of bargaining power in the triangular relationship between themselves and between each of them and the third party. The argument is not that unilateralism is never a good bargaining strategy but that third party pressure to this effect may be counter-productive.

There remains the symmetrical case, which invites both parties to act so as to avoid compromise while seeking to make the third party blame the adversary. The object of each of them is to make the demand of the third party asymmetrical to their own advantage and hence to exploit the intervention of the third party to improve their own bargaining position before a deal is struck. Both contenders are encouraged to engage in posturing rather than in constructive negotiation – to do what they can to appear more conciliatory than the adversary while not conceding anything of substance. Accommodation is unlikely unless and until the competition over the preferences of the third party has led to a definite result.

Summary

In summary, Proposition Ia is that international opinions are likely to have an impact by virtue of their substantive persuasiveness, their legitimacy, and their strategic implications. Proposition IIa is that such opinions will have little effect, since they lack substantive persuasiveness and legitimacy and since their strategic implications are marginal to what is at stake in international politics; this may not fully apply to international opinions at the official level, however. Proposition IIIa is that whereas international opinions lack persuasiveness and legitimacy, their strategic implications may be significant; however, by complicating the bargaining processes into which they seek to intervene they are apt to be counter-productive.

If the propositions about formation and those about impact are combined, as in Table 3.2, we can see more clearly what is special about the beliefs of internationalists concerning world opinion. The issue is whether international opinions can be counted on to strengthen peace and security. Internationalism presumes that such opinions are likely to be formed when needed and that they are likely to have an impact. For a 'realist' like Morgenthau, cited at the beginning of this chapter, international opinions are irrelevant; such opinions are unlikely to be formed and unlikely to have an impact even if formed. There is also a third position: opinions will indeed have an impact but this poses a threat to international peace and security, since international opinions are biased, counter-productive, or both. This thought has a long history in so far as it can be traced back to the classical view of public opinion as a constraint on the rational conduct of foreign policy and to the old notion of democracy as a security problem.[6]

Table 3.2 Propositions about the implications of international opinions for peace and security

Will opinions form?	Will opinions be effective?		
	Yes	*No*	*Counter-productive*
Yes	Positive	Nil	Negative
Yes, but biased	Negative	Nil	Negative
No	Nil	Nil	Nil

Setting the three views against each other in this fashion serves to emphasize that this is the outline of a research programme more than anything else. Just as little research has been done about the formation of international opinions and its conditioners, whether general or nation-specific, little research exists about their impact. The case study about to be reported should be seen against this background. The US-Soviet treaty on intermediate-range nuclear forces, known as the INF Treaty and signed in Washington on 8 December 1987, was widely hailed as historic.[7] At issue is whether this historic result – a turning-point in the nuclear arms race – was attained because of, regardless of, or in spite of massive protests against nuclear armaments around the world. The interaction that took place in the 1980s between US-Soviet negotiations about nuclear weapons and the formation of an international opinion against such weapons thus provided a rare test of the notion that world opinion can be mobilized to support international peace and security in a decisive way – an opportunity for what Eckstein calls a plausibility probe with regard to Propositions I and Ia (Eckstein 1975: 109).

Note that this is a hard test from the point of view of internationalism. The INF issue, first of all, was of great importance for the national security policy of many countries. This, if anything, would seem apt to make opinion formation conditioned by nation-specific factors (Proposition III) and to make governments unlikely to consider public opinion to be an essential consideration (Proposition IIa). The context, on top of this, was one of bargaining. Indeed, the outburst of anti-nuclear activity was arguably an expression of despair over the arms race more than a demonstration of support for a specific demand. The contingency, in other words, was one in which an international opinion is least likely to have an impact, as argued above.

Therefore, if it can be shown that nation-specific factors did not inhibit the formation of an international opinion even in this case, and if it can be demonstrated that the mobilization of an international opinion was effective in producing a historic nuclear disarmament treaty, this would go a long way towards indicating that internationalist optimism is justified.

THE INF CASE

Intermediate-range nuclear missiles were an issue in East–West relations for a period of ten years.[8] The starting-point is often considered to be a speech given in October 1977 by Helmut Schmidt, the West German Chancellor. Schmidt gave voice to a growing European concern over the implications of US-Soviet parity with regard to strategic nuclear weapons, especially in view of the deployment, begun in 1976, of the SS-20s – a new generation of Soviet missiles targeted on Western Europe (Garthoff 1985: 856, 870–86).

NATO in 1977 began to study the need to deploy missiles that could reach Soviet targets from bases in Western Europe; this was considered important to avoid the 'decoupling' of the US deterrent (Garthoff 1985: 854–65, SIPRI 1982: 26). This led on to the famous 'two-track decision' of December 1979. One 'track' was to prepare for deployment within 4 years of 108 Pershing IIs in Germany and a total of 464 Tomahawk cruise missiles in 5 NATO countries. The other 'track' was for the USA to negotiate with the Soviet Union about reductions in intermediate-range missiles. The idea was not to strive for an agreement eliminating such missiles from Europe: some NATO deployment was considered necessary in any event (Haslam 1990: 105; Talbott 1985: 39).

The negotiations came to be conducted in two phases. The first phase, which began in 1980, ended in November 1983 when the deployment of NATO's missiles began and Soviet representatives walked out of the talks. The second phase began in March 1985 and resulted in the signing of the INF Treaty in December 1987.

While this went on in government quarters, remarkable developments occurred in public opinion. The movement of public protest against nuclear weapons arising at the end of the 1970s was unprecedented. It originated in Northwestern Europe but spread to other parts of the continent as well as to North America, Japan, Australia, and New Zealand. Singularly spectacular rallies were held in many cities. Established institutions such as churches and unions played a leading part, and it was common for political parties to take steps to accommodate this vast opinion (Everts 1990; Robertson 1992; Rochon 1988; Wittner 1988).

The anti-nuclear weapons movement – alternatively called the peace movement and the anti-missile protest in what follows – satisfied both criteria for an 'international' opinion: it was concerned with an international issue, and it was held in very many countries. It may be argued that the protesters had little in common except their dislike of nuclear weapons; if what appeared as a unified movement was in fact a loose coalition of diverse organizations and views, it may be misleading to speak of a single international opinion. Still there was a common element, and it would be peculiar not to regard this wide-ranging expression of concern with the nuclear arms race as a single opinion, especially since the participating organizations tended to work together and to be perceived as a single phenomenon by others as well as by themselves.

This opinion was international not merely in terms of its object and scope but also with regard to the dynamics of its formation; this was an instance not just of an international opinion but also of international opinion formation. Peace movement documents included myriads of references to peace campaigners abroad. Foreign participants were a standard feature of the rallies (36 groups from 11 foreign countries participated in the Bonn demonstrations of October 1981). Many of the peace groups belonged to international organizations or networks and participated in international conferences of activists. The Campaign for Nuclear Disarmament (CND), although essentially a British organization, had strong transnational features.[9] Moreover, the churches, which were important both as participants in the movement and as arenas for its activities, had their own international networks (Robertson 1992: 43–4). It is difficult to envisage a better example of what internationalists have in mind when they put their faith in the transnational mobilization of a non-official opinion in support of peace and security.

This remarkable event will now be set against the propositions introduced earlier in the present chapter. The propositions are meant as ideal types to which a case such as that of the INF negotiations may be compared in all its complexity and ambiguity, thus facilitating the task of assessing the plausibility of internationalist assumptions about opinion formation as a feature of international politics.

The protest[10]

The occurrence of the anti-nuclear protest supports Proposition I, according to which there is a significant probability that unbiased international opinions will be formed – but only insofar as the opinion was in fact unbiased, and only insofar as nation-specific factors did not interfere with the process of opinion formation. The issue is therefore the extent to which there is evidence in support not just of Proposition I but also of Propositions II and III.

Biases?

Proposition II is that opinion formation on international issues is systematically biased. A case to the effect that there was a systematic bias in the international opinion against nuclear weapons would rest on three assumptions, it appears: (1) there was a demand for unilateral Western concessions and not for mutual and agreed disarmament; (2) this asymmetry was due to media coverage; and (3) this coverage was misleading. None of these assumptions is easy to substantiate.

The common denominator of the peace movement was the protest against the NATO's intended deployment of Pershing II and cruise missiles. A nuclear freeze was what many demanded: the West was urged to compensate neither for the large deployment of Soviet ICBMs that had taken place in the 1970s, nor for the on-going Soviet deployment of SS-20s aimed at Western Europe. Indeed, when in 1981 the United States launched a proposal for a 'zero solution', by which there were to be no intermediate-range land-based missiles on either side, this was rejected by anti-nuclear activists as unrealistic or unfair (there will be more about the 'zero solution' below). Those who perceived the peace movement as opposing Western but not Soviet nuclear weapons had a point.

This was not the whole story, however. Peace movement activities often indicated an opposition to nuclear weapons in general, both Soviet and Western, even though the immediate objective was to stop NATO from deploying more of theirs. More fundamentally, what was known as the peace movement comprised organizations and groups with different ideological traditions (Everts 1990: 21–2) and differing conceptions of how to bring about peace (Robertson 1990; Rochon 1988: 21). Furthermore, consciousness-raising and information rather than traditional political activity was the preferred tactic of much of the peace movement (Robertson 1992: 58–9), and less precision about what one wants to attain is called for in the former case than in the latter.

Indeed, in the perspective of 'new social movement' theory, much of the peace movement was engaged in 'neo-romantic protest' against Western civilization and industrial growth. Seen in this way, the Pershing II and cruise missiles were merely symbols of a greater malaise, and the anti-nuclear protest was directed against 'the instrumental rationality of the apparatus of domination' rather than against the deployment of 572 missiles (see Robertson 1992: 51). The bottom line is the difficulty of determining what was in fact the precise standpoint of the peace movement with regard to nuclear weapons.

As regards media coverage, we may depart from an assertion commonly made at the time to the effect that the peace movement was inspired, supported, and exploited by the Kremlin (e.g. Clemens 1985). These efforts may have gained support from the propensity of Western mass media to dramatize and personalize politics and hence to emphasize the destructiveness of nuclear weapons, near-accidents in surveillance systems, and Ronald Reagan's trigger-happiness rather than the fact of Soviet rearmament. Was this in fact the case?

What we know about this matter is that the Soviet Union did use the World Peace Council to promote what it conceived as a 'peace offensive' in the West (Haslam 1990: 111–12, 115–17, 125). Whether it was successful in this endeavour is a different matter. So far as media coverage of the nuclear weapons issue is concerned, there seems to be no evidence that can be cited. Assuming that the anti-nuclear opinion was in fact unilateralist to the detriment of the West, it remains to be investigated whether this may have been due to the way in which Western media reported the issue or whether it was for other reasons.

Suppose for the sake of the argument that there was in fact a tendency in the media to emphasize whatever might suggest that nuclear war was approaching and to ignore information suggesting that deterrence remained necessary and was likely to work. Would this imply that media coverage was misleading? That would not be easy to determine. It is a truism that it is difficult to compare media reporting with reality because it is difficult to determine what 'reality' is like. It has been argued that since nuclear war had become far less likely than previously by the 1980s, the anti-nuclear opinion was based on an irrational Third World War scare (Sabin 1986). Reasonable and knowledgeable men and women can disagree about this, however. The issue at bottom is whether nuclear deterrence is easy or difficult, as Buzan has put it (Buzan 1987: 167–72), and this has long defined a fundamental division among strategic analysts. There just is no way of determining whether the anti-nuclear opinion of the 1980s was biased in the way Proposition II suggests.

National differences?

Proposition III is that opinions on international issues tend to be nation-specific. This was not literally the case with regard to the INF issue; if it had been, there would have been no international opinion to consider. The image of a broad opinion putting forward the same anti-nuclear demands across the Western world may have been exaggerated, however. The more nation-specific factors interfered with the process of opinion formation, the less persuasive the claim that this event demonstrates the plausibility of the theory of internationalism.

Alexa Robertson has compared organized anti-missile opinion in the UK and West Germany and has shown that there were significant differences (Robertson 1992: 55–62). Remember that it was a matter of public opinion in two neighbouring countries responding to what was precisely the same issue: NATO's decision to deploy intermediate-range missiles in both countries in response to a presumed common threat. In spite of this, the activities spearheaded by the Campaign for Nuclear Disarmament (CND) in the UK[11] were different in several ways from those of the efforts coordinated by the *Koordinationsasschuß* in West Germany. Not only did they differ in focus; the former were less successful than the latter.

The CND tended to operate as a traditional single-issue pressure group militating for nuclear disarmament by the use of conventional political methods such as lobbying, petitioning, and appealing to the government and the political parties. The *Koordinationsasschuß*, on the other hand, was a loose collection of groups with a variety of objectives and with a preference for non-traditional political methods. What is more, whereas the CND focused on nuclear disarmament, West German activists tended to link this issue to broader concerns. In particular, they viewed their protest as a defence of democracy and humanism. As Günter Grass put it, '[a] people that after fifty years is still suffering the consequences of its failure to resist Hitler's seizure of power ought to have learned to recognize different but comparable dangers before it is too late and thus look upon the right to resist as a democratic imperative' (Grass 1987: 141). Thus the characterization of the anti-nuclear protest as a 'new social movement' in the sense of a protest against Western society in general, while not irrelevant in the case of the UK was more pertinent in the West German case. These were dissimilar phenomena.

They also differed in the degree to which they succeeded in mobilizing popular and organized opinion in support of their aims. Robertson conceptualizes this in terms of the concept of salience, defined in terms of 'conspicuousness' and 'importance' (Robertson 1992: 9). She argues that the anti-nuclear opinion in West Germany was more salient than that in the UK in both respects. It was more conspicuous in that it attracted more attention and led to a deeper and more forceful public debate, and it was more important in the sense that it was perceived as the more capable of changing established patterns of domestic politics and foreign policy. There was an increasing questioning of NATO membership in the German debate, whereas nobody took the possibility of British neutrality seriously.

The difference can be substantiated in several ways. By 1982 and 1983, when the protests culminated, polls showed Germans to be far more favourable toward the peace movement and its ideas than British respondents (Table 3.3). The assumption that this was related to peace movement activities gains support from the fact that time series data show British attitudes to be more stable than German views: whereas Germans unexpectedly became more optimistic about international relations and less fearful of nuclear war as soon as the deployment of NATO missiles had begun and the protests had ceased, no similar change occurred among the British.[12] Organized opinion thus appears to have had a greater, albeit a temporary, impact on popular opinion in West Germany than in the UK.

So far as the mobilization of organized opinion is concerned we may first consider the churches. Churchmen came to play an important part

Table 3.3 Views about nuclear weapons and the peace movement in West Germany and the United Kingdom

	West Germany	UK
Perception of international relations, Oct. 1982 (% 'troubled' – % 'peaceful')[a]	+46	+23
Fear of nuclear weapons is among the 'greatest concerns for yourself and your country', March 1993 (%)[b]	42	32
Support for deployment, Oct. 1983 (%)[c]	39	62
View of peace movement, April 1982 (% approve – % disapprove)[d]	+36	−6

Notes:
[a] Eurobarometer 18, cited from Robertson 1991: 14
[b] Den Oudsten 1988: 11
[c] Robertson 1991: 29–30
[d] Eurobarometer 17, cited from Robertson 1992: 64–5

in the European peace movement during the 1980s, and the churches came to form an important battlefield in the anti-missile struggle. Protestant churches proved to be more receptive to the peace movement than catholic churches in both West Germany and the UK. However, whereas the Lutheran Church in West Germany decided to sanction steps toward unilateral nuclear disarmament, the Church of England Synod rejected unilateralism and took the position that it remained the government's duty to maintain forces adequate to guard against nuclear blackmail (Robertson 1992, ch. 3).

The Socialist parties – the SPD in West Germany, Labour in the UK – formed another battlefield. Both had pro-NATO leaders at the end of the 1970s. Both included sizeable groups critical of traditional stances on NATO and nuclear deterrence. Both, furthermore, came to adopt policies acceding to the demands of anti-nuclear activists: a Labour Party conference in 1980 committed the party to unilateral disarmament, and a SPD conference in 1983 came out against the deployment of NATO missiles and called for a nuclear-weapon-free zone in Central Europe.

Still there were differences between British and West German politics. In the SPD, the change in nuclear weapons policy heralded a break with the past. The Atlanticist Helmut Schmidt was dethroned, and the party set out to integrate peace movement issues with their programme and to win over public opinion in support of them. It did this in competition with another party, the Greens, that had made it into the Bundestag and was a radical presence in the peace movement. A West German government depending for its survival on the support of peace movement causes was within the realm of the possible.

The Labour party did not have to depose its leader, since CND supporter Michael Foot had already replaced Atlanticist James Callaghan by 1980. It had instead to contend with its right wing, which finally left it to set up a party of its own. Labour was thus challenged from the right instead of the left. Furthermore, Labour had little hope of influencing governmental policy other than by winning an election, and this it resoundingly failed to do. After having suffered its worst electoral defeat ever in 1983, losing to a conservative party led by such a staunch supporter of nuclear deterrence as Mrs Thatcher rather than to a moderate advocate of a continued *Ostpolitik* like Dr Kohl, unilateralism was played down at the 1984 party conference and disappeared from the party platform later on. Thus, whereas the anti-nuclear opinion had a relatively lasting impact on West German politics and came within reach of political power, its intervention in British politics was a catastrophe (Robertson 1992, ch. 4).

This situation reflected the differences in foreign policy orientation: a non-nuclear, divided Germany, potentially a nuclear battlefield, on the one hand, a nuclear UK with its insular location and its special relationship with the USA, on the other. The process of opinion formation, furthermore, was affected by features of the respective political systems: proportional representation, a multiparty system, and coalition politics, on the one hand; majority voting, a two-party system, and single-party rule, on the other. Digging just a little deeper, the differences in the degree of success of anti-nuclear opinion formation parallelled a difference between post-1945 political culture in Germany and post-imperial sentiment in the UK: the motto *Nie wieder Krieg von deutschem Boden* came to be set against the values and emotions aroused by the Falklands war.[13]

A further observation is of particular interest from the point of view of opinion formation about international issues, and that is the existence of a substantial difference between West German and British mass media in their news coverage of the anti-nuclear protests. Alexa Robertson has made a detailed content analysis of four 'quality' newspapers (two liberal papers, *Frankfurter Rundschau* and *The Guardian*, and two conservative papers, *Frankfurter Allgemeine Zeitung* and *The Times*) during the 'Hot Autumn' of October and November 1983, when the anti-nuclear protests peaked. She has supplemented this with an examination of the way in which key events between October 1981 and November 1983 were reported in a wider sample of newspapers and in the ARD's *Tagesschau* and the BBC's *Nine O'Clock News* and *News Review*. The conclusions drawn on the basis of the former study were essentially confirmed and amplified by the latter (Robertson 1992, ch. 5). Among Robertson's findings are these:

1 War-and-peace news items were twice as common in the German quality papers than in the British. The number of such items per day in October–November 1983 was 11.3 in *Frankfurter Rundschau* and 9.5 in *Frankfurter Allgemeine Zeitung* as against 5.8 in *The Guardian* and 5.3 in *The Times* (p. 161).

2 What went on within the churches and in the socialist parties (SPD and Labour), whose support was essential for conferring respectability on the peace movement, was reported to a much larger extent in German than in British newspapers. For example. in October–November 1983, *Frankfurter Rundschau* included 1.1 items per day about the socialists and *Frankfurter Allgemeine Zeitung* 1.7, in contrast to The *Guardian* with 0.2 items per day and *The Times* with 0.3 (p. 164).

3 The amount of attention given to the peace movement was more

a function of ideology than of nation (pp. 165–6), but German coverage tended to be more favourable than British, regardless of ideology. For example, the law-and-order aspect of the protests (police intervention, security measures, court actions) was given far more attention in British than in German media (pp. 179–80). German and British media, furthermore, gave different images of what sort of people the protesters were. British media thus tended to portray the protesters largely as women, if not as incidental to the women's liberation movement, whereas German media pictured them as serious and knowledgeable people (clergy, Christians, trade unionists, professionals, writers, intellectuals, journalists, civil servants, politicians, and Nobel laureates; see Table 3.4).

4   The most profound difference noted by Robertson concerns the relationship between the peace movement and society. There was a tendency in British media to set nation and society against the protesters; comments were cited in which nuclear unilateralism was equated with the appeasement of Hitler in 1938. German media rather tended to present the anti-nuclear movement as a legitimate participant in the democratic process and suggested on occasion that the protests, rather than the missiles, were comparable with resistance against nazism, just as did Günter Grass in the speech quoted above (pp. 187–91).

Table 3.4   The sort of people identified as protesters in peace movement reports, October–November 1983 (per cent of total types identified in each paper)

	Frankfurter Rundschau	Frankfurter Allgemeine Zeitung	The Guardian	The Times
Women	11%	6%	46%	41%
Serious and knowledgeable people	38%	42%	25%	22%

Source: Robertson 1992: 181

The reason why British and German media differed in their coverage of the protests may have been that the British peace movement was in fact different from the German. The issue of nuclear weapons may have attracted different kinds of people and been defined in different ways in West Germany and the UK for reasons having to do with differences in foreign policy and domestic politics, as suggested previously.[14] A reason to hypothesize that the media nevertheless may have exerted an independent influence is the difference in journalistic tradition. British and West German journalists have been found to differ in their role perception, 'a neutral role traditionally having greater importance in British journalism and a pronounced commitment to journalism-of-opinion characterizing German journalism' (Köcher 1986: 60, quoted from Robertson 1992: 146). This goes along with the characterization of West German mass media as generally more politicized than media in Britain. Differences such as these may have made British media likely to report on war and peace and on the anti-nuclear protests in a conventional and apparently detached fashion, whereas West German media may have been more likely to question established policies and to take the side of whom they defined as the underdogs.

It may not be possible to distinguish between media and other influences on opinion formation in this fashion, however. All three background variables discussed in this chapter – foreign policy, domestic politics, and the media – may interact with each other and reinforce each other. Maybe they are best seen as three aspects of a single phenomenon: national political culture in an extended sense.

Seen from this perspective, the media reflect as well as reinforce international-political and domestic-political influences on the formation of opinions about international issues. Their combined influence on opinion formation is threefold: they jointly determine whether an opinion will be formed in a country in response to an international situation or event; what direction it will take if formed; and the extent to which original opinion-holders will succeed in mobilizing others in support of their views. Because political cultures differ, a situation or event will have different repercussions in different countries. A given situation or event is likely to evoke a response only in some countries, and an international opinion that is formed about this situation or event; will be weaker and less international as a consequence. Furthermore, the national opinions that will in fact be formed will be dissimilar, and this will make the resulting international opinion – the lowest common denominator – more of a general mood than a specific demand.

This seems a reasonable interpretation of what took place in public opinion with regard to nuclear weapons in the early 1980s. Thus the final conclusion of this section is that a substantial international opinion was in fact formed about a crucial war-and-peace issue (Proposition I), that it is difficult to determine the extent to which it was biased (Proposition II), and that nation-specific factors intervened to make it weaker and less coherent than it might have been (Proposition III). Whether this reflects a general pattern cannot be determined on the basis of a single case.

The impact of the protest

The mobilization of an international opinion against nuclear weapons coincided, more or less, with the first phase of the INF negotiations. The USA and the Soviet Union came to negotiate about nuclear weapons against the background of escalating anti-nuclear protests. The climate was different during the second phase: after NATO had begun to deploy the missiles with which the protests had primarily been concerned, the peace movement ceased to be a 'coalition movement' and returned to being essentially a 'prophetic minority' (Everts 1990: 22–4). Thus the accommodative phase of the negotiations did not begin until the protesters had gone home. Whether this indicates a causal relationship or was a coincidence will now be considered.

Some of the main bargaining events during the first phase were these:

The freeze proposal On 23 February 1981, Brezhnev took the opportunity of the 26th Party Congress in Moscow to announce a Soviet proposal for a moratorium on the deployment of 'new nuclear missile systems of medium range' in Europe, that is, a 'freeze in quantitative and qualitative terms' of the existing level of such systems, 'including, of course, the USA's forward-based systems in this region'. The Soviet Union presumed that both sides would end 'all preparations towards the deployment of corresponding supplementary systems, including the American missiles, "Pershing-2", and strategic ground-launched Cruise missiles' (Haslam 1990: 111).

The zero option Some of Ronald Reagan's people thought that the two-track decision (the commitment to negotiate, not the decision to deploy new missiles if negotiations failed) had been a mistake, but the new president decided, under European pressure, to resume negotiations with the Soviet Union (Haslam 1990: 110–12, SIPRI 1982: 38; Talbott 1985: 43–9). When preparing for the negotiations, the Reagan administration came to make a major change in the American position. The idea of a *Null-Lösung* (no land-based, intermediate-range missiles on either side) had been discussed within the West German Social Democratic Party (Haslam 1990: 113; Talbott 1985: 56). Even though 'heavily loaded to Soviet disadvantage' (Garthoff 1985: 1023–4), it failed to solve the problem of 'decoupling' that had prompted the two-track decision and was first opposed by both the State Department and Pentagon.[15] Both came to accept it later on, however, and the controversy in Washington came to concern 'zero plus' versus 'zero only'. 'Zero plus', which was advocated by the State Department, meant that the USA should remain committed to equal limits on land-based intermediate-range missiles; the new element was to be the proposal that the limit be set at the lowest possible level and preferably, but not necessarily, at zero. However, 'zero only', which was a more radical departure from the original position and was favoured by the Pentagon, won the debate in Washington.[16]

Reagan launched the 'zero option' in a speech given on 18 November 1981. The key sentence was simple: the USA 'is prepared to cancel its deployment of Pershing II and ground-launched [cruise] missiles if the Soviets will dismantle their SS-20, SS-4 and SS-5 missiles' (Haslam 1990: 113; SIPRI 1982: 39; Talbott 1985: 80).

The Soviet proposal for moratorium cum denuclearization The Soviet reply was given on 23 November by Brezhnev to an audience in Bonn and elaborated in an announcement by the Soviet Government a week later. It amounted to a four-point amplification of the Soviet freeze proposal: (1) a moratorium on the deployment of medium-range weapons in Europe; (2) negotiations toward 'substantial reductions'; (3) a reduction to zero of all medium-range systems 'threatening Europe'; and (4) the elimination from Europe of shorter-range nuclear weapons. Brezhnev also offered an initial unilateral Soviet reduction if there were agreement on a moratorium (Haslam 1990: 113–14; SIPRI 1982: 39; Talbott 1985: 90). The proposal, as seen from the vantage point of Western defence ministries, would deprive France and Great Britain of their nuclear capability and 'decouple' Europe from the United States while retaining for the Soviet Union superiority in conventional forces and a large nuclear arsenal.

When the negotiations were resumed, the Soviet side further amplified Brezhnev's plan. They added, among other things, a proposal for gradual reductions of medium-range systems in 1985 and 1990 to levels high enough to let the British and French keep theirs (SIPRI 1983: 10–11; Talbott 1985: 95–6). The need to retain compensation for French and British systems had by now become the centrepiece of the Soviet position: the USSR might be prepared to go to zero, albeit keeping enough to offset the British and French forces (Haslam 1990: 118; Talbott 1985: 106).

A unilateral Soviet moratorium In March 1982, Brezhnev announced a unilateral moratorium on the deployment of medium-range weapons in the European part of the Soviet Union. Western governments maintained that the Soviet Union did not live up to this promise (SIPRI 1983: 9–10; Dean 1987: 131).

The Walk-in-the-Woods episode There was little movement during the first half-year of the resumed negotiations. An attempt made in mid-1982 by the chief US negotiator, Paul Nitze, to break the deadlock resulted in the famous Walk-in-the-Woods episode. Nitze and his Soviet counterpart Yuli Kvitsinsky made a secret, tentative agreement by which 75 SS-20s would be retained in Europe to be matched by 75 Tomahawks. No Pershing IIs would be deployed and this was significant, since the Soviet side considered the Pershing IIs to be particularly threatening (Haslam 1990: 123; Talbott 1985: 126–8).

This very feature of the Nitze-Kvitsinsky agreement proved to be Ronald Reagan's chief objection to it. The final US decision was taken at a meeting of the National Security Council on 13 September 1982, during which the president concluded that any compromise would have to retain Pershing IIs (Talbott 1985: 142–7). The deal was thereupon also rejected by the Soviet Union, the main reason apparently being the failure to include British and French forces (Haslam 1990: 124).

Andropov's offer On 21 December 1982, Yuri Andropov, the new Soviet leader, offered to reduce the number of Soviet medium-range missiles in Europe to the level of the French and British missile forces, if there were no NATO deployment (Haslam 1990: 127; Talbott 1985: 61–2).

Reagan's interim proposal There was by now an increasing European pressure on the United States to compromise with the zero option. NATO's Secretary General told a news conference in late 1982 that 'we never said [the zero option] was the only solution' (SIPRI 1983: 15). In West Germany, the SPD began to suggest that it was not unreasonable to take British and French forces into account (Haslam 1990: 127). During the West German election campaign in early 1983, Foreign Minister Hans-Dietrich Genscher began to advocate a *Zwischenlösung*, an interim solution, with equal ceilings at a level above zero, and CSU leader Franz Josef Strauss dismissed the zero solution as unattainable if not absurd. Margaret Thatcher also suggested that in the absence of zero, a 'balance' had to be sought at a higher level (Haslam 1990: 127–9; Talbott 1985: 172). After winning the election, West German Chancellor Helmut Kohl concluded that a compromise was possible and that the USA had to move; a similar message came from London (SIPRI 1983: 15; Talbott 1985: 177–8).

Accordingly, on 30 March, Reagan announced what was termed a new proposal. He repeated that so far as intermediate-range missiles in Europe were concerned, 'it would be better to have none than to have some'. He added, however, that he hoped that the Soviet Union would join the United States in an interim agreement that would reduce these forces to equal levels on both sides. Thus Reagan substituted 'zero plus' for 'zero only'. The offer was rejected in Moscow. The United States, for its part, kept rejecting demands for the postponement of deployment (Talbott 1985: 181–7).

In the last hectic weeks, both sides did what they could to see to it that blame was put on the adversary (Dean 1987: 133–5; Talbott 1985: 197–205). On 22 November, however, the Bundestag approved the deployment of Pershing IIs, and the next day the first missiles reached a US brigade at Mutlangen. The Soviet side discontinued the negotiations and lifted its moratorium. The first phase of the negotiations was over.

The second phase began fifteen months later, after the Soviet Union had given up its refusal to negotiate as long as NATO missiles were deployed. A new factor was the United States' SDI programme; the Soviet Union initially made an INF treaty contingent on an agreement prohibiting weapons in space. In the new round of negotiations, both sides initially took up positions on the INF issue similar to those they had held in 1983 (Dean 1987: 139; Haslam 1990: 152–3). Some of the steps leading from there to the INF treaty were the following:

Moratorium on the deployment of SS 20s On 7 April 1985, Mikhail Gorbachev announced a unilateral moratorium on the deployment of further medium-range missiles in Europe and urged the USA to do the same (Dean 1987: 139–140; Haslam 1990: 152).

Gorbachev in Paris On 3 October 1985, in a speech to the French National Assembly, Gorbachev announced that the Soviet Union would render non-operational its SS-20s capable of reaching Western Europe in excess of the number deployed in November 1983. He also suggested separate negotiations about British and French forces and indicated a willingness to set the INF problem apart from the issue of space weapons (Dean 1987: 140; Haslam 1990: 157).

Gorbachev's proposal for nuclear disarmament. On 15 January 1986, Gorbachev published a proposal for eliminating all nuclear weapons in three stages. The first stage would include 'the complete elimination of medium-range missiles of the USSR and the USA in the European zone' – the zero option. This was a major Soviet concession insofar as the insistence on compensation for existing British and

French nuclear forces was dropped. However, Great Britain and France were to 'pledge not to build up their respective nuclear arsenals', and the USA would 'undertake not to transfer its strategic and medium-range missiles to other countries'. There was US interest in the proposal but it was rejected at European insistence (Dean 1987: 143–7; Haslam 1985: 159–62; SIPRI 1987: 326–7).

Compensation dropped A breakthrough came during Soviet-American meetings in August and September 1986: the Soviet side definitely dropped its insistence that French and British nuclear forces be taken into account in an INF agreement (Haslam 1990: 165; SIPRI 1987: 329).

The Reykjavik summit At the summit meeting in Reykjavik on 11–12 October 1986, Gorbachev proposed an agreement to set a global limit of 100 missiles on each side, with no missiles deployed in Europe. British and French forces would not be included in the agreement, which Gorbachev characterized as a 'very big concession'. Reagan accepted this, as well as Gorbachev's proposal for cutting strategic nuclear weapons by half in five years. However, Gorbachev also proposed an ABM treaty which would put an end to the SDI programme and insisted that this was an 'organic' part of the package. This Reagan refused to accept (Carter 1989: 209–10; Haslam 1990: 166–7).

Final Soviet concessions In February 1987, Gorbachev dropped the link between INF and SDI. In March the Soviet side accepted on-site inspections. In April they agreed to a global zero. Verification procedures were negotiated, and the treaty was signed in December (Carter 1989: 210, 215–16; Haslam 1990: 169–72).

The INF negotiations were complex; only the barest outline has been provided here. The main course of events was obvious, however. The Reagan administration changed the US position fundamentally at an early date when adopting 'zero only' and then modified it only marginally. The Soviet Union, on the other hand, conducted a gradual retreat from its original stance and finally accepted 'zero only'.[17] The result was an agreement to destroy about 850 US and 1,750 Soviet missiles – the first nuclear disarmament treaty.

The precise role that international public opinion played in the considerations of the two sides during the INF negotiations cannot be determined on the basis of the available source material. However, something can be said about the extent to which each of Propositions Ia,

IIa, and IIIa is compatible with what took place. Was this international opinion effective, irrelevant, or counter-productive?

Effective?

An interpretation of the INF case in support of Proposition Ia, according to which international opinions are effective, begins with the failure to deploy the so-called neutron bomb in 1977. This incident demonstrated to the NATO governments that there was reason to expect an uproar against any deployment of new nuclear weapons. In the absence of this demonstration the two-track decision might not have been dual: NATO might have decided on deployment without even proposing to negotiate with the Soviet Union about the matter. If public opinion had not been mobilized against the two-track decision, furthermore, the Reagan administration would have postponed the negotiations for a long time or even indefinitely (Haslam 1990: 110); or the negotiations would have been interrupted earlier and would not have been resumed; or the Soviet Union would not have realized the futility of continuing to fuel the arms race; or the United States would not have adhered to the zero option once it became clear that the Soviet government was about to accept it. Thus an international opinion against nuclear armaments proved to be effective in causing the superpowers to produce an outcome in accordance with its demands.

The main evidence in support of this interpretation is the correlation between public demand and political result. There are two problems with it, however: the difficulty of determining whether the INF Treaty was what had been demanded, and the ease with which the outcome can be explained in other ways.

Thus, as we have seen, what was known as the peace movement in the singular form comprised organizations, groups, and individuals of different ideological traditions and with different national perspectives. True, there was the common denominator of opposition to the deployment of NATO missiles; the INF Treaty accorded with this demand. The treaty also scrapped the SS-20s, however, and in this regard the demand of the anti-nuclear opinion was more difficult to determine.

A symmetrical stance was taken by those who protested against the nuclear arms race as such and demanded that the parties do whatever it took to reverse it. The INF Treaty was clearly a success from their point of view, but only from their point of view. Otherwise the question of success or failure was less clear.

A genuinely asymmetrical stance on the INF issue was justified in several different ways. Some opposed NATO's projected deployment because of their conviction that the specific features of the missiles that NATO planned to deploy, especially the Pershing IIs, made them more destabilizing than other nuclear weapons; those who took this position had reason to be satisfied with the final outcome, since the specific missiles to which they were opposed were among those to be destroyed. For others the objective was less to stop nuclear armaments than to weaken NATO; they cannot have been satisfied with watching the Soviet Union capitulate and accept an American proposal. Still others accepted the Soviet claim that there existed a nuclear balance in Europe by 1980, that this balance would be upset if the NATO missiles were deployed, and that these missiles were motivated by the destabilizing nuclear designs of the United States; such a well-known institution as the Stockholm International Peace Research Institute (SIPRI) maintained that the rationale of the missiles was to increase the strategic threat to the USSR in accordance with the countervailing strategy (SIPRI 1982: 29–34). From their point of view, presumably, the INF Treaty had both advantages and disadvantages; the US was deprived of its missiles, but what they took to be an East–West balance was to be undermined by parallel disarmament on the part of the USSR.

There remained those who did not oppose the NATO missiles per se but thought it necessary to cancel deployment in order for Soviet-Western arms reductions to be possible. The Soviet Union, during the first phase of the bargaining, offered to talk if there was a moratorium on deployment and refused to talk if the missiles were deployed; part of the public demanded that the offer be accepted. This was archetypical spurious asymmetry: a unilateral measure was advocated as a means to obtain a bilateral result and not because it was considered to be valuable in itself.[18] Those who took this position joined forces with those who opposed the zero solution, but not because they found a zero solution *à la* Ronald Reagan to be unfair or destabilizing but because they were convinced that the Soviet Union would never accept it and that arms control would suffer. Much of the opposition to the deployment of NATO missiles would seem to have been of this kind. These people won a tactical defeat but a strategic victory, as it were: their objective was attained but by means they had taken to the streets to protest. It is paradoxical to regard the implementation of a proposal (the zero solution) as a victory for those who have worked against it.

The variety of views about the objective to be attained thus complicates the task of determining whether the anti-nuclear movement was effective. The other problem for Proposition I is that the outcome (the INF Treaty) can be explained convincingly without reference to an international opinion. I am referring, of course, to *perestroika*. A common assumption is that the state of the Soviet economy made détente and arms reductions imperative for the Soviet government, that this motivated major departures from previous foreign-policy positions, and that one was to withdraw opposition to the zero solution. The 'new thinking' in Soviet foreign policy, in another interpretation, resulted from the fact that the people Gorbachev brought with him (Eduard Shevardnadze, Aleksandr Yakovlev, the 'institutchiks') were inspired by Western centre-left politicians and peace researchers to oppose the politics of the Brezhnev period and to adopt the notion of 'common security' (Risse-Kappen 1991); this influence, rather than problems in the Soviet economy, produced the turnabout on the INF issue, according to one line of thought. Still the explanatory factor is something other than the mobilization of an international opinion.

It has been suggested that by the time the Soviet Union had accepted the zero option, European governments had returned to their fear of 'decoupling' and that they would have opposed the treaty, if it had not been for the the fact that public opinion welcomed it (Carter 1989: 226; Everts 1990: 97–8). What can be said about this is that, regardless of public opinion, it would have been difficult for the United States to withdraw from a position it had itself proposed and to which it had committed itself as strongly as the zero option. Gorbachev is reported to have reproached Reagan at the Reykjavik summit for suggesting to abandon his own proposal (Haslam 1990: 166). Once the Soviet Union had accepted the zero option, the INF Treaty would seem to have been more or less inevitable, with or without second thoughts on the part of governments in Western Europe.

Irrelevant?

Proposition IIa was clearly disconfirmed by the INF case. It is debatable whether public opinion was effective in this case, but this is not to say that it failed to produce effects. The evidence is strong that the perception of public opinion in Western Europe had an impact on the US side, and it has been common to interpret the first phase of the negotiations as a struggle over public opinion.

First and foremost, the zero option was launched with public opinion uppermost in the minds of the Reagan administration. The object was to appease the anti-missile movement and to make deployment politically easier for the European governments; what made it acceptable was the conviction that the Soviet Union would reject it. It was launched in a way that made it clear to whom it was directed. The date – 18 November 1981 – was determined by the fact that Brezhnev was about to begin a visit to West Germany. The occasion was such an important public event as the delivery of a speech to the National Press Club in Washington. The speech was held at 10 am – late afternoon in Europe. The US International Communication Agency paid for live satellite transmission (Haslam 1990: 113; Talbott 1985: 79–80; see also Risse-Kappen 1991).

Brezhnev replied a few days later by calling for a moratorium on deployment in the city that was becoming the focus of the peace movement, namely, Bonn. He received a sympathetic hearing in the West German opposition, and leading people such as Willy Brandt now indicated that the deployment deadline might be extended. Helmut Schmidt is reported to have told Paul Nitze that if no progress had been made by the autumn of 1982, West European support for deployment, and even for US policy generally, would crumble. This prompted Nitze to take the initiative that led on to the Walk-in-the-Woods deal. Nitze appears to have thought that European popular opposition to deployment might paralyse NATO and to have argued in the White House that the Walk-in-the-Woods deal was a good one because it would defuse European opposition to deployment (Talbott 1985: 90–2, 116–18, 131, 136).

After the deal had been rejected, concern grew in Washington over European perceptions of the USA as overly intransigent. Soviet moves were thought to reinforce the impression that while the Soviet Union was searching for a compromise, the USA refused to contribute (Talbott, 1985: 153, 161–6, 181–7). Both the British and the West German governments appeared to need US flexibility for domestic-political reasons, and a modification of the US position was urged by top leaders in both countries. The softening of the zero option announced in early 1983 was a response to European demands for a *Zwischenlösung* (Haslam 1990: 127–9; SIPRI 1983: 15; Talbott 1985: 172, 177–8).

This should suffice as a reminder of what most observers have taken for granted, namely, that some of the main moves during the INF negotiations were motivated by concern over public opinion. Public opinion, far from being insignificant, was a major factor in the INF case.

Counter-productive?

There is a correspondence between the two phases of the INF negotiations and the division of bargaining into a coercive phase and an accommodative phase. A case can be made that as long as the Soviet Union had reason to believe that Western opinion would prevent NATO from carrying out its projected deployment of intermediate-range missiles, it had no reason to concede anything; the United States, by the same token, had reason to demonstrate intransigence. Both had reason to conceal their intransigence behind posturing designed to mislead public opinion; the process was prolonged by the uncertainty about the strategic implications of an on-going mobilization of support for ill-defined demands. Only after NATO had demonstrated its firmness, some NATO missiles were in place, and the public had resigned or lost interest, could accommodation be substituted for posturing (Carter 1989: 223). According to this interpretation, then, the mobilization of public opinion against nuclear weapons was counterproductive in the sense of complicating the negotiations and delaying the agreement.

Public posturing did characterize the first phase of the negotiations. There can be little doubt that the public features of the negotiations made it difficult to come to an agreement.[19] However, the rejection of the Walk-in-the-Woods deal suggests that quiet diplomacy might not have succeeded either. One must not lose sight of the intricacy of the substantive issue: the Reagan administration and the Brezhnev government considered the matter to be so important and defined their respective interests so differently that it would have been difficult to arrive at a mutually acceptable compromise in any case – unless and until one side fundamentally revised its entire outlook, which of course is what happened later on (this point is made in Risse-Kappen 1991).

The suggestion that the mobilization of public opinion discouraged concessions applies to the Soviet Union in the first instance. We know that the Soviet Union actively used the World Peace Council to promote a 'peace offensive' in the West (Haslam 1990: 111–12, 115–17, 125). We also know that it was feared in Washington that because of Western European opinion, the USSR would merely have to prolong the talks and the NATO missiles would never be deployed (Talbott 1985: 91). It has been argued, furthermore, that the neutron bomb episode affected Soviet thinking about the new missiles: in 1977, public protests fuelled in part by the World Peace Council had caused President Carter to retreat, and there was reason to believe that the success could be repeated and that deployment of new missiles could be prevented by combining negotiations with propaganda. It is argued in the literature that Soviet bargaining behaviour during the first phase of the INF negotiations resulted from a failure to realize the weakness of the Soviet position and that this failure was due to illusions about the strength and impact of the peace movement in Western Europe (Haslam 1990: 96–105, 110, 139). There is evidence suggesting that as late as the Reykjavik summit meeting, Gorbachev calculated that West European opinion would turn against Reagan's refusal to give up the SDI project and that there was surprise in Moscow when West European governments proved to be relieved that no INF agreement was made (Haslam 1990: 167–8).

Most of this is inferential, however. I have no direct evidence supporting the contention that the Kremlin abstained from making significant concessions because public opinon in the West was thought to make them unnecessary. Nor have I found anything to prove that the White House turned down compromise proposals for fear of appearing to give in to public opinion; when Reagan rejected the Walk-in-the-Woods formula, this seems to have been for other reasons (Talbott 1985: 142–4). The final Soviet turnabout, furthermore, need not have been due to the failure of public opinion to prevent NATO from deploying the new missiles; *perestroika*, of which the acceptance of the zero solution was a part, was likely to have been due to other factors. It seems obvious that the anti-nuclear opinion complicated the negotiations and increased the difficulty of coming to a result, but it cannot be confirmed that the effect was dramatic.

Summary

This interpretation of the INF case can be summarized thus. The mobilization of an international opinion had two effects in particular: it impaired the conditions for accommodative bargaining, on the one hand, but caused one party to launch the proposal that was incorporated in the final agreement, on the other. The former accords with Proposition IIIa and the latter essentially with Proposition Ia. This is not an illogical combination: it may be difficult for a third party to enforce his views on two adversaries without complicating their interaction in the short term.

A thought must be added, however. If it had not been for the unforeseen phenomenon of Gorbachev's 'new thinking', the complications introduced by massive public protest might have proven fatal to the negotiations; the Deadlock-type features of the situation might have been cemented rather than softened by the appearance of an international opinion (on the game of Deadlock see Snyder and Diesing 1977: 45–6, 124–9). The process had paradoxical features, moreover: the zero solution was proposed by the United States in the expectation that it would help the West European governments by appeasing public opinion but that it would be rejected by the Soviet Union and hence never implemented. Instead West European opinion turned against it – most of the major rallies took place after it had been put forward – while the Soviet Union came to accept it; the West European governments, for whose sake it had been launched, had second thoughts about it because of their fear of 'decoupling'; thus nobody was satisfied with the final result except some of those who had previously taken to the streets to protest against it. Unpredictability is a major lesson of the INF case. More about this in the next section.

World opinion and international peace: lessons from the INF case

It remains to consider what may be learnt from the case of the INF Treaty about the validity of the theory of internationalism. Two preliminaries must first be disposed of.

One is to emphasize that a strong international opinion was in fact formed in the INF case and that it had a major impact on superpower action with regard to a key issue in international politics. The least that can be said about this is that the feasibility of influencing world politics by international opinion formation has been convincingly demonstrated. This may be important enough. The INF case, as pointed out previously, is a difficult test of the assumption that international opinion matters, and therefore the rejection of Proposition IIa is significant. The contention that non-official international opinions do not matter when supreme national interests are at stake has been put into serious question.

The other preliminary is to take note of the reminder that the assumption of unbiased opinion formation is essentially untestable. A case may be made that the protesters overestimated the probability of nuclear war (this is my own view) or that they underestimated the extent to which Soviet missiles were a threat to the West; both errors of judgment may have been caused by biases in media reporting about war-and-peace issues, including a tendency on the part of the media to overdramatize and underanalyse. It is difficult to see how this could be proven, however, especially since deterrence theory is controversial among specialists.[20] For centuries internationalists have expressed themselves as if they took it for granted that public opinion is bound to be based on a correct understanding of the issues at the crucial moments. Whether this is in fact the case may be unknowable in a specific instance, as demonstrated by the INF case.

So much for the obvious. There are three further observations about the role of international opinion formation in world politics that may be made on the basis of the INF case. They relate to the diversity of political culture, the limited need for democracy, and the unpredictability of effects.

The diversity of political culture

Anti-missile opinion gained more salience in West Germany than in the United Kingdom in spite of the fact that both countries were faced with the same problem. The difference, it has been suggested here, can be traced back to a difference in political culture in an extended sense. Now if this was the case between countries as similar as West Germany and the UK, diversity in political culture would seem to be a major conditioner of the formation of international opinions, a main reason why the vision of a world opinion responding when needed to events and situations so as to uphold international peace and security may be unrealistic.

First of all, if political culture in an extended sense is important, there is reason to expect the propensity to respond to a situation or an event to vary between countries. Whereas in one country a small number of concerned opinion-holders may succeed in winning over a large part of organized opinion and maybe even a popular majority, thus putting their government under pressure, all of this may fail in another country, where opinion-holders may remain a small minority. In one country a peace movement may develop into a major 'coalition movement' under the pressure of what is perceived as a threatening development, while in another it remains a 'prophetic minority'. This sets a limit to the degree to which opinions may become international.

Second, even if people in several countries were to respond significantly and in a similar way to a situation or an event, they are likely to differ on detail, and 'details' are not always unimportant. Thus, whereas a specific demand may gain massive support in one country, public opinion in another may rest content with voicing an unspecified concern. To the extent that specific demands are put forward, moreover, they are likely to vary between countries. In particular, the supporting arguments may differ, and hence the quality of the message sent to decision-makers; *Nie wieder Krieg von deutschem Boden*, maybe the key to the success of the peace movement in West Germany, did little to move the public in countries where concerns were different. An international opinion – what the opinion in several countries has in common – is apt to be ambiguous or even inconsistent and to be more of a mood than a demand, to repeat a phrase already used.

Sizeable political coalitions consist of disparate elements. Every sizeable political opinion is a coalition. Add national differences in political culture, and it is easy to see why international opinions are even more likely than intranational ones to give voice to moods rather than demands.

These are thoughts suggested by the case of the INF Treaty. If they hold more generally we are approaching an outer limit of the internationalist programme. Internationalists cannot advocate homogeneity in political culture, if they are to remain true to their ideals. Their object is to safeguard peace and security in a system of diverse states; it is not the unrealistic one of replacing this system with a single world political culture. Indeed, internationalists may argue that their programme is being increasingly challenged by the emergence of a biased world media culture and that the preservation of pluralistic diversity is the only remedy. This testifies to the difficulty of making a system of independent states function in a way similar to a single nation without actually transforming it into one.

The limited need for democracy

The idea of large-scale autonomous opinion formation at the non-official level presumes a degree of political freedom for which democracy would seem to be a precondition. The more widespread the democratic form of government, the more plausible the expectation that strong international opinions will be formed when needed. This is obvious.

Is democracy equally necessary in order for a non-official international opinion to have an impact on governmental action? If yes, the internationalist programme arguably presumes not just widespread but universal democracy. International institutions can hardly be expected to remain effective, if non-compliance is costly only to some. Efforts to influence bargaining by opinion formation, by the same token, may have peculiar effects unless opinions are capable of influencing both sides. Internationalism presumes fairness, it may be argued, and fairness presumes that all states and not just some are accessible to manifestations of international concern.

There is something to be learned from the case of the INF Treaty in this regard. Asymmetry in political system was an essential feature of the INF case. It was widely argued at the time that because one side was democratic and the other authoritarian, the impact of the anti-nuclear protest was bound to be asymmetric regardless of whether this was the intention. What actually took place was less straightforward, however.

Presently available data suggest that the main reason why the anti-nuclear protests were thought to be important in Washington and Moscow was their presumed effect on the governments of the deployment countries in West Europe. The credibility of NATO's projected missile deployment was taken to be crucial, and public opinion in the deployment countries was taken to undermine its credibility – this appears to have been the chief way in which the mobilization of an international protest against nuclear weapons affected Soviet-American bargaining. The concern in Washington and Moscow was not primarily about what they themselves would 'look like in the eyes of world public opinion', as Mikhail Gorbachev put it to Margaret Thatcher (Gorbachev 1987: 245). They were more concerned about what the governments of the deployment countries would be like in the eyes of their respective domestic opinions and hence with the way in which their own behaviour would affect the domestic opinions of a handful of other countries.[21]

Assuming that the object of an international opinion is to influence the behaviour of one or several governments, this can be done in three different ways shown in Figure 3.4. The notion that world opinion is important often seems to imply that its impact is direct: the influencee listens to the message and is impressed by its substantive contents, its democratic authority, or its strategic significance. Believers in world opinion thus tend to presume that its role is comparable to that of public opinion in the domestic politics of democracies. When Proposition Ia was introduced earlier in this chapter, the implication of the argument was similar. The case for Proposition IIa is that the assumption that international opinion has a direct impact on governments is fallacious and that this is due to the structural differences between international and domestic politics.

Two indirect possibilities also exist, however. One, shown to the left

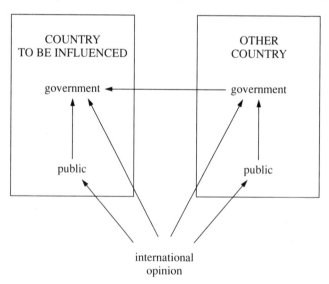

Figure 3.4 The direct and indirect impact of international opinions

in Figure 3.4, is that the influencee's own public is influenced by opinions from abroad and that this gives him a domestic-political, strategic incentive for doing what world opinion wants. The other, shown to the right in the figure, is that an international opinion has an impact, directly or indirectly, on other governments and that this in turn gives the influencee a strategic incentive to do what is demanded. An example of the former may be what many West Europeans tried to achieve when protesting against US warfare in Vietnam; an important idea was to change United States policy by supporting the anti-war movement inside the US. The INF case is an example of the latter.

Judging from the INF experience, then, an international opinion may matter primarily because of its role as the domestic opinion of governments that are important to the influencee. In each situation some governments are more important than others; opinions matter to the extent that they can influence or constrain the important governments (those of West Germany and the UK rather than India or Sweden in the case of US-Soviet bargaining over nuclear weapons). It is not necessary that an international opinion has a direct effect on anybody in the country whose government it tries to influence. It may have significant consequences nevertheless.

The indirectness of the effects of international opinions implies that the assumption of a need for global democratization is an exaggeration. What matters, it appears, is the political system of the few countries that are strategically important in the specific situation; these countries, rather than the influencee, need to be democratic in order for public opinion to have an impact on foreign policy. The strategically important countries are not necessarily the opinion's targets, and therefore asymmetry in political system between two contenders does not necessarily imply asymmetry in vulnerability to international opinions. By the same token, the role of world opinion as a general feature of international politics is not necessarily proportional to the spread of democracy. What matters is whether the consequential states are democratic, regardless of whether they are the targets of international opinions or not. This is the case with North America, most of Europe, and Japan, and therefore one condition for international opinions to have an effect obtains to a very considerable extent.

The unpredictability of effects

A feature of the case of the INF Treaty is that few anticipated the outcome. The INF case suggests three reasons why international opinion formation may lead to unexpected results.

First, background conditions may change in unexpected ways. What may have been a sensible third-party demand (that the USA renounce the zero option so that at least something may be obtained) at one stage may prove to have been ill-considered at a later stage (when the weakness of the Soviet Union has become obvious).

Second, the less precise the position taken by an opinion, the more unpredictable the behaviour of those who think it necessary to take it into account. Broad international opinions at the non-official level, as has been pointed out, are likely to consist in coalitions of diverse views sharing a mood rather than a demand. A mood has less substantive interest and probably less legitimate authority than a demand. Its strategic implications, furthermore, are unclear: a mood is more likely than a specific demand to create uncertainty about the balance of bargaining power and to make adversaries believe that they can change this balance in their favour. This is an invitation to attempts at manipulation rather than to submission and suggests that international opinion formation may risk bringing about the opposite of what it is intended to do. This is not inevitable, however; the argument is that the effects of weakly specified opinions are difficult to predict and not that they are necessarily counter-productive.

Third, and regardless of whether the position taken by an opinion is precise or imprecise, it is difficult to predict how a move by a third party will affect on-going bargaining between others. There is a tendency in bargaining theory to de-emphasize deterministic models and to stress the role of communication and perception. The dynamics of bargaining is often intractable, especially to non-participants such as third parties who wish to influence the outcome.

The INF case took place at an unusual time. Few in the West anticipated in the first half of the 1980s what Soviet arms policy would be like in the latter half. The situational context of an influence attempt is not always radically different at a late stage from what it was at the outset; we should hesitate to generalize from such an exceptional decade as the 1980s. Yet it may be inevitable that a broad international opinion of the non-official type is characterized by imprecision. Limited predictability, moreover, would seem to be an inescapable feature of such an interactive phenomenon as bargaining. Therefore, international opinion-formers and opinion-holders will often be wrong about the impact their opinion will have on those they mean to influence.

Conclusion

The case of the INF treaty, in summary, supports the assumption that strong international opinions can be formed on key issues in international politics and that they may have a significant impact on governmental action. It suggests, furthermore, that this is contingent on widespread rather than universal democracy and thus that the validity of this aspect of the internationalist programme does not hinge on universal democratization. On the other hand, we have been reminded of the fact that the assumption that international opinions are unbiased is essentially untestable. There is reason to believe, moreover, that national political culture in an extended sense exerts a strong influence on the formation of opinions about international issues. This in turn may contribute to making the effects of international opinion formation unpredictable, especially since the political process, into which the opinion is an input, is often interactive and dynamic in a way that itself tends to make the outcome unpredictable. What this means for the validity of the internationalist programme for peace and security will be considered in Chapter 6. It is obvious, however, that the making of peace by international opinion formation risks becoming a haphazard activity – a well-meaning bull in the china shop of international diplomacy.

4 Cooperation and war

The object of this chapter is to consider the plausibility of the proposition that cooperation between adversaries in international politics tends to inhibit war between them. The proposition is not merely that joint measures to inhibit war tend to be effective. Nor is the proposition limited to the truism that peaceful agreement on an issue makes it less likely that war will occur over that issue. We will be concerned with a bolder claim in this chapter: cooperative interaction of whatever kind tends to reduce the probability of war over any issue, and thus the cumulative effect of sustained cooperation is to make war unlikely. This proposition is essential to internationalism, as pointed out previously.

The literature on international integration, interdependence, regime formation, and other forms of advanced international cooperation is mainly concerned with explaining how and why cooperation comes about and is sustained. That is not the issue raised here. Experience has proven internationalism to be realistic when assuming far-reaching international cooperation to be feasible. What needs to be demonstrated is that war tends to disappear as a result. Authors in the field of international cooperation have less to say on this point.[1] Some in fact make it clear that they do not assume a straightforward negative relation between cooperation and conflict. Keohane and Nye thus admonish us in *Power and Interdependence* 'to be cautious about the prospect that rising interdependence is creating a brave new world of cooperation to replace the bad old world of international conflict' (Keohane and Nye 1977: 10). Zacher, who argues that states are becoming enmeshed in a 'network of interdependencies and regulatory/collaborative arrangements from which exit is generally not a feasible option', goes on to emphasize that 'there will continue to be a great deal of conflict in the world' albeit in a different setting (Zacher 1992: 61). The least one can say about the literature on international cooperation is that the precise way in which cooperation may make war unlikely is not always spelled out.

The first half of this chapter, therefore, is devoted to outlining a general theory of the relationship between sustained cooperation and major conflict at the international level. An attempt will be made to make a convincing case for the proposition that cooperation tends to inhibit war. Then, in the second half, the weaknesses of this theory of international cooperation will be considered. The chapter concludes with an assessment of their implications for the theory of internationalism.

Three introductory comments must be made, however: first on the concepts of cooperation and conflict, second on empirical testability, and third on foreign policy as action.

INTRODUCTORY COMMENTS

Cooperation and conflict

It is difficult to distinguish clearly between cooperative and conflictive behaviour, as many have discovered. The distinction presumably is one between the addition and the deprivation of value. One difficulty, however, is whether cooperation and conflict should be defined in terms of the intentions of actors, the perceptions of targets, or the final outcomes. Another is the tendency of interaction to be characterized by a mixture of value-addition and value-deprivation. Apart from this there is the issue of whether cooperation should be defined as joint or collaborative action (Eduards 1985: 12) or more broadly as non-conflictive interaction (Nygren 1980) and whether conflict should be defined in terms of interests, objectives, behaviour, attitudes, or a combination of these (Wiberg 1989: 8–10).

Since the object is to explicate internationalist thinking, it is not necessary to go into matters such as these in the present study. The theory of internationalism is concerned with factors that may inhibit two kinds of behaviour, namely, escalation and war. The problem that needs to be considered is whether conflictive behaviour in this sense is inhibited by international exchange and communication as well as by the setting up of international institutions. The former is what is here called conflictive behaviour and the latter cooperative behaviour, and the present chapter is concerned with the relationship between cooperative and conflictive behaviour in this simple sense.

The problem of the relationship between cooperation and conflict exists at all levels of social relations. Organizations – political parties, associations of employers and employees – may come to confront each other in conflicts of interest resulting from the structure of the system to which they belong, as pointed out previously (Chapter 2). The issue in all such cases is whether cooperation helps to avert major conflict in spite of the fact that underlying conflicts of interest cannot be fully resolved. Looked at in this way, the issue raised by internationalism is but a special instance.

Of course, whereas there is a tradition of advocating international cooperation for the sake of inhibiting major conflict such as war, it has been considered less self-evident that major conflict among interest organizations and political parties must be avoided. Rather, cooperation may be opposed on the ground that were major conflict implausible, one's interest organization or party would lose its *raison d'être*. What stands out as an opportunity at the international level may appear at other levels as a risk. The causal issue is the same, however: is it true that sustained cooperation tends to reduce the likelihood of major conflict?

It has been tempting to conduct the present analysis in terms general enough to encompass all of these cases. I have decided against it, however. An analysis in such general terms, apart from being pretentious, would be problematic precisely because of the difficulty of defining the very concepts of cooperation and conflict. This difficulty, more than anything else, makes it questionable to move between contexts and systems in the way a general argument presumes. What follows is thus limited to a consideration of cooperative and conflictive interaction among states. This does not exclude that the insights that may be gained are relevant for systems of interest organizations, political parties, or other types of actors.

Testability

The proposition that cooperation inhibits war concerns an empirical relationship. Yet no attempt will be made in this book to subject it to empirical testing. This needs justification.

A proposition that is not about a determinate relationship assumed to obtain under specified conditions but merely about a general tendency in international relations cannot be confirmed or disconfirmed by reference to single historical cases. In the case of an underresearched topic, such as the impact of international opinion formation on world politics, case studies may be useful for specifying the problem and suggesting hypotheses, but when, as in the present case, the issue is well understood and is one about relative frequency and degree of explanatory power, more is required for empirical confirmation.[2] The problem is the ease with which apparent 'cooperation successes' (cooperation and no war) as well as apparent 'cooperation failures' (war in spite of cooperation) can be explained away.

The problem with 'cooperation successes' is to prove that the association between cooperation and the lack of war is not spurious. There is reason to suspect that the opposition between the parties must be small in order for sustained, far-reaching cooperation to be possible. But then the non-occurrence of war may be due to the former just as well as to the latter. Developments in Western Europe after 1945 can be seen as a uniquely ambitious effort to carry out the internationalist programme in a region plagued by war throughout history. It stands out as a great cooperation success, since war now seems to have become permanently unthinkable in this part of the world. The sceptic, however, may argue that this development took place under special historical circumstances such as those created by the perception of an immediate, common threat; the case of Western Europe thus cannot be assumed to be representative of the universe to which the proposition is meant to apply. He or she may argue, more generally, that the fact that war has ceased to be a serious possibility among Western European countries may be due to insufficient conflict just as well as to the cooperative network that has been set up between them, that the lack of conflict may be a condition for the cooperative developments that have occurred,[3] and that it is impossible to control for the former variable in an attempt to test the impact of the latter.[4]

Perhaps because extensive cooperation is unlikely to develop between adversaries liable to go to war with each other, clear 'cooperation failures' are difficult to find. What has occurred in Sino-Vietnamese relations may be seen as such a failure, however.[5] There was traditional rivalry between the two countries, but this came to a halt in the 1940s, when communist regimes were established in both capitals, thus setting the stage for the kind of peace-building between adversaries that internationalism is about. The two communist parties were not just of the same ideological persuasion, but also had a long history of cooperation (Salisbury 1967: 180–1; Turner 1975: 23, 79–86, 103–4, 120–1, 292, 295–8). An 'atmosphere of warm friendship and co-operation developed between the two countries that shared similar security concerns and the same anti-imperialist goals' (Hung 1979: 1038). Then, in the Vietnam War, China and Vietnam were like 'lips and teeth' (Hung 1979: 1037). China was North Vietnam's chief source of foodstuff and consumer goods and a major provider of small arms, mortars, and other weapons, as well as of bicycles and trucks. Moreover, China had given North Vietnam considerable aid in developing a railroad system and helped keep railroads going during the war

(Salisbury 1967: 181–3). And yet, just a few years after the war was over, both countries began to militarize the border area, and on 17 February, 1979, China invaded Vietnam. This may appear to be convincing evidence against the proposition under review.

Internationalists could try two lines of defence. They may suggest that Sino-Vietnamese relations, even though cooperative, came nowhere near what is required to prevent war; lasting peace requires more than ideological friendliness and comradeship in war. They may add that since the proposition is probabilistic, single counter-instances do not prove anything. Both points illustrate the difficulty of determining the issue raised in this chapter on the basis of the study of single cases. What is needed is something else: a statistical design.

Some such studies of the relationship between international co-operation and conflict have been made. They essentially suggest that international organization and international economic exchange do reduce the likelihood of war, albeit modestly or under special conditions (Nye 1971; Gaisorowski 1986; Domke 1988). This evidence is not conclusive, however, and further efforts at the collection and analysis of data are unlikely to improve the situation more than marginally. This is so for two reasons. One is the problem of validity that must be faced when it is a matter of translating complex constructs, such as the amount of cooperation between states, into observational indices or, conversely, when it is a matter of the theoretical interpretation of the kind of statistical analysis that is operationally possible. The other is the fact that statistical analysis, however sophisticated, is as vulnerable as case studies to the objection that the invariances of yesterday may not obtain tomorrow, a major consideration when it is a matter of evaluating a political programme.

The limited empirical testability of one of its key assumptions is one of the weaknesses of internationalism. It remains to seek to assess its validity by conceptual analysis.

Foreign policy as rational action

Many thoughts have been put forward about the way in which co-operation between nations may reduce the likelihood of conflict. One object of the chapter is to bring this variety of thought together in a common framework so that its basic features can be seen more clearly and evaluated more easily. The proposition that cooperation inhibits conflict in international politics will be taken to rest on two assumptions, one about images and the other about interests.

First, an actor's choice between cooperative and conflictive action is presumed to be affected by his image of the adversary. An unfavourable image promotes conflictive action, on this assumption. Cooperation makes the contenders view each other more favourably, internationalists may be taken to believe, thereby inhibiting conflict.

Second, cooperation is presumed to create values that would be endangered by war. Against the adversity between the contenders is set a growing common interest in preserving the fruits of cooperation. Cooperation renders conflict more costly and hence less likely, internationalists may be assumed to think.

The proposition is thus presumed to be one about action that is rational in the sense that it results from decision-makers' evaluations of alternative courses of action and their choice of what they think is best for them. Cooperation between adversaries is presumed to make their relationship decreasingly war-prone by affecting their choices between conflictive and non-conflictive action. It is difficult to see how the proposition that cooperation inhibits conflict could be explicated without some such assumption. Even if the rationality assumption is part of the hard core of 'realist' theory, it has been argued, it must be retained in any theory of the impact of international structure on foreign policy, since without it 'inferences from structure to behavior become impossible without heroic assumptions about evolutionary processes or other forces that compel actors to adapt their behavior to their environments' (Keohane 1986: 194).

It may be important to emphasize what the assumption of rationality does and does not imply. This is old stuff, but misunderstandings keep coming up and must be anticipated at the risk of stating the obvious. The rationality assumption implies two things: (a) that governments do what they consider best under the circumstances as they perceive them; and (b) that changed circumstances are apt to change their objectives and perceptions and hence their actions in a predictable direction. It does not imply that governmental objectives are always characterized by narrow self-interest but only that governments have objectives. Nor does it imply that governmental perceptions are always correct and that governments always agree about objectives and perceptions. Hence there is no assumption to the effect that changed circumstances, such as those following from sustained co-operation, will necessarily have a particular impact. Rationalistic theory of the kind to be outlined in this chapter is not deterministic. Thus what is assumed here is that it is useful to conceive of foreign policy in terms of bounded or subjective rationality, and this is different from assuming perfect or objective rationality (Simon 1957: 196–206, 241–56). The theory of internationalism is taken to belong to that vast category of social science theory in which it is assumed that the subjective rationality of actors will be sufficiently similar to the objective rationality of the analyst in order for its propositions to be worthy of interest. If this assumption is problematic, so is internationalism, a matter to which we will return.

EXPLICATING THE PROPOSITION

The proposition that cooperation inhibits war, as interpreted here, is concerned with four aspects of an interaction sequence: pre-decision relations between the contenders, a decision situation defined in terms of their preferences, the decisions they make in this situation, and the resulting outcome (Figure 4.1). According to the proposition, the preferences of the parties and their perceptions of one another are affected by the degree to which their previous relationship has been cooperative. Their preferences define the decision situations that arise between them. The actions they actually take result from the decision situation defined in terms of preferences and from their mutual perceptions. Therefore, the outcome depends on the degree to which pre-decision relations have been cooperative.

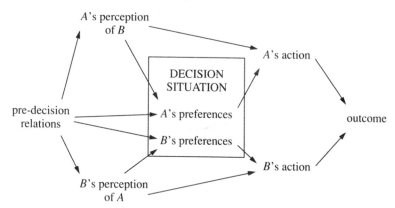

Figure 4.1 Cooperation and war: framework of analysis

The latter part of this sequence – from decision situation to outcome – will be explored with the help of elementary game theory, which provides what is needed: a theory about outcomes as functions of decisions made in situations defined in terms of the preferences of interdependent actors. Game-theoretical models, as interpreted here, describe constraints on the players' choices that reward or punish them in certain ways and therefore induce them to behave in certain ways rather than others (Snyder and Diesing 1977: 83). The notion to be explored is that cooperation changes the constraints and hence the resulting behaviour. Just as changing external circumstances may affect the deliberations of rational actors and hence their actions in a predictable fashion, a change in the game-theoretical structure of a relationship between actors may change their actions *vis-à-vis* one another in a way indicated by the theory of games.

Somebody may be tempted to object that game theory cannot be used in the present context, since it is inherently incompatible with the proposition being explicated. It has been common to associate game theory with 'realism' (Jervis 1988) and the use of this analytical tool may seem to be biased against phenomena like trust, altruism, and norms and, therefore, to be incapable of doing justice to the thought that cooperation inhibits war. In particular, a game-theoretical perspective on institutions may seem to be inherently structural (decisions are determined by situations) and unable to accommodate the cognitive dimension (actions result from knowledge and purpose; see Chapter 2); the change in mentality which is part of what internationalism is meant to bring about cannot be understood in terms that take the egoistic rationality of a 'realist' approach to international politics for granted, it may appear.

This thought is doubly mistaken. First of all, to use game theory is not to rule out the possibility of altruistic and universalistic considerations on the part of governments. Rationality and egotism are not the same, as pointed out previously. The assumption that needs to be made is that actors strive to maximize whatever they consider important. No assumption is made about what they consider important. The conjunction of game theory and narrow self-interest, even though common, is not necessary (Axelrod 1984: 6–7).

Second, even if it had been true that game theory assumes not merely rationality but also egotism, this would not have made it unsuitable for exploring the validity of internationalism. As repeatedly emphasized, internationalism accepts much of the 'realist' view of the problematic of politics in a system of independent states. The starting-points of internationalism are: (1) the observation that relations between states have often been hostile; (2) the assumption that this is due in part to the features of politics in a system of independent states; and (3) the objective of solving or ameliorating this problem without replacing the independence of states with a world state. What the theory of internationalism needs to show is that sustained cooperation will reduce inter-state hostility between adversaries that will remain separate states with separate national interests that are not fully compatible. Thus, if game theory runs parallel with 'realist' analysis to some extent, it is for this very reason useful for the purpose of explicating the theory of internationalism.

True, the process of change that internationalism aims at promoting cannot be accounted for in game-theoretical terms alone. Game theory is essentially static and does not concern itself with changes in mentality of the kind that internationalists have in mind. The proposition that cooperation inhibits conflict will be taken to suggest that cooperation, or at least sustained cooperation, tends to change the kind of game that will be played as well as the way in which some games will be played; the result, according to the proposition, is to make war a less likely outcome for reasons given in the theory of games. However, game theory, while helpful for exploring the implications of given preferences and perceptions for actions and outcomes, is less useful for answering what some consider to be the more important question: how preferences and perceptions are formed and how they are changed (Jervis 1988: 322–9) – how they are affected, for example, by sustained cooperation.

In what follows, therefore, game-theoretical concepts are used to formulate a set of assumptions about the relationship between decision situation, action, and outcome. The subsequent consideration of the ways in which cooperation may change preferences and hence decision situations, actions, and outcomes necessarily draws on other kinds of reasoning.[6]

Decision situations and outcomes

Six games

It is convenient to begin with the standard two-by-two matrix shown in Table 4.1. The matrix assumes that we are dealing with a relationship between two contenders, each of whom has a choice between two strategies, one of which is to cooperate (C) and the other to defect (D). 'Defection', in the kind of situation with which the theory of internationalism is concerned, typically means beginning to wage war, escalating a conflict, or refusing to make concessions. 'Co-operation' in this context typically means stopping on-going warfare, de-escalating a conflict, or making concessions in order to accom-modate the adversary.

There are four possible outcomes, which are conventionally denoted CC, CD, DC, and DD. They will here be called compromise (CC), confrontation (DD), and capitulation (CD, DC). Compromise, depending on the circumstances, may be anything from an agreement resolving the point at issue to the mere continuation of the status quo; one result of previous cooperation may be to increase the perceived likelihood of the former relative to the latter. Confrontation, again depending on the circumstances, may mean war as well as a lesser form of escalation or merely the interruption of efforts at conflict resolution. Regardless of what cooperation and defection mean concretely in a specific context, the way in which the contenders rank the outcomes defines the decision situation and helps to determine whether the outcome will be compromise, confrontation, or capitulation. This simple tool should suffice for the limited purpose of explicating the proposition under consideration.

Table 4.1 The cooperation-defection matrix

Own options	Other's options	
	Cooperate	*Defect*
Cooperate	compromise (CC)	own capitulation (CD)
Defect	other's capitulation (DC)	confrontation (DD)

There are literally hundreds of ways in which the preferences of two players can be ordered in a two-by-two game (Fraser and Kilgour 1986). Most of the present argument, however, will be limited to situations in which both parties prefer DC to all other outcomes, that is, situations in which the most-preferred outcome of both is to maximize their own values, whether egoistic, altruistic, or universalistic, with the acquiescence of the adversary. The proposition that cooperation inhibits war is taken to mean that sustained cooperation will reduce the probability of conflictive behaviour even if the acquiescence of the other party remains the most-preferred outcome of the parties in the ensuing decision situations. The possibility that cooperation may cause the parties to set compromise or even their own capitulation before getting their own way will be considered later on, but for the moment DC is assumed to be their first choice.

Assuming further that CD is not the second choice of either party[7] and that indifference is ruled out,[8] four possibilities remain for each contender:

    (I)   DC > DD > CC > CD
    (Ia) DC > DD > CD > CC
    (II) DC > CC > DD > CD
    (III) DC > CC > CD > DD

In the first two alternatives, defection – obstinacy, escalation, war – is unambiguously preferred to cooperation. The difference between them is unimportant for the problem considered here, and Case Ia will not be discussed further.

Cases I, II, and III have in common the fact that the capitulation of the adversary (DC) is preferred to compromise (CC) and compromise (CC) to one's own capitulation (CD) – a standard situation in politics, it would appear. The variation concerns confrontation (DD). An actor in Case I prefers confrontation to compromise. An actor in Case III seeks to avoid confrontation at all costs. Case II is intermediate: there is on the one hand a preference for compromise over confrontation, but on the other hand a preference for confrontation over capitulation.

The three preference orderings can be paired in six different ways, thus producing six well-known games. Assumptions will now be spelled out about the way in which actors are induced to behave in the six situations. They are for the most part commonplace in the game-theoretical literature and need not be elaborated here. The object is not to contribute to the game-theoretical analysis of international relations, which can be very sophisticated, but to draw on some familiar implications of elementary game theory to explicate a proposition about cooperation and war so as to improve our insight into its strengths and weaknesses.

Game 1. Both parties: DC > DD > CC > CD

This situation has been named Deadlock (Snyder and Diesing 1977: 45). Defection is the dominant strategy of both parties. Hence, to the extent that the nature of the situation determines what the parties will do, confrontation (DD) will result.

Snyder and Diesing's *Conflict among Nations* is a useful source of illustrative examples, because the games they analyse are historical rather than hypothetical and are identified by the independent study of perceptions and preferences rather than inferred from the outcomes they are supposed to explain. Their main instance of Deadlock is US-Japanese relations in 1940–41. Their analysis of the road to Pearl Harbor leads them to conclude that the efforts of soft-liners on both sides to resolve the situation peacefully were doomed to fail because of the Deadlock-type features of the situation; 'the inevitable occurred, but only after a tremendous amount of frantic, confused negotiation' (Snyder and Diesing 1977: 129).

Game 2. Both parties: DC > CC > DD > CD

This, of course, is the famous Prisoners' Dilemma, in which both parties have incentives to defect in spite of the fact that both prefer compromise (CC) to confrontation (DD). In classical game theory, confrontation is the expected outcome of a Prisoners' Dilemma because of it being a so-called Nash equilibrium: neither player could do better by switching to another strategy. The logic of the argument has seemed sufficiently persuasive to make it remarkable that major crises of the Prisoners' Dilemma type have occurred without leading to war. Snyder and Diesing consider several such cases, including the superpower confrontations over Berlin in 1958–1962 and over the Middle East during the Yom Kippur war in 1973 (Snyder and Diesing 1977: 92–3, 103–5, 447–50). The United States and the Soviet Union found themselves in a Prisoners' Dilemma *vis-à-vis* each other in both Berlin and the Middle East, according to their analysis, and yet superpower war was avoided in both instances.

Much of the game-theoretical literature, as a matter of fact, has been concerned with explaining why Prisoners' Dilemmas often lead to compromise rather than confrontation in spite of the apparent logic of such situations. Two thoughts about this are of particular interest for explicating the assumption that cooperation inhibits war. It has been shown, among other things, that confrontation is the logical outcome of a Prisoners' Dilemma only if binding agreements cannot be made, and only if the game is played once or a known number of times.

Binding agreements If binding agreements can be made, confrontation can be avoided – this is probably the point most commonly made about cooperation in Prisoners' Dilemmas. It is not enough that the parties can communicate, it has been argued, since there are built-in incentives to break an agreement they might reach. Both parties must reckon with the fact that the adversary has an interest in violating such an agreement, and it therefore remains rational for both to defect. A mere agreement is not self-enforcing, as it has been put (Harsanyi 1977: 110).

The key concept when its comes to the effects of cooperation would seem to be trust rather than enforceability, however. The decisive question is whether mutual promises not to defect are mutually credible. Third-party enforcement need not be the only factor that can produce this result. A possible effect of sustained cooperation, it will be suggested, is to increase mutual trust and hence to increase the likelihood that compromise will be substituted for confrontation in Prisoners' Dilemmas.

Iterated play It has long been pointed out that compromise may be an equilibrium outcome in iterated Prisoners' Dilemmas (Shubik 1970). Axelrod has shown how stable cooperation can develop under such conditions. The core of the argument is that the players have reason to assume that their adversary's way of playing future games depends on their own way of playing the current game. If the future does not cast its shadow over the present it is rational to defect, but if the contenders have an interest in avoiding future confrontations, they both have an interest in abstaining from defection in the current game (Axelrod 1984).

Hence, whether defection is rational in Prisoners' Dilemmas depends, among other things, on what Axelrod terms the size of the shadow of the future, that is, on the significance the contenders ascribe to future games relative to that of the current game. This means, furthermore, that the choice between cooperation and defection is rationally affected by the size of the differences in utility between outcomes: the larger the superiority of compromise over confrontation, and the smaller its inferiority in relation to capitulation, the greater the likelihood of cooperation (Axelrod 1984: 59, 133–4; Oye 1985: 9). A possible effect of sustained cooperation, it will be suggested, is to increase the importance of the future relative to that of the present. Another is to increase the utility of compromise relative to other outcomes. Both should reduce the propensity to defect in Prisoners' Dilemmas.

Game 3. Both parties: DC > CC > CD > DD.

Here we have what is known as the game of Chicken. Its basic feature is usually suggested to be its indeterminateness, since there are two Nash equilibria: both CD and DC. The outcome implied in the structure of the game is the capitulation of one party to the other, and neither compromise nor confrontation. There is, however, no way of deducing from the game itself who will capitulate to whom.

This, it has been suggested, depends on the balance between the parties' willingness to take risks, that is, on their relative resolve (Powell 1987). One strategy is to rush to be the first to defect. This is sensible if the adversary can be relied upon to prevent a confrontation from resulting. A preferable alternative in some Chicken-type situations is for the parties to postpone the choice between cooperation and defection and try instead to act so as to impress the adversary with their resolve in other ways. A competition in risk-taking followed by capitulation is the kind of behaviour encouraged by Chicken-type situations, it will be assumed here. Whereas DD or CC are the characteristic outcomes of Prisoners' Dilemmas, DC or CD are those of games of Chicken – but only after some degree of confrontation, a mini-DD as it were.

The Munich crisis of 1938 and the Berlin crisis of 1948 are among the situations Snyder and Diesing consider to be of the Chicken type (1977: 111–15). In both cases both sides were anxious to avoid confrontation, and yet the outcome, after a period of intense crisis, was more nearly the capitulation of one party than a balanced compromise.

Note that the shadow of the future has a different meaning if the parties believe the future to consist of games of Chicken rather than of Prisoners' Dilemmas. If you expect to play Chicken tomorrow, this is a reason for demonstrating resolve rather than cooperativeness today. Repeated play, in other words, does not induce cooperation in this case. Trust, moreover, does not play the same role in games of Chicken as in Prisoners' Dilemmas. The question in Prisoners' Dilemmas is whether the outcome will be confrontation or compromise; the issue in games of Chicken is who will capitulate to whom.

Game 4. One party: DC > DD > CC > CD.
              Other party: DC > CC > CD > DD.

We now come to the first of three asymmetrical games. In Game 4, the preferences of one party are of the Deadlock type whereas those of the other party are of the Chicken type. The position of the former is stronger than that of the latter, due to their different evaluation of confrontation. The weak party must assume that the strong will defect and therefore has reason to cooperate. The expected outcome is that the weak capitulates to the strong. Snyder and Diesing's main example is the Fashoda crisis in 1898, which was a British-French confrontation over the Upper Nile in which France had to give in (Snyder and Diesing 1977: 123–4).

Game 5. One party: DC > DD > CC > CD.
              Other party: DC > CC > DD > DC.

This is a less drastic form of Game 4. Here the preferences of the weak party are of the Prisoners' Dilemma type rather than the Chicken type. The outcome in this case will be confrontation. The weak party must assume the strong party to defect, and since he himself prefers confrontation to capitulation, he also has reason to defect.

This, according to Snyder and Diesing, was the situation obtaining between the Central Powers and the Entente in 1914 (Snyder and Diesing 1977: 94–5). Explanations of the outbreak of World War I, of course, vary from an emphasis on long-term shifts in the balance of power to a stress on misperceptions during the weeks preceding the war and on the semi-automatic character of the mobilization plans. If Snyder and Diesing are correct in their game-theoretical account of the decision situation resulting from these and maybe other factors, this explains why war was inevitable by August 1914.

Game 6. One party: DC > CC > DD > DC.
            Other party: DC > CC > DC> DD.

Here we have an encounter between a party with preferences of the Prisoners' Dilemma type and one with preferences of the Chicken type. The former must be expected to defect. The latter therefore has reason to cooperate. The expected outcome is the capitulation of the party fearing confrontation the most. The Cuban Missile crisis of 1962 stands out as a prototype case in Snyder and Diesing's analysis (Snyder and Diesing 1977: 115–16).

Misperception and lack of clarity

The argument so far presumes that the parties perceive each other's preferences correctly. It is useful for a consideration of the proposition that cooperation inhibits war to see what happens, if this assumption is relaxed. Each party in effect plays his own game, defined by his own preferences and the preferences he ascribes to the adversary, and the previous argument has been concerned with the special case in which both players play the same game. Taking misperception into account increases the number of possible situations from six to forty-five. Table 4.2, in which the six original games are marked out, shows the expected outcome – confrontation, compromise, capitulation, or competition in resolve followed by capitulation – in each of the forty-five situations. The chief points are as follows.

Compromise is never the uniquely expected outcome and is a serious possibility only in special circumstances. One is a correctly perceived, symmetrical Prisoners' Dilemma (Game 2.4). The other is an asymmetrical Prisoners' Dilemma / Chicken that is misperceived by the strong party to be symmetrical (Games 6.4 and 6.5). In the former case compromise, if it occurs, results from the parity inherent in the situation. In the latter case it would be a mistake; it would result from the strong party's mistakenly believing the situation to be balanced and the weak party therefore being in for a pleasant surprise.

Capitulation, according to the assumptions shown in Table 4.2, is the plausible outcome of most asymmetrical games of Chicken; a partial exception is the case just discussed, when the stronger party mistakenly believes the situation to be a symmetrical Prisoners' Dilemma.

Competition in resolve demonstration followed by the capitulation of the party that proves to be weakest is the expected outcome of all symmetrical games of Chicken, regardless of whether they are perceived correctly or incorrectly. The reason for the competition is that both contenders have an interest in convincing the adversary that they themselves do not prefer anything to confrontation. The reason for the capitulation is that one contender proves more successful than the other in this regard. This is the plausible result not only when one or both contenders decide to demonstrate their resolve but also in the peculiar case when both capitulate by mistake (Games 3.1, 3.2, and 3.4) because they both misperceive a symmetrical game of Chicken to be asymmetrical to their disadvantage. The assumption made here is that in such situations, the capitulation of the adversary is taken by both to show that they have misperceived the situation and that the game is in fact symmetrical. Compromise, in other words, is presumed to be an unstable outcome in this peculiar case.

Confrontation, first of all, is inevitable in symmetrical Deadlocks, whether correctly or incorrectly perceived, and in some situations of the Deadlock / Prisoners' Dilemma type; it may also result from misperceived symmetrical Prisoners' Dilemmas. In all remaining Prisoners' Dilemmas and Prisoners' Dilemmas / Deadlocks, confrontation is one of two alternatives.

So much for misperception. Another simplifying assumption also needs to be relaxed: the assumption that the parties have a clear view of how they themselves as well as the adversary evaluate all outcomes in relation to each other. This can be done with recourse to the notion that decision situations may vary in clarity.

Thus the implications of the various outcomes may be more or less

Table 4.2 Outcomes as a function of own preferences and adversary's preceived preferences

Game no.	A's preferences	B's perceived preferences	B's preferences	A's perceived preferences	A's action	B's action	Outcome
1	**Deadlock**						
1.1	I	I	I	I	D	D	confrontation
1.2	I	I	I	II	D	D	confrontation
1.3	I	I	I	III	D	D	confrontation
1.4	I	II	I	II	D	D	confrontation
1.5	I	II	I	III	D	D	confrontation
1.6	I	III	I	III	D	D	confrontation
2	**Prisoners' Dilemma**						
2.1	II	I	II	I	D	D	confrontation
2.2	II	I	II	II	D	C or D	confrontation or capitulation
2.3	II	I	II	III	D	D	confrontation
2.4	II	II	II	II	C or D	C or D	confrontation or compromise
2.5	II	II	II	III	C or D	D	confrontation or capitulation
2.6	II	III	II	III	D	D	confrontation
3	**Chicken**						
3.1	III	I	III	I	C	C	competition → capitulation
3.2	III	I	III	II	C	C	competition → capitulation
3.3	III	I	III	III	C	Dem	competition → capitulation[b]
3.4	III	II	III	II	C	C	competition → capitulation
3.5	III	II	III	III	C	Dem	competition → capitulation[b]
3.6	III	III	III	III	Dem	Dem	competition → capitulation
4	**Deadlock/Chicken**						
4.1	I	I	III	I	D	C	capitulation
4.2	I	I	III	II	D	C	capitulation
4.3	I	I	III	III	D	Dem	capitulation[a]
4.4	I	II	III	I	D	C	capitulation
4.5	I	II	III	II	D	C	capitulation
4.6	I	II	III	III	D	Dem	capitulation[a]
4.7	I	III	III	I	D	C	capitulation
4.8	I	III	III	II	D	C	capitulation
4.9	I	III	III	III	D	Dem	capitulation[a]

Table 4.2 (cont.)

Game no.	A's preferences	B's perceived preferences	B's preferences	A's perceived preferences	A's action	B's action	Outcome
5	**Deadlock/Prisoners' Dilemma**						
5.1	I	I	II	I	D	D	confrontation
5.2	I	I	II	II	D	C or D	confrontation or capitulation
5.3	I	I	II	III	D	D	confrontation
5.4	I	II	II	I	D	D	confrontation
5.5	I	II	II	II	D	C or D	confrontation or capitulation
5.6	I	II	II	III	D	D	confrontation
5.7	I	III	II	I	D	D	confrontation
5.8	I	III	II	II	D	C or D	confrontation or capitulation
5.9	I	III	II	III	D	D	confrontation
6	**Prisoners' Dilemma/Chicken**						
6.1	II	I	III	I	D	C	capitulation
6.2	II	I	III	II	D	C	capitulation
6.3	II	I	III	III	D	Dem	capitulation[a]
6.4	II	II	III	I	C or D	C	compromise or capitulation
6.5	II	II	III	II	C or D	C	compromise or capitulation
6.6	II	II	III	III	C or D	Dem	[competition→]capitulation[a,b]
6.7	II	III	III	I	D	C	capitulation
6.8	II	III	III	II	D	C	capitulation
6.9	II	III	III	III	D	Dem	capitulation[a]

Notes:

[a] This presumes that if one party defects and the other merely demonstrates, this will lead on to the capitulation of the latter.

[b] This presumes that if one party cooperates and one demonstrates, the former will realize his mistake and take demonstrative counteraction.

I = DC>DD>CC>CD	D = defection
II = DC>CC>DD>CD	C = cooperation
III = DC>CC>CD>DD	Dem = demonstration
	→ = followed by

difficult for the contenders to assess; it may be difficult, for example, to determine whether DD entails a large or a small risk of catastrophe, or whether CC entails a large or a small chance of acceptable agreement. Moreover, the differences in utility may be found to be small as well as large, with indifference as the limiting case. The adversary may similarly be thought to be more or less uncertain about his priorities. The clarity of a decision situation, then, is a function of: (1) the extent to which the implications of the outcomes are thought to be known; (2) the magnitude of the differences in utility; and (3) the perception of the decision situation of the adversary with regard to (1) and (2). I shall assume that the less clear a situation, the smaller its impact on the outcome, and the larger in consequence the impact of non-situational factors. Clear situations impose themselves on decision-makers more than unclear situations do, according to this assumption.

The proposition reformulated

The proposition that cooperation affects perceptions and preferences and thereby the likelihood of war can now be reformulated. According to the proposition, sustained cooperation reduces the likelihood of confrontation in subsequent decision situations:

1 by reducing the relative utility of confrontation. Sustained co-operation, according to this line of thought, renders the contenders decreasingly likely to rank confrontation second and increasingly likely to rank confrontation last. Unclear Deadlocks are substituted for clear Deadlocks; situations in which compromise can occur (Prisoners' Dilemmas) are substituted for situations in which confrontation is the only possibility (Deadlock); and situations in which confrontation is not just avoidable but implausible (Chicken) are substituted for situations in which it remains a serious possibility (Prisoners' Dilemmas). Furthermore, Prisoners' Dilemmas in which the superiority of the adversary's capitulation over compromise is small and that of compromise over confrontation is large are substituted for those in which the adversary's capitulation is much superior to compromise and compromise only moderately superior to confrontation.

2 by changing the way in which the contenders perceive each others' preferences. Sustained cooperation, according to this line of thought, makes the contenders decreasingly likely to believe that the adversary ranks confrontation second and hence helps to reduce the likelihood that Prisoners' Dilemmas are misperceived as Deadlocks.

3 by reinforcing trust. Sustained cooperation, according to this line of

thought, increases the credibility of the adversary's promises to cooperate in Prisoners' Dilemmas. Compromise is thereby encouraged, and confrontation is discouraged.

4 by increasing the significance of the future. Sustained cooperation, according to this line of thought, makes future games an increasingly important consideration in Prisoners' Dilemmas. This also helps to encourage compromise and discourage confrontation.

Points 1 and 4 reflect changes in the overall preferences of the contenders, and points 2 and 3 in their overall perceptions of each other. The game-theoretical argument suggests why it is reasonable to expect such changes to reduce the likelihood of war. It remains to be considered why sustained cooperation may be taken to have this impact on preferences and perceptions.

Cooperation and decision situations

The outbreak of war may be explained in two ways, as suggested in Chapter 2: by reference to a basic incompatibility between the parties, and in terms of the process of interaction between them. The former explanation may be termed structural and the latter processual. The proposition that cooperation inhibits war may be taken to presume that sustained cooperation has the double effect of changing the structure of a relationship so as to reduce the incompatibility between the parties and of inhibiting escalatory interaction so as to make autonomous processes of conflict less likely.

Cooperation, just as war causation, can be viewed from two perspectives: as a process and as a structure. A cooperative act – the making of an agreement, the setting up of an institution, a meeting at the summit – can be seen as a link in an action-reaction chain, and it can be regarded as a contribution to cooperative structure-building. The issue in the former case is how the sending of cooperative signals affects the likelihood of war. The issue in the latter case is how the existence of a cooperative structure affects the likelihood of war. In the older international relations literature, the former thought is exemplified by Charles Osgood's concept of 'Graduated Reciprocation in Tension Reduction' (GRIT; see Frei 1980) and the latter by Karl Deutsch's theory about the formation of security communities (Deutsch *et al.* 1957). Both thoughts are central to the question of the relationship between cooperation and conflict.[9]

The two distinctions are combined in Table 4.3. Four links between cooperation and the avoidance of war are thus defined. The links are

Table 4.3 Four ways in which cooperation may inhibit war

Cooperation	Causation of war	
	Structure	*Process*
Process	'mutual understanding'	'accommodative bargaining'
Structure	'complex interdependence'	'détente'

represented in the table by catchwords meant to hint at four familiar thoughts about the way in which sustained cooperation may inhibit conflict that have not previously been brought together in this fashion: (1) by promoting 'mutual understanding' between the contenders; (2) by encouraging accommodative rather than coercive bargaining; (3) by producing a state of 'détente' in the sense of peaceful coexistence between fundamental adversaries; and (4) by establishing a relationship of 'complex interdependence' between contenders whose adversity is becoming less fundamental. Each link is outlined in what follows, in an amplification of some of the argument in Chapter 2.

'Mutual understanding'

The first thought to be considered here is that the fact of cooperation between time t_1 and time t_2 reduces the likelihood that the parties will go to war with each other at t_2, since they are brought to see each other in a new light and to revise their views of each others' characteristics. This is what internationalists like to conceive of as increased mutual understanding, which is an important concomitant of cooperation, in the perspective of internationalism. The presumed improvement may be cognitive as well as affective: cooperation may render the views the parties have of each other less prejudiced as well as more friendly. The incompatibility between their long-term interests or objectives will diminish, and this in turn will change the type of decision situation in which they are likely to find themselves *vis-à-vis* each other in a way making conflictive action less likely, on this line of thought.

Suppose that we are concerned with two parties apt to find themselves in symmetrical Deadlocks or asymmetrical Deadlock/Prisoners' Dilemmas *vis-à-vis* each other because of the scope of the underlying cleavage between them. These are the situations most liable to result in confrontation (Table 4.2). Deadlocks may be rooted in hate and fear; if the adversary is thought to be the incarnation of evil, or if he is regarded as a threat that must be contained at every juncture, this cannot but reinforce the view that unless you have his capitulation, confrontation is preferable to compromise in most situations.

Cooperation-induced mutual understanding, according to the thought pursued here, is apt to make the advantages of confrontation over compromise appear less obvious and thereby to substitute situations in which compromise can occur for those in which confrontation is more or less inevitable. Unjustified or exaggerated hate and fear will disappear and hence the likelihood of war will diminish. In the future, the build-up of confidence between Israel and the PLO after their mutual recognition in 1993 may come to be cited as an example.

A continuing process of cooperation may further deepen the mutual understanding of the parties and convince them that compromise is vastly rather than marginally preferable to confrontation, perhaps even that capitulation is preferable to confrontation when it is a matter of an opposite number for whom you have come to have respect and affection. Even if the capitulation of the other side remains your first choice, confrontation then has become your last. If such a shift from Deadlock-proneness to Chicken-proneness takes place, the risk of deliberate confrontation has been not just reduced but averted, according to the argument outlined in the previous section.

Would it be reasonable to take the further step of suggesting cooperation-induced mutual understanding to make the parties inclined to set compromise or even their own capitulation before the capitulation of the adversary? Even strong believers in international cooperation for the sake of mutual understanding may hesitate to go this far. A claim that sustained cooperation may lead to such profound changes in perceptions of basic interests or objectives is more likely to be defended with reference to the impact of cooperation-based structures than to the mere fact that there has been cooperation; see below.

'Accommodative bargaining'

We now turn from underlying incompatibilities to processes of escalation. States often have to decide whether to take escalatory action or not. This problem is integral to bargaining.

A process of bargaining, as suggested in Chapter 3, may be taken to comprise a confrontation stage and a resolution stage. In the former, bargaining is essentially coercive. Its function is to clarify the relative bargaining power of the contenders. Resolution can begin only after this has been achieved. In the resolution stage, bargaining is essentially accommodative (Snyder and Diesing 1977, esp. p. 249).

Escalation is a feature of coercive bargaining. A likely consequence of deliberate escalation, which may be unintended and unwanted but may also be what is meant to put pressure on the adversary, is an increase in the probability of autonomous conflict. The thought considered here is that if the contenders cooperate between t_1 and t_2, they are likely to escalate less at t_2. Bargaining behaviour, in other words, is thought to be affected by the degree to which previous interaction between the parties has been cooperative. The proposition that cooperation inhibits war is taken to imply, among other things, that the more the parties have cooperated between t_1 and t_2, the less likely it is that their bargaining will be coercive later on.

As before, the hypothesized effect of cooperation has to do with the contenders' mutual images. However, whereas previously it was a matter of the adversary's basic characteristics – whether there was reason to hate and fear him – here it is a matter merely of the way in which he is likely to bargain. A common history of cooperation suggests an adversary intent on compromise and anxious to avoid dangerous situations, that is, a basically accommodative bargainer. The assumption is that if the parties grow used to seeing each other as basically accommodative, this will inhibit escalation.

Thus one way in which sustained cooperation may have an effect is by modifying what the parties expect from CC when a new decision situation has arisen. If the adversary is thought to be intent on accommodation, it may be found unnecessary to escalate in order to compel him to make a deal; CC may be seen to offer an opportunity for agreement rather than a mere standstill. By demonstrating that it is possible to do business with the adversary, sustained cooperation may increase the perceived utility of compromise relative to that of confrontation, thereby reducing the likelihood of Deadlocks and increasing the likelihood of cooperation in Prisoners' Dilemmas.

If the parties are apt to find themselves in symmetrical Prisoners' Dilemmas, this leads on to the question of how cooperation affects trust. Axelrod's well-known finding is that the evolution of stable cooperation benefits from the parties' adhering to strategies that are 'nice' and 'forgiving' as well as 'provocable' (Axelrod 1984). The role of cooperation – this is suggested by Axelrod's argument – is to increase the credibility of niceness and forgiveness. Cooperation today provides evidence that cooperation will be reciprocated tomorrow. Cooperation is self-reinforcing. Axelrod's analysis supports the proposition, or intuition, that cooperation today inhibits escalation tomorrow.

'Détente'

The third thought to be considered here is that sustained cooperation inhibits escalation by weaving a constraining network of norms and dependencies. Cooperation, according to this notion, helps to establish rules of conduct that the parties are unwilling to violate and exchange structures that they are unwilling to put at risk just to gain a bargaining advantage. This causes them to interact in a more civilized way than they would otherwise have done and to abstain from threats and provocations. The idea is reminiscent of what became known as East–West *détente* in the 1960s and 1970s, that is, the notion of embedding an adversary relationship in a network of norms and exchanges, thus reducing the probability of conflict. The term is used here for lack of an alternative to denote cooperation-based structures of norms and dependencies taken to inhibit escalation between adversaries that might otherwise go to war against each other.[10]

The reinforcement of customary norms against escalation would seem to be a minimum result of sustained cooperation. Formalized rules to this effect may also be established; they may take the form, for example, of the Basic Principles Agreement that Richard Nixon and Leonid Brezhnev signed in Moscow in 1972. The effect of anti-escalation norms on the decision situations that arise between adversaries may be conceived both as a decrease in the relative utility of confrontation and as a reinforcement of trust. One is reminded of Richard Nixon's claim that the Yom Kippur war of 1973 might have led to a major US–Soviet confrontation but that 'with detente, we avoided it' (George 1983: 148).

It is not necessary to consider in detail the concept of dependence for the limited purposes of this chapter. My usage needs to be clarified in one respect only. Dependence can be defined in two principal ways, one broad and one narrow. Dependence in the broad sense is a matter of need: if one actor controls what another actor needs, the latter is dependent on the former. Such dependence can exist regardless of whether the parties have cooperated or not. What I am after in the present study is more limited: the additional dependence that co-operation can create. Cooperation may render non-cooperation increasingly costly because the parties adapt structurally to continued cooperation.[11] Dependence in this more narrow sense may serve as a link from cooperation to the inhibition of escalation and war.

Cooperation-induced dependence thus results from adaptation to a continuing exchange. Nations adapt their economies to continuing imports and exports – this is a prime example of cooperation-induced dependence. The argument is that governments are unwilling to put cooperation-based relationships at risk and that this renders them reluctant to escalate. Cooperation-induced dependence, just as co-operation-based norms, is presumed to decrease the relative utility of confrontation as well as to reinforce trust. Rules and dependencies thus combine to inhibit escalation, according to this line of thought.

A marriage of convenience of this kind is initially fragile but may grow stable over time. The way in which this may occur is discussed in detail elsewhere (Goldmann 1988). Adversaries may be assumed to embark on policies of détente toward each other under the impression of a particular situation. The question is whether these policies will prove resistant to pressure for change from varying circumstances, indications of failure, or other stresses to which they will be exposed. This I have suggested to depend on the extent to which 'stabilizers' have developed to protect them against stress. Stabilizers of foreign policies may be cognitive as well as domestic-political and administrative. The theory of internationalism may be taken to include the assumption that ongoing processes of *détente* are likely to gain increasing protection against pressure for change by becoming embedded in the thinking as well as in the domestic politics and the bureaucracies of both sides.

'Complex interdependence'

It remains to consider the thought that sustained cooperation may create a structure in which the underlying incompatibility between long-term interests or objectives is decisively reduced. The new structure would have three features: very extensive exchanges of goods and services, a multiplicity of communication channels, and common institutions. This is sufficiently similar to the phenomenon Keohane and Nye call complex interdependence for their label to be used here (Keohane and Nye 1977: 24–5).

The exchange structure associated with complex interdependence is a farther reaching version of that mutual dependence which has already been considered; it must be farther reaching in order to affect the basic incompatibility between the parties and not just their propensity for escalation. The establishment of institutions serves to reinforce the expectation that the relationship will remain cooperative and that cooperative solutions will be found to problems that may arise. This, among other things, helps to deepen and lengthen the shadow of the future and, hence, to increase the propensity for cooperation in Prisoners' Dilemmas. The communications structure is highly trans-national and transgovernmental (Keohane and Nye 1977: 33–5). Such a multiplicity of communication channels is apt to make it difficult for governments to control the foreign relations of their countries and to mobilize internal support for external conflict, thus making confrontation more costly and risky.

Institutions are of particular interest in this context. The essential feature of an institution, according to a definition cited previously, is that it comprises rules for what are allowable alternatives and eligible participants. The creation of institutions in this sense is a possible result of sustained cooperation. The essence of '*détente*' is that rules are established that exclude some conflictive options from the set of allowable alternatives. The institutions that form part of 'complex interdependence' are more advanced in also encompassing rules about eligible participation and in regulating allowable alternatives in more detail. It is now a matter not merely of anti-escalatory rules of conduct but of institutions for the making of common decisions. Advanced institution-making, which thus is a plausible long-term result of sustained cooperation, may be taken to reinforce trust in Prisoners' Dilemmas and maybe even to make confrontation the least-preferred outcome for both parties.

The order in which the four links between cooperation and conflict have been discussed does not necessarily represent a temporal sequence and still less a causal one; they may be conceived of as parallel but separate concomitants of ongoing cooperation between adversaries. Still, what has here been called complex interdependence stands out as the crowning achievement of successful accommodative internationalism. It should serve in various ways to make confrontation not just avoidable but also implausible and to form the strongest and most stable link between sustained cooperation and the inhibition of war. It is difficult not to consider community-building in Western Europe after World War II as a case in point. Interdependence, furthermore, may shade into integration, and a concomitant of integration is arguably that the capitulation of the other party ceases to be the most-preferred outcome in the decision situations that arise. Sustained cooperation thus carries the ultimate promise, or threat, that the parties will merge into one. Post-Maastricht debate about the future of the European Community comes to mind.

It is not clear whether internationalists find such merger to be undesirable or merely implausible, as pointed out in Chapter 2. Internationalism, at any rate, is a programme for peace and security among states that remain independent to a significant extent, and the theory of internationalism is meant to explain how this can be achieved. If all states were to merge into a world state, the programme would lose its relevance and the theory would lose its applicability.

This concludes the presentation of the proposition that cooperation of any kind tends to inhibit war. The objective has been limited to laying bare the central features of the argument, thus making it easier to see what is problematic with this body of thought. To consider what is problematic is our next task.

THE WEAKNESSES OF THE PROPOSITION

Civil war and intervention

The proposition that cooperation inhibits major conflict such as war is concerned with inter-state relations. It may have broader applicability and may be taken to suggest that closer relations between structural adversaries of any kind reduces the likelihood that major conflict will break out between them – not just between states but also, for example, between interest organizations and political parties. Its relevance for civil war, and intra-organizational strife in general, is more limited.

Civil war may thus be traced back to the closeness of the relationship between the contenders rather than to the separation between them. It results from a wish to break out of an existing political community rather than from a lack of community, or from competition over the control of common institutions rather than from a lack of common institutions. The source of the incompatibility between the parties in such cases is the existence rather than the absence of a cooperation-based structure. Whether there is a tendency for sustained cooperation to avert war between states is a question worth pursuing; it is obvious that the link between cooperation and conflict is different within states.

We encounter here a limitation of the scope of the internationalist programme. Internationalism as conceived in this book is concerned with reducing the likelihood of inter-state war through measures aimed at making inter-state relations more cooperative and institutionalized. The idea is to retain the 'virtues of anarchy' (Waltz 1979: 114–17) while minimizing its vices. It can be taken for granted, however, that internationalists are concerned with ridding the world of large-scale violence in general, whether inter- or intra-state. There is a tension between their tendency to concern themselves with the human condition in general and the tradition of theorizing mainly about the conditions for inter-state peace and security. Thus the proposition that cooperation inhibits war, which is a fundamental assumption of internationalism, is essentially irrelevant when it comes to preventing the outbreak of hostilities within states.

Much international warfare is of a third type, however, and consists in the intervention of a state in hostilities that are already in progress between others, either within another state or between other states. Can it be maintained that sustained cooperation tends to decrease the likelihood of intervention in on-going wars?

Not as a general rule – not if the argument outlined in the previous section is a valid explication of the proposition that cooperation inhibits war. The very closeness to which sustained cooperation is presumed to lead may encourage just as well as discourage intervention. Whether it does one or the other would seem to depend on the specifics of each case, including the specific pattern of cooperative and conflictive relations among the original contenders, potential interveners, and potential counter-interveners. One is led in the direction of structural balance theory, which purports to show how the stability of a positive as well as a negative bilateral relationship depends on the overall pattern of positive and negative relationships (Harary *et al.* 1965). It is not a plausible generalization that increased cooperation between a state and its adversaries tends to make it less inclined to intervene in wars between others.

The proposition that cooperation inhibits war is thus plausible only with regard to part of the world's violence. An increase in international cooperation, even if effective in reducing the probability of war, will only affect the probability of some warfare. It is difficult to assess how much this reduces the scope of the proposition, if only because the line between inter-state and other sorts of war can be drawn in different ways, as can the line between original participation and subsequent intervention.[12] Of wars in progress in the early 1990s, only a small portion – maybe less than 20 per cent – appeared to fall within its scope.[13] At the time of writing, it is difficult to avoid being impressed by the fact that war and the threat of war in post-Cold War Europe is in large measure such as to render the idea of peace and security by sustained cooperation irrelevant. The internationalist programme is concerned with peace and security in a system of well-established, long-existing, integrated states. Its accommodative dimension would seem to lack relevance when the issue is the break-up of the components of the states system rather than the incompatibilities obtaining between them.

Preferences and perceptions

The proposition that cooperation inhibits war, as interpreted here, presupposes that cooperation affects preferences and perceptions, and hence actions, in a particular way. Several more or less familiar questions can be raised on this point – questions about cognitive constraints, about the difference between individuals and nations, and not least about the inherent utility of confrontation. These matters will be considered in the present section. The main thread is that there may be such a large discrepancy between what is objectively rational according to the theory and the subjective rationality of actors that a rationalistic argument of the kind outlined above lacks predictive utility.

The proposition also presupposes that if in fact perceptions and preferences change as expected, this will make escalation and war unlikely. Here it is important to consider two complications that are evident in a game-theoretical perspective: the problem of deterrence and the possibility of autonomous conflict. They are taken up in a subsequent section.

Cognitive constraints

The proposition that cooperation inhibits war shares with rational deterrence theory and other thoughts about international relations the assumption that decision-makers are capable of making a correct interpretation of what is going on between themselves and their adversaries (on rational deterrence theory see Achen and Snidal 1989). This assumption has been challenged with particular persuasiveness by Jervis, generally in his seminal work about the psychological aspects of international relations and specifically in a criticism of game-theoretical analyses of cooperation under anarchy (Jervis 1976, 1988, 1989, Jervis *et al.* 1985). Statesmen, Jervis argues, are constrained and conditioned by psychological factors in their perceptions and calculations of utility. They are, among other things, prone to underestimate the extent to which their actions threaten or harm others and to overestimate the hostility implied in actions directed against themselves. Mutual misperception is likely to result; both sides are likely to believe that whereas they themselves cooperate, the adversary responds by defecting. Imperfect information, as a matter of fact, has been shown to diminish radically the probability of compromise in Prisoners' Dilemmas (Downs *et al.* 1985).

There is indeed reason to question the validity of propositions about the foreign policy impact of structural changes and interactions in which cognitive constraints are ignored. Specifically, psychological factors may prevent sustained cooperation from having the expected effect on the preferences and perceptions of adversaries. Trust, understanding, and the recognition of a mutual interest in avoiding confrontation may be overly difficult to attain between nations facing each other in a 'security struggle' (this term is from Buzan 1983: 157).

The argument is twofold: (1) any proposition to the effect that a specific structural change or a specific interaction event will affect action in a specific way is weak, since psychological factors may prevent decision-makers from perceiving the change or the event in the expected way; (2) the kind of misperception that is typical in international politics is apt to make it especially difficult to diminish the mutual perception of hostility between adversaries. The former points at a problem common to much international relations theory and is as relevant for 'realism' as it is for internationalism. The latter is specific to internationalism and similar reasoning and implies that the expected change in preferences and perceptions is not just uncertain but unlikely.

The strength of this as an argument against the proposition that cooperation inhibits war – whether it is devastating or merely a reminder of its limited explanatory power – cannot be determined. What can be said is that if psychological factors intervene to undermine the plausibility of the proposition that deterrence inhibits war, this applies *a fortiori* to the proposition that war is inhibited by sustained cooperation.

Individuals versus states

Suppose now that the preferences and perceptions of people who take part in cooperation are affected in the presumed way, in spite of the cognitive constraints that may obtain. However reasonable this presumption may be at the individual level, there are question marks at the level of collectivities. The proposition that sustained cooperation inhibits war assumes in effect that states are like individuals. It has long been taken for granted among analysts of international relations that the so-called unitary actor approach is misleading (the standard reference is Allison 1971).

Thus, even if individual statesmen come to understand each other better and to like each other, and even if they grow used to regarding each other as sensible people intent on accommodation, it is uncertain how much of this remains when these particular individuals have left the scene and been replaced by others. It is a pertinent question to what extent organizations such as states 'learn' from and 'remember' the experiences of the individuals that represent them. Moreover, even if transgovernmental and transnational cooperation multiplies, the effect that preferences and perceptions at these levels have on foreign policy decision-making is uncertain. It cannot be assumed that there is identity in perceptions and preferences between those who cooperate across borders and those who decide about matters of peace and war. There is, furthermore, the possibility that some members of a society lose from the international activities of other members. It is not self-evident that governments will be constrained by the interests of those who gain from international cooperation but not by the interests of those who lose; cooperation, as is often pointed out, may cause new tensions and not just reduce old ones. The relationship between individual experiences, on the one hand, and collective preferences and perceptions, on the other, is complex.

The general problem encountered here is the one of the role of domestic politics in theories of international systems. No criticism of international systems theory is more familiar than the one that such theory standardizes states unduly. One cannot assume states to have the same interests regardless of political system and domestic-political context, critics argue. This criticism is routinely levelled against the view that the conflictive features of international politics are due to features of the international system (e.g. Keohane 1986: 158–203). It is equally valid with regard to the proposition that cooperation inhibits war. Internationalism, no less than 'realism', presumes factors at the systemic level to have a uniform impact.

The inherent utility of confrontation

The proposition under review presumes that the views the contenders have of each other and of their mutual relationship determine their choices between cooperation and defection. This is not necessarily the case. Confrontation may be placed before compromise because it is regarded as advantageous in itself. One reason for a government wanting a crisis to escalate or even war to break out is that this is thought to increase internal cohesion; external confrontation may be a vehicle of internal statecraft, cynics have argued for hundreds of years. Just as the demands of domestic politics may lead to deterrence failures (Jervis *et al.* 1985), then, they may cause 'cooperation failures'.

Perhaps less obviously, escalation may serve to clarify the distribution of bargaining power. It is a chief feature of Snyder and Diesing's analysis that this is a prerequisite of accommodation. How much confrontation is required for this purpose may vary, but it is difficult to see why there should be a uniform tendency for the need for confrontation to be reduced by cooperation. Sustained interaction may simplify the clarification of the balance of bargaining power should the need arise, but conflictive interaction is apt to serve this purpose at least as well as cooperative interaction.

These observations need not imply that the proposition that co-operation inhibits conflict is invalid, but they do imply that its explanatory power is limited by yet another factor. Even if sustained cooperation were to have the expected effect on perceptions and preferences in spite of the intervention of cognitive and domestic-political variables, this may be insufficient to produce cooperative action because of the importance of other factors tending toward conflictive action.

Summary

The proposition is that cooperation between t_1 and t_2 reduces the probability of war at t_2 because of its impact on the perceptions and preferences of the contenders. Three problems with this thought have now been pointed out. First, cognitive constraints may intervene to prevent perceptions and preferences from changing as expected. Second, states, like other organizations, are not unitary actors responding in a uniform and predictable way to their environment. Third, a government's choice between cooperative and conflictive action *vis-à-vis* an adversary depends on more than the extent to which pre-decision relations between them have been cooperative. All three problems are typical of systemic theory of international relations. The bottom line is that the proposition that cooperation inhibits war shares with 'realist theory' the fact that there is reason to suspect its explanatory power to be modest.

Deterrence and autonomous conflict

The use of two-by-two games to explicate the proposition that sustained cooperation inhibits war can be criticized on at least three grounds: (1) Such simple games misrepresent the way in which real decision-makers perceive real situations. (2) Game theory, by assuming options and preferences to be stable, fails to take the dynamics of bargaining and decision-making into account. (3) Particular assumptions about games such as Prisoners' Dilemma and Chicken are not the only ones that can be made. These are standard criticisms of the use of game theory in international relations research (e.g. Jervis 1988).

They are not fully convincing in the present case, however. With regard to (1): the proposition under review cannot be explicated without making simplified assumptions about decision situations. It may be debatable whether the particular simplifying assumptions made here succeed in doing justice to the proposition, but simplification is a feature of the proposition and is a reason for being sceptical about it, as shown in the previous section.

With regard to (2): the proposition as interpreted here is indeed concerned with the dynamics of perceptions and preferences, but these have not been represented in game-theoretical terms in the above analysis. Game theory has been used for a different purpose: to identify the implications of given perceptions and preferences and hence the consequences of changes in perceptions and preferences. If even this is unrealistic because of a tendency for perceptions and preferences to be unstable, this too is a weakness in the proposition under review and not in the method used to explicate its meaning.

With regard to (3): the assumptions made above about rational action in six specific games are commonplace and obvious, given the logic of standard game theory. If they have to be rejected on the ground that this logic is not so clear – if, in other words, we cannot predict the outcome even of these extremely simple, ideal-type situations – we have a further reason for scepticism with regard to a proposition to the effect that if preferences and perceptions change in a particular way, we can count on this to make war a less likely outcome of future encounters.

Now if the proposition is rejected on the ground that there may be too large a gap between objective and subjective rationality, as suggested in the previous section, this ends the argument. That is also the case if the proposition is rejected on the basis that we cannot determine what is objectively rational even in highly simplified circumstances. If however the gap between objective and subjective rationality is taken to be sufficiently modest for a rationalistic argument to be meaningful, and if the game-theoretical argument pursued earlier in this chapter is presumed to be basically sound, then there is something to add. Just as game theory may be useful for explicating a proposition to the effect that a specific outcome will result, if the perceptions and preferences of interacting decision-makers are changed in a specific way, it may help to focus attention on some problematic features in the relationship between individual decisions and collective outcomes, and hence in the proposition that cooperation inhibits war. One such problem relates to the credibility of deterrence and another to the avoidance of autonomous conflict.

The credibility of deterrence

Compromise is an alternative to confrontation in Prisoners' Dilemmas. Whether the outcome will be one or the other hinges not just on trust but also on deterrence. A result of cooperation may be that the credibility of deterrence is undermined.

One of Axelrod's results, as mentioned already, is the demonstration of the dual nature of the requirements of stable cooperation. It is essential, Axelrod shows, for the parties to be not merely 'nice' and 'forgiving' but also 'provocable'; both should pursue a strategy of cooperation as long as the adversary refrains from defecting, but of defection if the adversary defects (Axelrod 1984). Axelrod's analysis suggests that if, in a Prisoners' Dilemma, one party lacks credible provocability, the other will defect. A condition for an actor to remain credibly provocable is presumably that he remains capable of defecting in retaliation for defection by the adversary, that is, that he remains capable of seeing to it that in the next game the outcome will be confrontation rather than capitulation. Zagare, in his analysis of deterrence as a sequential Prisoners' Dilemma, comes to a similar conclusion: whether the final outcome will be compromise rather than confrontation hinges on the continued ability of the parties to defect (Zagare 1987).

Sustained cooperation may undermine or be perceived to have undermined this ability. If a state, or another organization, habitually behaves in a cooperative fashion toward another, it may become difficult for it to switch to conflictive behavior, and to maintain the credibility of this option. There is inertia in organizations. There is a tendency for organizational policies to become stabilized, that is, increasingly resistant to pressure for change.[14] It is difficult to increase trust without undermining deterrence.

Indeed, cooperation may undermine the credibility not just of the adversary's ability to retaliate but of his desire to do so. This is the case when a party to a Prisoners' Dilemma comes to believe that the preferences of the adversary are in fact of the Chicken type, that is, that the adversary prefers capitulation to confrontation. If a symmetrical Prisoners' Dilemma is misperceived in this fashion, confrontation will result (Table 4.2, Games 2.3 and 2.6). Just as sustained cooperation may encourage trust, it may come to be interpreted as an indication that the adversary no longer prefers confrontation to capitulation. These are two sides of the same coin. If cooperation does change preferences in the way that the proposition under review is taken to presume, it is reasonable to expect it to change perceptions of adversaries' preferences in the same way.

It is not a valid objection to this argument that the rationalistic analysis of deterrence has proven to be mistaken. Rational deterrence theory, to be sure, has been difficult to reconcile with the results of empirical case studies (see, e.g., George and Smoke 1989; Lebow and Stein 1987, Jervis 1989, Jervis, Lebow, and Stein 1985). However, if rational deterrence theory is weak on this score, so is the equally rationalistic proposition that cooperation inhibits war. Conversely, if this proposition is thought to have merit, there is reason to take the possibility that cooperation undermines deterrence seriously.

A more pertinent objection is that the deterrence argument applies only to Prisoners' Dilemmas and that a likely effect of sustained cooperation is to make Prisoners' Dilemmas unlikely. As cooperation continues, both contenders are increasingly likely to consider confrontation to be their worst outcome, according to this line of thought; the likely decision situation will be Chicken rather than a Prisoners' Dilemma. Indeed, as cooperation deepens and broadens even more, the parties need no longer be presumed to set the capitulation of the other side before other outcomes. Cooperation is thus apt to make deterrence unnecessary. Look at France and Germany since World War II, look at Scandinavia over the last hundred years. Sustained cooperation may lead to the creation of security communities in Karl Deutsch's sense – communities in which war has ceased to be a possibility and deterrence of war is no longer needed.

The plausibility of this thought can hardly be denied. It is not convincing to presume the need for credible deterrence to be unaffected by ongoing cooperation between what used to be adversaries.

This does not suffice to rid the theory of internationalism from its problem with deterrence, however. A distinction must be made between the short and the long term. Maintaining the credibility of deterrence may be a marginal problem in the long term but this need not be the case in the short term. It remains a reasonable thought that cooperation undermines deterrence, and hence peace and security, when cooperative peace-building is at an early stage. There is no getting away from the need for balancing the creation of trust against the maintenance of deterrence, with a significant probability of failure; this is a cardinal problem with war-avoidance by cooperation. This problem may become decreasingly serious as cooperation progresses, but short-term success is a condition for success in the long term.[15]

The United States pursued a remarkably cooperative policy towards its adversary Iraq throughout the 1980s, including the selling of arms and the provision of substantial credit guarantees. On 25 July 1990, the famous or infamous meeting took place between Saddam Hussein and the US Ambassador, April Glaspie, at which the ambassador informed Saddam Hussein that she had 'a direct instruction from the president to seek better relations with Iraq' (Sifry and Cerf 1991: 128). This was barely a week before Iraq invaded Kuwait and six months before a major war broke out between Iraq and the USA. The Iraqi invasion that unleashed the Gulf War was widely blamed on 'the confused semiotics of American diplomacy' (Christopher Hitchens in Sifry and Cerf 1991: 115). Confused semiotics may be a concomitant of the early build-up of cooperation between adversaries.

The possibility of autonomous conflict

Suppose now that cooperation has brought about a situation in which the preferences of both contenders are of the Chicken type. Deliberate confrontation is implausible in this situation, as argued previously. Both contenders have reason to demonstrate their resolve, however. If both do, the autonomous dynamics of escalation may come into play. Hence, the implausibility of deliberate confrontation under Chicken-type conditions is bought at the cost of an increase in the likelihood of autonomous conflict.

What is counter-intuitive here is the suggestion that both parties will deliberately escalate to increase the likelihood of confrontation, in spite of the fact that this is the least-preferred outcome of both. To see their problem, consider coercive bargaining – resolve demonstration – under Chicken-type conditions. Both contenders fear above everything else the increased risk of war that might follow from an intensification of their confrontation. Both, however, have reason to exploit the adversary's fear by playing on the 'threat that leaves something to chance', to use Schelling's famous phrase (Schelling 1960). The suggestion made here is that when caught in this dilemma, which should be as pressing as that of the prisoners, the contenders will strike a balance and take action meant to convince the adversary of their greater willingness to run the ultimate risk while increasing this risk only marginally. What cannot be taken for granted is that they will succeed in finding the point where one must capitulate to the other while pressures for further escalation remain manageable. There is room for misperception and miscalculation. It may prove difficult to limit conflict even when – indeed, because of the fact that – deliberate war is unthinkable.

In fact, to encourage escalation, the expectation that Chicken-type situations will occur in the future is sufficient. Then, even if the current situation is a Prisoners' Dilemma, the interest of the parties in proving themselves trustworthy is not so clear. If the future casts its shadow over the present, they also have an interest in demonstrating their resolve. Previous cooperation may indeed have made them credibly trustworthy; this, if anything, gives them reason to prove that they remain resolute. Thus, if the contenders believe Chicken-type situations are likely to occur later on, the utility of defection in a current situation of the Prisoners' Dilemma type is increased, as is the likelihood of an autonomous, conflictive development.

I have now outlined the case for worrying about the risks inherent in MAD, that is, in that mutually assured destruction on which stability was thought to rest during the Cold War. The advantage of MAD is (or was) that deliberate war is more or less unthinkable. The disadvantage is (or was) that because deliberate war is more or less unthinkable, inadvertent war is a serious possibility in a crisis. This is the cardinal problem with the proposition that nuclear deterrence makes peace secure. The suggestion that the same applies to the proposition that cooperation inhibits war may seem preposterous. Is it really a plausible thought that inadvertent war may occur between the Scandinavian countries or between France and Germany?

The answer must be taken to be 'no' in these cases; a reason for this will be indicated later on. What needs to be considered at this point is whether it is out of the question in all circumstances that cooperation between adversaries places them in Chicken-type situations in which autonomous war is a serious possibility. The distinguishing feature of MAD is (or was) extreme mutual dependence between adversaries capable of inflicting extreme damage on one another. It is not entirely inconceivable that a similar situation might result from extreme economic interdependence. Economic exchange does not presuppose friendly feelings, only that each side considers its own gains to exceed the costs. OPEC–Western relations in the 1970s are suggestive of the possibility that states with incompatible interests may become so dependent on continuing an economic exchange that their relationship could be described as MAD-like. By the same token, speculation about the possibility of another war between Japan and the United States (Friedman and Lebard 1991) should perhaps not be dismissed out of hand as nonsensical.

CONCLUSION

If international relations become more cooperative, the likelihood of war will diminish – this proposition has been shown in the present chapter to be plausible insofar as it can be given an interpretation in rationalistic terms. One weakness of the proposition is its limited empirical testability. Its claim to general validity, moreover, has been shown to be implausible on several grounds: (a) its scope is limited to the outbreak of war between states; it applies neither to the outbreak of civil war nor to intervention in war that is already in progress; (b) governmental choices between cooperative and conflictive action are affected by a variety of psychological, domestic-political, and international factors in addition to previous interaction with the adversary; (c) the effect of cooperation is not necessarily to reduce the likelihood of war but may also be to increase it, especially by undermining the credibility of deterrence but perhaps also by encouraging action apt to increase the likelihood of autonomous conflict.

To show this is not to force an open door, since the internationalist programme is based on an optimistic assessment of the general utility of cooperation for averting war between adversaries. The main point, however, is not to demonstrate that cooperation cannot always be counted on to do this but to pave the way for a consideration of when it can. Even if the general validity of the proposition is in doubt, it may remain plausible with regard to particular circumstances and particular contenders. Now that the general argument has been sorted out it is easier to see what particulars to consider. Two will be taken up here: type of cooperation, and type of contender.

Type of cooperation: organization, communication, and multidimensionality

One problem with the proposition that cooperation inhibits war, I have argued, is the dilemma between trust and deterrence. Another may be the dilemma between deliberate and autonomous conflict. The issue in the former case is the extent to which credible deterrence will remain necessary in an increasingly cooperative relationship. The issue in the latter case is the extent to which the parties will be inclined to escalate in spite of the increasing cooperativeness of the relationship. Cooperation may make deterrence unnecessary and autonomous conflict implausible in some contexts but not in others.

Some forms of cooperation, first of all, seem less likely than others to lead to dilemmas of this kind. The suggestion I wish to make is that international law and exchange do less to solve the dilemmas than international organization and communication. Law, in order to be effective among states, would seem to require credible provocability in Axelrod's sense (see above); rule-making does not obviate deterrence. Exchange creates mutual dependence, and the result in the extreme case is not unlike mutual nuclear deterrence: both sides will have reason to avoid confrontation but also reason to exploit the adversary's fear of confrontation. International organizations, in contrast, may be set up to avoid, manage, and resolve conflict; if successful, this may reduce the need for deterrence and the incentives for escalation. Transnational communication, furthermore, may help to constrain the kind of behaviour that would need to be deterred as well as the freedom of action of those who might escalate.

This suggestion goes along with a tendency in the academic literature of the 1980s to emphasize the roles of international organization for coordinating expectations and channelling interests toward specific outcomes. An illustration is Keohane's *After Hegemony,* in which the approach set against 'realism' was called 'institutionalism' (Keohane 1984: 7) The invention of the concept of international regime as an aid in the analysis of problems in international political economy was essential for the renewal of institutionalism (Krasner 1983; Haggard and Simmons 1987). This led to an inclination among analysts to emphasize organization rather than interdependence as a means of alleviating the negative consequences of international anarchy (Snyder 1990).

This is not to suggest that international organization will help where interdependence will fail. What I am suggesting is merely that some objections against the proposition that cooperation inhibits war are less pertinent in the former case than in the latter. Organization and communication may still be insufficient to safeguard peace and security. A multidimensional process like the one in Western Europe seems particularly likely to avoid the dilemmas associated with establishing peace by sustained cooperation between adversaries. Mere organization may prove to be as inconsequential as mere communication. The combination of rules and exchange with organization and communication may be needed. There is reason to pose the question whether simpler patterns of international cooperation suffice to bring peace and security. Maybe the internationalist programme needs to be implemented thoroughly and *in toto* in order to work. The argument about the two dilemmas, which seems to have merit in the case of a selective cooperative relationship, is less convincing if it is a matter of a multidimensional build-up of cooperation, however incompatible the original interests of the parties.

Type of contender: democracy and peace

The cognitive argument against the proposition that cooperation inhibits war is in essence that people cannot be presumed to perceive their environment correctly and are particularly likely to misperceive decreases in hostility. The issue in the present context is whether this is true not just of individual leaders and citizens but also of collectivities like states. That would seem to depend on one factor at least: whether there is competition over the definition of the situation. If some have an interest in taking note of decreases in hostility, and if definitions of the situation are publicly debated, sustained cooperation may be more likely to change preferences and perceptions in the way presumed in the theory of internationalism than if this is not the case. Pluralism reduces the impact of cognitive constraints and makes sustained cooperation more likely to affect choices between cooperative and conflictive action – this is one hypothesis that may be put forward.

What may be called the organizational argument against the proposition is in essence that those who cooperate, or who benefit from cooperation, need not be those who make the choice between cooperative and conflictive action on the part of an organization. The argument is twofold: a set of leaders need not inherit the perceptions and preferences of their predecessors, and they need not be influenced in their decision-making by the preferences and perceptions of particular constituencies.

This must be taken to vary between organizations, however. There is variation between countries in the degree to which those who decide on foreign conflict need to take those with transgovernmental and transnational experiences and interests into account. Proponents of the proposition that cooperation inhibits war seem to take it for granted that governments are responsive to those with such experiences: international cooperation is thought to embed governments in a constraining web of interests, concerns, and loyalties across borders. This is more plausible with regard to some countries than to others. A further hypothesis, then, is that governmental responsiveness helps to increase the impact of sustained cooperation on the propensity for conflictive action.

The argument about the inherent utility of conflict is also twofold: external conflict may strengthen one's internal position, and conflict may be a feature of successful bargaining. The latter cannot be helped, but the former may. The more easily governments can obtain internal legitimacy without external conflict, the smaller the inherent utility of external conflict and the larger the inhibiting effect of sustained cooperation – this is a further thought that seems to be plausible.

These suggestions point in the same direction: democracy is essential if cooperation is to inhibit war. Democracies are more pluralistic than non-democracies; democratic governments are more responsive than the governments of non-democracies; democracy provides a degree of governmental legitimacy lacking in non-democracies. Some of the criticisms that can be levelled against the proposition that cooperation inhibits war thus seem less compelling if it is a matter of democratic states. Add this to the role of international opinion formation in the theory of internationalism.

The thought that domestic democracy is essential for international peace-building is commonplace and is often traced back to Kant's presumption in *Zum ewigen Frieden* that peace presupposed not only the establishment of a federation but also that the states were 'republican'. But then it needs to be asked whether effective peace-building is feasible only when it is not needed. Maybe domestic democracy is a sufficient condition for war avoidance. Maybe international peace-building is superfluous where it might succeed.

The fact that democratic states do not fight each other has been characterized as 'one of the strongest nontrivial or nontautological generalizations that can be made about international relations' (Russett 1990: 123). The absence of war between democratic states, in the words of another scholar, 'comes as close as anything we have to an empirical law in international relations' (Levy 1989: 270; for more sceptical views see Cohen 1992 and Gleditsch 1992). The association between democracy and absence of war cannot be accounted for in terms of variables like wealth, economic growth, and common alliances (Maoz and Russett 1991, 1992); insofar as can be ascertained, the absence of war between democracies is in fact related to the democratic form of government.

It is not obvious what it is about democracy that inhibits war between democracies. The end of the Cold War placed this issue at the top of the research agenda but even if much of the academic literature is recent, the debate has a long history.

The traditional view is that democracies are peaceful because this is in the interest of the majority. This is how Kant put it two hundred years ago:

> If . . . the consent of the citizens is required to decide whether or not war should be declared, it is very natural that they will have a great hesitation in embarking on so dangerous an enterprise. For this would mean calling down on themselves all the miseries of war. . . . But under a constitution where the subject is not a citizen . . . it is the simplest thing in the world to go to war. For the head of state is not a fellow citizen, but the owner of the state, and war will not force him to make the slightest sacrifice so far as his banquets, hunts, pleasure palaces and court festivals are concerned.
>
> (Doyle 1986: 1160)

When democracy was afforded a crucial role in nineteenth- and early twentieth-century pacifism, the basic idea remained that peace was in the interest of the people more than in that of the rulers, and therefore a 'greater popular voice in the conduct of foreign affairs would prevent governments from making commitments likely to lead the country into war' (Beloff 1955: 20). Democracy, as it was typically put in 1915, 'is anti-militarist: because the people as a whole do not believe any advantage, moral or material can be gained by war. . . . A State will become militarist in proportion to the degree in which it can succeed in eliminating the democratic element' (Ponsonby 1915: 115–16).

The argument in its present-day version is made in terms of institutional constraints rather than the will of the majority: the division of powers, the presence of checks and balances, and the need for public debate 'make it difficult for democratic leaders to move their countries into war' (Ember *et al.* 1992: 576).

This view is open to two objections. Democracies on the whole do not seem to pursue less violent foreign policies than non-democracies and have waged war about as frequently as other states.[16] This, it has been argued, 'cannot simply . . . [be] blame[d] on the authoritarians or totalitarians'; 'aggression by the liberal state has . . . characterized a large number of wars' (Doyle 1986: 1157). What is special is the lack of violence between democratic states.[17] Moreover, it is common for democracies to make foreign policy in a way that differs from their policy-making in other issue areas; the difference between democracy and non-democracy sometimes seems to be smaller so far as foreign policy-making is concerned than with regard to other issue areas (this thought is considered in Goldmann, Berglund, and Sjöstedt 1986).

An explanation of the fact that democracies behave peacefully towards each other but not always towards others has been suggested in terms of the democratic ethos. Politics within democracies, according to this line of thought, are characterized by norms of mutual respect, tolerance, and moderation. Democratic peoples expect such norms to prevail between their own state and the states of other peoples sharing the same ideals. 'Within a transnational democratic culture, as within a democratic nation, others are seen as possessing rights and exercising those rights in a spirit of enlightened self-interest. Acknowledgement of those rights both prevents us from wishing to dominate them and allows us to mitigate our fears that they will try to dominate us' (Russett 1990: 127). Hence war does not occur between democracies. This same factor is a source of tension *vis-à-vis* non-democracies. Just as democrats trust fellow democrats to be intent on resolving conflicts of interest in a spirit of mutual respect, tolerance, and moderation, they regard the rulers of non-democracies with distrust. '[F]ellow liberals benefit from a presumption of amity; nonliberals suffer from a presumption of enmity'

(Doyle 1986: 1161). An attempt to test the arguments in terms of institutional structure and normative ethos against each other found support of both models, but the support of the normative argument was more robust and consistent (Maoz and Russett 1992).

Thus there is evidence supporting the assumption that the democratic form of government itself is indeed the determining factor, and not international peace-building. Peace-building takes place domestically rather than internationally, it appears. There remains a third possibility, however, and that is that the network of inter-state and transnational relations is decisive, just as internationalists presume, but that this network is difficult to twine and is unlikely to inhibit war except between democracies. What matters, according to this argument, is the ability of impulses from abroad to penetrate national borders and gain a foothold within societies. There is some limited empirical evidence pointing in this direction (Holsti and Sullivan 1969). The idea has been characterized as a mere variant of the institutional approach (Ember *et al.* 1992: 577) but this is misleading. Democracy, according to the line of thought now pursued, is not a sufficient condition for international peace and security. It may not even be strictly necessary. The pre-requisite of war-avoidance may not be a particular form of government but a sufficient degree of openness – *glasnost* rather than democracy, so to speak. Openness and democracy tend to go together, but the correlation is not perfect, and the distinction may be crucial in some cases, such as in parts of Europe by the early 1990s.

It is difficult to determine on the basis of the historical record whether democracy or maybe openness is sufficient to inhibit war between societies that are democratic or at least open, or whether close cooperative relations are also necessary. The reason for the difficulty is that democracy, peace, and close cooperation have tended to go together.[18] What can be said is this: whereas there is reason to question whether cooperation between a non-democracy and other states affects the likelihood of war, the matter is less obvious so far as relations between democracies, or open societies in general, are concerned.

If it is openness rather than democracy that is a condition for the internationalist programme to be effective, then the programme stands out as that much more realistic. Add to this the observation made at the end of Chapter 3 to the effect that it is not necessary that all or even most states are democratic in order for internationalism to work. Inter-nationalism does not stand out as utopian in this perspective. Universal democracy, even if ideal, may not be necessary in order for the internationalist programme to work. Widespread openness may suffice.

These are matters about which we can only speculate. The bottom line of the argument therefore is to emphasize the need for research about the way in which inter- and transnational relations interact with domestic structures to produce policy outcomes.[19] The old issue of cooperation and war is linked to one that is more up-to-date: the internationalization of domestic politics and the domestic-politicization of international politics. The more politics become what Putnam calls a two-level game (Putnam 1988), and the more intertwined international and domestic politics become in other ways, the greater the likelihood that peace and security will be affected by international cooperation. By the same token, the more we learn about the links between politics at the international and national levels in different types of political systems, the greater our ability to specify the conditions under which cooperation will play a part in inhibiting war.

5   The ethics of internationalism[1]

If the sanctity of human life is an overriding moral concern, and if altruism is a feature of moral principle, then the case for regarding internationalism as a moral obligation has been outlined. Internationalism is a programme for saving human life on a grand scale by setting universal peace and security before short-term national interests. To refute the claim that there is a moral obligation to pursue the internationalist programme it is insufficient to point out that there are questions and uncertainties in the underlying causal theory: certainty may not be necessary for a moral claim to hold, and the validity of a moral claim may even be independent of causality. This is why the moral status of the internationalist programme needs to be examined.[2]

Moral conviction is part of the internationalist tradition. It has been common to regard internationalist reform as morally compelling rather than as merely expedient (Smith 1992). This has come out not only in Richard Cobden's rhetoric and Immanuel Kant's philosophy but also in the writings of contemporary international relations scholars. Stanley Hoffmann, for example, argues in *Duties beyond Borders* that the ethics of the statesman 'ought to be guided by the imperative of moving the international arena from the state of a jungle to that of a society' (Hoffmann 1981: 35), and Joseph Nye outlines in *Nuclear Ethics* a number of 'ethical maxims' that include the reduction of 'reliance on nuclear weapons over time'; his long-term programme to this end is not unlike Hoffmann's movement from jungle to society (Nye 1986: 99, 130). Hence the pertinence of considering the internationalist programme from a moral point of view.

The tension between the coercive and the accommodative dimensions of internationalism – what is here called the Internationalists' Dilemma – is an additional reason for considering internationalism from a moral point of view. The Internationalists' Dilemma may be seen as an instance of a common issue in moral debate: the tension between a strict adherence to principle and pragmatic manoeuvring for higher ends. There is reason to examine whether a solution in principle can be found to the dilemma between coercion and accommodation by considering internationalism as a moral issue.

THE CLAIM AND THE DILEMMA AS PROBLEMS OF RESEARCH

The moral claim

What it means to characterize a political issue as moral and a political standpoint as morally compelling is not obvious. Loosely speaking, to claim that an issue is of a moral nature would seem to mean that it ought to be decided on the basis of what is right rather than on the basis of what is useful or advantageous. Similarly, to claim that one's own position on such an issue is morally compelling would seem to mean that it represents what is right, in contrast to competing positions. This is not very clear, however. A distinction has been proposed between morality as concerned with 'existing rules and duties' and ethics as concerned with 'ideals and ends that go beyond these duties, and especially with the outcomes of action' (Nardin and Mapel 1992: 3–4). This distinction, however, fails to solve the problem of distinguishing between the ethical and the expedient and will not be adopted here. In the terminology of this book, 'moral' claims may be outcome-orientated as well as rule-orientated.

A non-specialist, as a matter of fact, may get the impression that it is less important in moral philosophy than in politics to devote attention to the difference between the ethical and the expedient. It is obvious that people of diverse persuasions – Christians and non-Christians, liberals and socialists – gain strength from the conviction that they are doing the right and not merely the useful thing in politics. It is obvious, furthermore, that it is considered advantageous in politics to have morality on one's side. There is a millennial tradition of debating peace and security in such terms (Teichman 1986). The presumed moral quality of this issue comes out in several ways: through explicit references to moral principles; through the legitimization of standpoints by professional moralists like bishops and academic philosophers; sometimes implicitly, such as when nuclear weapon-free zones or peace research are contrasted with the alleged propensity of national security policy or political science to be based on immoral *realpolitik*.

There are two reasons for examining such claims. The relationship between ethics and politics may be considered from two perspectives, one constructive and the other sceptical. The task from the former point of view is to increase our insight into how to behave morally – how to do what is right – in politics. Assuming that people are concerned with adopting a stance that can be justified on moral grounds and that the issue is complex enough to make it difficult to see immediately what is right and what is wrong, an analysis of the issue in ethical terms is a constructive contribution to opinion formation and policy-making. The task from the latter point of view is to scrutinize moral claims in a critical fashion. To claim that an issue has a moral dimension and that one's own position is morally superior to that of others is a tempting method for political manipulation, which is a reason for submitting such claims to critical analysis.

The task of examining internationalism can be undertaken both constructively and sceptically: to examine what a person intent on taking a moral stance on issues of war and peace ought to do, and to question the case for affording a moral quality to the internationalist programme. It will be argued in this chapter that the two perspectives, even if separate in principle, are intertwined in practice, since if it is difficult to determine what stance a person ought to take, the claim that a particular stance is morally compelling is undermined. This, it will be argued, is the way in which the problem posed by the Internationalists' Dilemma relates to the general issue of whether the internationalist programme is morally compelling.

A distinction may be made between two types of peace proposal: direct and indirect. Direct proposals for peace and security refer to preparations for war and the conduct of war. Both deterrence and disarmament are examples. The distance between such questions and moral precepts such as 'Thou shalt not kill' is small, since killing is the immediate issue.

Indirect proposals for peace and security refer to background conditions thought to be of consequence for the likelihood of war: proposals to alter individuals with information and education, to change states through democratization, or to transform the international system by internationalism.[3] The distance between the proposed measure and the prevention of killing is larger in this case, and that affects the moral argument.

The debate over the ethics of peace and security has mainly been concerned with the direct approaches. One result of the rise of an anti-nuclear opinion in the 1980s was an avalanche of academic analyses of the ethics of nuclear deterrence, arguably the largest moral challenge in the history of mankind. The issue of arms and ethics was brought to a head in this literature, which is the best recent source of well-considered ideas about how to analyse peace proposals from a moral point of view.

The indirect approaches have attracted less attention in the literature on the ethics of international relations. In what follows, therefore, the debate about nuclear ethics will be surveyed in a search for ideas that may facilitate the task of evaluating the moral status of internationalism and of resolving the Internationalists' Dilemma.

The Internationalists' Dilemma

The Internationalists' Dilemma follows from the tension between the coercive and the accommodative dimensions of the internationalist programme for peace and security; it follows from the fact that internationalists must be prepared both to ostracize and to empathize. The dilemma arises when internationalists are faced with a government violating or threatening to violate institutions that are vital in their conception of international order. Since institutions – norms and organizations – must be upheld and strengthened, it is necessary for internationalists to take a stand on who is right and who is wrong in international conflicts. The party which is right has a right if not a duty to be uncompromising,[4] and third parties have an obligation to support the just against the unjust. However, according to internationalist thinking it is also necessary to see every conflict from everybody's point of view and to seek resolution through compromise. This is necessary both to prevent the immediate conflict from escalating and with a view to the long-term building of an international society characterized by mutual understanding and accommodation. The proper role of a third party in this perspective is to avoid taking sides and to urge the contenders to negotiate and help them work out a settlement. This is the opposite of what is also needed. The dilemma thus follows from the fact that internationalists are presumed to make all and not just some of the assumptions outlined in Figure 5.1[5] which shows the Internationalists' Dilemma in graphic form.

It must be emphasized that the Internationalists' Dilemma is not merely a logical possibility but a real political problem. The choice facing internationalist-minded Westerners throughout the Cold War may be cited as an example. The choice was between opposing an adversary thought to be pursuing a policy at variance with the requirements of a peaceful international order, in spite of the fact that the act of opposing him implied great dangers to peace and security, or accommodating him, in spite of the fact that this would condone practices seen as incompatible with the requirements of a peaceful

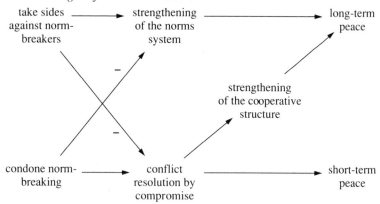

Figure 5.1 The Internationalists' Dilemma

international order. Much of the post-1945 Western debate over containment wrestled with the contradiction between the twin demands of international peace and security: adhering to principle and seeking a *modus vivendi*, bargaining from strength and making unilateral concessions, confrontation and cooperation, deterrence and détente. Internationalist principles failed to provide guidance, since internationalist arguments could be made on both sides.

A more specific example resulted from Iraq's invasion, occupation, and annexation of Kuwait in 1990. There can be no better illustration of the reality as well as the intractability of the Internationalists' Dilemma – of the difficulty, that is, of determining on the basis of internationalist principles what to do when international norms are violated. A reminder of the substance and tone of the US debate about the Gulf crisis may be helpful as a background to a consideration of internationalism in moral terms.

Few apart from Iraq and the PLO denied that Iraq had violated fundamental precepts of international law. The invasion was immediately characterized as a breach of international peace and security by the UN Security Council; the council, in its first resolution on the subject, condemned the invasion and demanded an immediate and unconditional withdrawal of Iraqi forces (Resolution 660, adopted on 2 August 1990). That was not the issue. The issue was whether to use military force to rectify the situation. Four views on this issue may be distinguished: coercive nationalism, coercive internationalism, accommodative nationalism, and accommodative internationalism (Table 5.1).

Table 5.1 Views on how to respond to Iraq's annexation of Kuwait

	Force should be used	*Force should not be used*
National perspective	coercive nationalism	accommodative nationalism
Internationalist perspective	coercive internationalism	accommodative internationalism

Here is, first, an argument of the coercive-nationalist type:

> The United States clearly has a vital interest in preventing Saddam Hussein from getting away with his invasion and annexation of Kuwait. An aggressive Iraq bent on the absorption of its neighbors represents a serious economic threat to American interests. A hostile Iraq armed with chemical, biological, and eventually nuclear weapons represents a 'clear and present danger' to American security. . . .
>
> If Saddam succeeds in incorporating Kuwait into Iraq, he will be in a position to control, by intimidation or invasion, the oil resources of the entire Gulf. This would enable him, and him alone, to determine not only the price, but also the production levels, of up to half the proven oil reserves in the world. This is not simply a question of the price of gas at the pump. It is a matter of the availability of the essential energy that we and our friends around the world need to heat our homes, fuel our factories, and keep our economies vigorous. . . .
>
> Far more important than the question of oil, however, is the extent to which, in American constitutional terms, Saddam is a 'clear and present danger.'. . . [Saddam] is determined to dominate the entire Middle East. . . . Like Hitler, Saddam has an unappeasable will to power combined with a ruthless willingness to employ whatever means are necessary to achieve it. . . . [I]f Saddam prevails in the current crisis, he might eventually pose a direct threat to the United States itself; it would be unacceptable to live in the shadow of an irrational man's nuclear arsenal. . . . If we do not stop him now, we will almost certainly be obligated to confront him later, when he will be chillingly more formidable.
>
> (Representative Stephen J. Solarz,
> Sifry and Cerf 1991: 269–71)

From an accommodative-nationalist point of view, however, military intervention would entail great costs to the United States:

> The war will most likely be bloody and protracted. Victory might

well entangle us in Middle Eastern chaos for years – all for interests that, so far as the U.S. is concerned, are at best peripheral.

Worst of all, the Iraq sideshow is enfeebling us in areas where vital interests are truly at stake. . . . Europe is far more essential to our national security than the Middle East.

And we confront urgent problems here at home – deepening recession, decaying infrastructure, deteriorating race relations, a shaky banking system, crime-ridden cities on the edge of bankruptcy, states in financial crisis, increasing public and private debt, low productivity, diminishing competitiveness in world markets. The crisis of our national community demands major attention and resources too. . . .

War against Iraq will be the most unnecessary war in American history, and it may well cause the gravest damage to the vital interests of the republic.

> (Arthur Schlesinger Jr,
> Sifry and Cerf 1991: 268)

The concerns were different from an internationalist point of view. The foremost coercive internationalist in the debate was President Bush:

[R]ight now Kuwait is struggling for survival. And along with many other nations, we've been called upon to help. The consequences of our not doing so would be incalculable, because Iraq's aggression is not just a challenge to the security of Kuwait and other Gulf nations, but to the better world that we all have hoped to build in the wake of the Cold War. And therefore, we and our allies cannot and will not shirk our responsibilities. The state of Kuwait must be restored, or no nation will be safe, and the promising future we anticipate will indeed be jeopardized.

> (News conference on 8 November 1990,
> Sifry and Cerf 1991: 229)

This is an historic moment. We have in this past year made great progress in ending the long era of conflict and Cold War. We have before us the opportunity to forge for ourselves and for future generations a new world order, a world where the rule of law, not the law of the jungle, governs the conduct of nations.

> (Speech on 16 January 1991,
> Sifry and Cerf 1991: 313)

The standard accommodative-internationalist argument was twofold: loss of life and damage to world order:

[T]he U.S. administration increasingly prepares for war, a war that could lead to the loss of tens of thousands of lives and the devastation of the region. . . .

In the face of such reckless rhetoric and imprudent behavior, as representatives of churches in the United States, we feel that we have a moral responsibility publicly and unequivocally to oppose actions that could have such dire consequences. . . .

We stand on the threshold of a 'new world order.'. . . There are present in this moment seeds either of a new era of international cooperation under the rule of international law or of rule based upon superior power, which holds the prospect of continuing dehumanizing chaos.

> (The National Council of Churches of Christ,
> Sifry and Cerf 1991: 231–2)

As for the new world order, the United Nations will be far stronger if it succeeds through resolute application of economic sanctions than if it only provides a multilateral facade for a unilateral U.S. war. Nor would we strengthen the U.N. by wreaking mass destruction that will appall the world and discredit collective security for years to come.

> (Arthur Schlesinger Jr,
> Sifry and Cerf 1991: 267)

The first [lesson to be learnt from the U.S. invasion of Panama] has to do with the limits of official foresight. Conservative ideologues talk about a 'law of unintended consequences', which means, roughly, that the effort to fix things sometimes worsens the damage.. . .

The second lesson is that however noble the ends, the use of force always entails one tragic and, realistically speaking, *intended* consequence, and that is the loss of lives. Maybe, if President Bush ever overcomes his obsession with Saddam, he might think about how to repay the estimated $1 billion in damage caused by his invasion of Panama. But the dead, whether they number in the thousands or 'only' hundreds, will not wake up to see that happy day. Nor will the tens of thousands who may die in a Gulf war – Americans, Iraqis, and others – ever stir again once the tanks have rolled away across the sand.

> (Barbara Ehrenreich,
> Sifry and Cerf 1991: 300–1, emphasis in original)

The point is that there were both national and internationalist arguments on both sides of the issue. This was not a confrontation between nationalists and internationalists. Debaters disagreed both about what the matter was like from the point of view of the US national interest and about what was the right thing to do from an internationalist point of view. It is worth mentioning that essentially the same internationalist arguments were put forward on both sides in the heated Gulf debate taking place in a country as remote from Middle Eastern power politics as Sweden, a debate that was very much one between internationalists (Liliehöök 1992).

From the perspective of internationalism, then, regardless of whether there is a national interest in going to war, there is an obligation to seek a peaceful solution. At the same time, regardless of the national costs – our boys will be killed, our money will be wasted – there is an obligation to do what it takes to maintain an international order based on the rule of law. Small wonder that Michael Walzer, author of *Just and Unjust Wars*, wrestled with the issue in an article appropriately called 'Perplexed'. Walzer characterized an attack on Iraq as 'just but dangerous':

> The aggressor, as Clausewitz wrote, is a man of peace; he wants nothing more than to march into a neighboring country unresisted. It is the victim and the victim's friends who must choose to fight. Most of us believe that aggression should be resisted and its victims rescued, whenever this is humanly possible. . . . It is very bad to make a deal with an aggressor at the expense of his victim. . . .
>
> [A]nd yet I feel little confidence in the argument and no readiness to join in the shouting, 'Let's fight.' There are a lot of good reasons to be afraid of fighting. The Middle East is a terribly volatile place in which to start a war: Who can say how far the violence will extend? Modern military technology is massive and unpredictable in its effects: How many of the targets that we aim at will we manage to hit? How many homes, schools, hospitals will we hit without aiming at them?
>
> (Sifry and Cerf 1991: 303–5)

As Stanley Hoffmann put it looking back on the Gulf War two years after the fact, 'minimizing violence in international affairs is no less important than resisting aggression', and yet 'there may well be instances in which such resistance, undertaken in the hope of minimizing future violence, can only take the form of force' (Hoffmann 1992: 56).

Two ways of ameliorating the Internationalists' Dilemma may be conceived of. One is to demonstrate that the internationalist programme is not morally compelling. This would reduce the problem from being one of moral incompatibility to one of political optimization. Examination of the strength of the claim that internationalism entails a moral obligation is one object of the present chapter.

The other possibility is to devise a principle for when to ostracize and when to empathize, that is, a plausible solution in principle to the

Internationalists' Dilemma. The Dilemma, as pointed out previously, may be seen as an instance of a common issue in moral debate about politics: the tension between the principle of upholding principles and the principle of doing whatever it takes in the specific case to attain an end deemed to be supremely important. I have made a distinction elsewhere between norms that are 'situation-orientated' and norms that are 'outcome-orientated' (Goldmann 1971: 21). Situation-orientated norms relate the acceptability of an action to a type of situation; whenever such a situation occurs, a particular action is prescribed or prohibited, regardless of the outcome. Outcome-orientated norms relate the acceptability of an action to the occurrence of a certain type of outcome, regardless of other aspects of the situation. The distinction may be useful for our present purposes. Situation-orientated norms are often set against outcome-orientated norms in moral debates over politics, such as in the opposition that may obtain between *ius ad bellum* and *ius in bello* (Walzer 1977). This is also the structure of the Internationalists' Dilemma. To be morally compelling, the internationalist programme needs what may be called a priority-creating norm, that is, a norm determining which of two or more other norms should be given priority, if they come into conflict with each other when applied to specific situations. To search for a priority-creating norm is another objective in what follows.

ETHICS AND POLITICS: THREE ISSUES

This chapter is about the difficulties that may arise for someone intent on forming an ethically-based opinion on a political issue or – which is the same in a different perspective – intent on scrutinizing political persuasion by moral argument. It appears that uncertainty or disagreement may arise in three respects when it is a matter of assessing alternative courses of action from a moral point of view: with regard to (1) the moral basis of the argument – its validity, implications, and consistency; (2) the practicability of proposed courses of action; and (3) the consequences of choosing one course of action rather than another.

The moral basis

Deontology versus consequentialism

The opposition between deontology and consequentialism is fundamental to moral debate. From a deontological point of view, the moral quality of an action is independent of its effects; motives are characteristically stressed instead of consequences. From a consequentialist point of view, the moral quality of an action is contingent on its effects. Some advocates of unilateral disarmament consider their position to be morally compelling because it is derived from a rule such as the Fifth Commandment: 'Thou shalt not kill', and hence you must not prepare for killing, period. The moral case for deterrence, on the other hand, is typically consequentialist: deterrence is permissible or even prescribed, since it may reduce the likelihood of killing. The opposition between deontology and consequentialism is an obvious source of disagreement and uncertainty with regard to the relation between ethics and politics.

Two other issues in political ethics do not run parallel to this opposition in spite of appearances. There is, first of all, no correlation between consequentialism and selfishness, and between deontology and unselfishness. Consequentialists are generally considered obliged to take everybody's well-being into account when assessing the consequences of a course of action, and not just their own or that of their own community.[6] On the other hand, deontologists who act in accordance with a principle whatever the consequences for others are arguably not unselfish. The case for deterrence may be made in terms of peace and security for mankind; the case for disarmament may be that one wishes to keep one's own hands clean.

Furthermore, consequentialism need not mean that there is no obligation to obey rules. Consequentialists may be as concerned as deontologists with the general adherence to a rule such as 'Thou shalt not kill', not because it is the Fifth Commandment but because it will be best for everybody in the long run if all act in accordance with it. That deontologists and consequentialists may differ about what principles to uphold is another matter.

Interpreting the principles

It is a feature of moral uncertainty that it is difficult to determine what a general principle implies in a specific case. Disagreement about this matter is a characteristic feature of moral debate. Two types of problem may arise when a general principle is to be applied to a specific case: problems of precision, which have to do with the meaning of the principle, and problems of information, which are concerned with the features of the specific case. The core principle of *ius ad bellum* is that war is justified in self-defence; few states enter into war with other states without claiming that they do it in self-defence. This typically leads to the problem of how to draw the line between attack and defence as well as to that of determining what course of events preceded the outbreak of war.[7] The debate over nuclear deterrence has similarly been much concerned with the precise meaning of principles for *ius in bello* as well as with the actual features of various deterrence postures.

Conflicting principles

A further concomitant of the moral consideration of politics is the problem of determining what to do when moral principles contradict each other. It is common to maintain that a moral system should be free of contradictions. It is obvious, however, that people may find contradictory demands to be obligating. You should not kill, according to the Fifth Commandment; you should honour your father and mother, according to the Fourth; some have found this to expose them to cross-pressure. A similar problem arises from the tension between *ius ad bellum* and *ius in bello*, as exemplified by the issue of whether the allied strategic bombing of Nazi Germany was justified (Walzer 1977: 255–63).

If there is no moral basis for giving one principle priority, such as the Fifth Commandment or *ius in bello*, all of the conflicting principles would seem to have been undermined. What remains is something less definite than a binding principle, namely, an obligation to engage in what may be called ethical optimization. As we shall see, one of the problems for a person who is neither an extreme deontologist nor an extreme consequentialist and who wants to take a morally-based stance on nuclear deterrence or to assess the stances of others from a moral point of view, is that deontological and consequentialist considerations lead to radically different results; this is apt to undermine the assumption that a moral case can be made with regard to nuclear deterrence. I shall argue that the Internationalists' Dilemma similarly undermines the moral case for internationalism.

The practicability of the alternatives

A further consideration, whether one's object is to take an ethically-based stance on political issues or to seek inoculation against moral persuasion, is whether proposed courses of action are practicable. The issue generally is whether this or that morally appealing course of action is 'realistic'. There is constant disagreement over what is humanly possible (viz. the endless argument about peace and human nature) as well as over what is technically possible (viz. the debate over the sufficiency of renewable sources of energy), not to mention perennial controversies over what is 'politically' possible.

The thought that a course of action must be practicable in order to be morally compelling presumes a distinction between (a) advocating a course of action; (b) the features of this course of action; and (c) the consequences of implementing it. Suppose that somebody proposes that the moon be brought down for the sake of international peace and security. This peace proposal may be 'realistic' insofar as little prevents us from advocating it or from organizing a campaign to attempt to mobilize support for it, but this hardy suffices to make it morally compelling. Its 'realism' may need to be questioned on other grounds: it may be debatable whether it is possible to bring the moon down, and it may be debatable whether peace and security would benefit if it were. The practicability of a course of action is here taken to depend on the former but not on the latter; the practicability of bringing down the moon for the sake of peace and security thus hinges on whether the moon can in fact be brought down but not on whether this would safeguard peace and security.

It is important for a consideration of the ethics of international relations whether nuclear disarmament, internationalism, and other schemes are feasible options in this sense or whether they are castles in the air. This will be kept separate in what follows from the question of what the consequences of implementing them would be. What makes this distinction important is that the question of practicability in the former sense would seem to be important for deontologists and consequentialists alike, but obviously not practicability in the latter sense.

The consequences

Consequentialists often face the additional problem of the consequences of taking this action rather than that being difficult to assess. Nobody can be more aware of the difficulty of forecasting in international politics than one professionally engaged in the study of the field. The management of uncertainty over consequences poses a major ethical problem with regard to both nuclear deterrence and internationalism, it will be argued in what follows.

THE ETHICS OF NUCLEAR DETERRENCE

The debate over nuclear ethics will now be surveyed. Nuclear deterrence may be a less urgent issue in the early 1990s than it was just a few years ago, but the moral issues brought to a head in this debate remain as pertinent as ever.

The object in what follows is to specify what may be problematic about forming an ethically-based opinion on nuclear deterrence – problematic in the sense that there are reasonable arguments in favour of more than one view or no conclusive argument in favour of any view. The method used is to compare the arguments of very serious participants in the debate with contrary views about nuclear weapons. An additional objective is to search for a solution in principle to problems reminiscent of the Internationalists' Dilemma.

The present approach to identifying what is 'problematic' in a political debate is not self-evident. The 'problematic' in effect will be equated with the controversial, and the consensual with the 'non-problematic'. This is to conceive of political debate as rational discourse among people sharing the objectives of analytic clarity and cumulative insight rather than as a confrontation between people with convictions that must be either accepted or rejected. Points of disagreement, in other words, are taken to suggest what is problematic to someone coming in from the outside to take a balanced and well-considered view of what is right and what is wrong. This goes along with the general approach of the book, which is to explore the pros and cons of the internationalist programme rather than to preach it or oppose it.

No attempt has been made to examine all of the extensive literature in which nuclear weapons are considered from a moral point of view. What follows is mainly based on two collections of articles by academic philosophers and political scientists, in which a variety of views are represented: *Nuclear Deterrence: Ethics and Strategy*, edited by Russell Hardin, John J. Mearsheimer, Gerald Dworkin, and Robert E. Goodin (1985) and *Nuclear Rights / Nuclear Wrongs*, edited by Ellen Frankel Paul, Fred D. Miller Jr., Jeffrey Paul, and John Arens (1986). Two oft-quoted monographs about the ethics of international relations, in which the issue of nuclear deterrence is considered, have also been consulted: Michael Walzer's *Just and Unjust War* (1977) and Stanley Hoffmann's *Duties Beyond Borders* (1981).[8] To this has been added Joseph S. Nye's *Nuclear Ethics* (1986). This should suffice to indicate the main concerns and cleavages in the discussion.

The debate departed from a strategic situation appropriately called MAD-plus (Art 1985). MAD, the most well-known acronym of the nuclear age, stands for Mutually Assured Destruction, that is, the situation resulting from the ability of both sides to inflict unacceptable damage on the adversary in a second strike. It became a common thought in the 1960s that the emergence of MAD would cause the probability of nuclear war to be infinitesimal, make arms control a reality, and pave the way for détente; what has become known as common security would be unavoidable in a condition of MAD, since both parties would be compelled to guarantee the security of the adversary for the sake of their own (Buzan 1987: 147–51).

Neither the West nor the Soviet Union were satisfied with MAD, however. In NATO, MAD was thought to be incapable of solving the problem of deterring the USSR from attacking West Europe; since the USSR could inflict unacceptable damage on the USA in retaliation, more than MAD was found necessary for credible deterrence. The Soviet Union, for its part, continued its build-up of nuclear weapons far beyond what was required for MAD. Hence MAD-plus was adopted by both sides.

In the debate over nuclear ethics, four postures in particular were advocated on the ground that they were morally superior to MAD-plus: (1) nuclear disarmament; (2) countercity retaliation, (3) limited counter-force; and (4) strategic defence. We may gain an insight into the moral problematic of nuclear deterrence by comparing the arguments given in support of each of them.

The moral basis

Deontological disarmament

It has been common to base the demand for nuclear disarmament on traditional notions of *ius in bello*. One such notion is the principle of proportionality, by which the damage inflicted by an act of war must be smaller than whatever may be gained by it. Another is the principle of discrimination, by which there is an obligation to discriminate between combatants and noncombatants, or between the guilty and the innocent, since noncombatants or innocents have a right to immunity. The interpretation of the principles and their application to concrete situations have long been debated, but nuclear disarmers maintain that this is irrelevant in the case of nuclear weapons. However the principles of proportionality and discrimination are interpreted, the conduct of nuclear war would violate them in the most obvious way imaginable, it has been argued – even if it is a matter of self-defence (Donaldson 1985) and even if an effort is made to limit devastation to military targets (Roszak 1985).

The principles of proportionality and discrimination are concerned with actual warfare rather than with deterrence, however, and this is wherein the problem lies. Proponents of nuclear deterrence mostly agree that the occurrence of nuclear war would be a moral catastrophe.

The very purpose of deterrence is to prevent the catastrophe from occurring, in their view. They find the moral difference between warfare and deterrence to be fundamental. Their challenge to the deontological disarmer is not to show that nuclear warfare is evil but to demonstrate that it follows from the evilness of nuclear warfare that the mere possession of nuclear weapons or at least their deployment for deterrence is evil.[9] Four ways of doing this are tried in the literature.

The traditional approach is to argue that the intent to commit an evil act is evil in itself (e.g. Dworkin 1985). This, it has been suggested, is 'the most familiar and probably the most widely accepted moral objection to the policy of nuclear deterrence' (McMahan 1985: 141) and has remained 'popular with the anti-nuclear public' (Lackey 1986: 156).

Moral philosophers have come to consider this thought untenable. An alternative that has been suggested is to depart from the concept of risk rather than from that of intention: 'it is wrong, other things being equal, to risk doing that which it would be wrong to do and wrong to support a policy which carries a risk of wrongdoing' (McMahan 1985: 159). What is to be assessed from a moral point of view thus is not the intention but 'the act of risk creation' (Lackey 1986: 159).

Goodin has proposed a third solution to the problem of relating the (obviously immoral) act of nuclear war to the (less obviously immoral) act of nuclear deterrence. Its essence is that since probabilities cannot be computed, there is an obligation to dispose of the very possibility of conducting nuclear war (Goodin 1985).

A fourth solution has been proposed by Hoekema. He has formulated what he calls the Wrongful Threat Principle: 'to threaten to do what one knows to be wrong is itself wrong'. The principle is not categorical; there are conditions under which a threat that would normally be illegitimate would be just. Hoekema argues that they do not obtain with regard to nuclear deterrence, however (Hoekema 1986).

A problem with forming an ethically-based opinion on nuclear deterrence thus concerns the link between the use and the mere possession of nuclear weapons. Given the common assumption that nuclear warfare is immoral in all circumstances, the morality of deterrence hinges on this link. How to forge the link is controversial among those who base their demand for disarmament on the presumption that the link can be forged.

Deontology versus consequentialism

The radical moral alternative to deontological disarmament is consequentialist countercity deterrence, that is, the threat of retaliation against civilian targets. It is difficult to imagine a more drastic challenge to traditional conceptions of *ius in bello*, since the essence of this nuclear posture is to have the conditional intention of killing incomprehensible numbers of people – combatants and noncombatants, 'guilty' and 'innocent', born and unborn. And yet this has been the position of doves in their polemics against hawks. Its moral basis is the assumption that countercity deterrence – MAD in essence – makes nuclear war unthinkable and can be maintained with relatively small nuclear forces, thus inhibiting both crisis instability and arms races.

The conflict between the obligation to adhere to the basic rules of ius *in bello* even, and especially, when it is a matter of nuclear weapons, and the obligation to prevent war from occurring, especially nuclear war, is for some the heart of the ethical problem of nuclear deterrence. This is largely a tension between deontology and consequentialism: the proscription of the massive killing of noncombatants is usually thought to be valid regardless of consequences, and the obligation to do whatever it takes to inhibit nuclear war is quintessentially consequentialist. Not everybody sees this as a dilemma; some give absolute priority to the former obligation and others to the latter. The debate between 'philosophers' and 'strategists' suggests this to be uncommon, however. Deontologists in the nuclear debate tend to concern themselves with consequences, and consequentialists seem anxious to remain faithful to deontological principles. Hence a dilemma.

One attempt to manage the conflict between deontological and consequentialist reasoning has been to make a moral distinction between first and second strike. The principle of discrimination, like other ethical principles, ceases to be binding under extreme conditions, it has been argued; 'in such circumstances killing the innocent would not be unjust because nothing would be unjust' (Morris 1985: 88). A nuclear attack would bring about what otherwise does not exist in modern international politics: a Hobbesian state of nature.

The basis of this view is contractual. Referring to Rawls, Morris writes that 'circumstances of justice' obtain 'only if there exists the possibility of mutually beneficial interaction' (Morris 1985: 91). This is no longer the case if somebody already has taken the morally unacceptable step of returning to a state of nature. Then principles that are otherwise valid have lost their validity and massive retaliation has become permissible.

Other authors have put forward similar thoughts. Mack argues that if an agent is presented with 'an inescapably perilous condition which imposes on him an inevitably fatal . . . choice', the responsibility may not be his but that of the one who has created the situation

(Mack 1986: 25). The concept of supreme emergency also plays an important part in Walzer's analysis of the application of *ius in bello*; so far as nuclear deterrence is concerned, 'supreme emergency has become a permanent condition' (Walzer 1977: 274).

A related line of thought is pursued by Gauthier, who departs from Rawl's idea of society as 'a cooperative venture for mutual advantage'. Herein is 'a baseline condition for social interaction: no person or other social actor is entitled to benefit at the expense or cost of another, where both benefit and cost are measured against a no-interaction baseline'. To threaten a nuclear first strike is incompatible with this condition, according to Gauthier. But not a threat of retaliation, since this is 'directed at upholding, rather than subverting, the requirement that human society be a cooperative venture for mutual advantage'. Thus nuclear deterrence is 'a moral policy – a policy aimed at encouraging the conditions under which morally acceptable and rational interactions may occur' (Gauthier 1985: 118–19).

So much for the attempt to show that the threat of countercity retaliation can be maintained without abandoning traditional principles of *ius in bello* altogether. A second way of trying to resolve the conflict between deontology and consequentialism has been to advocate limited counterforce. This nuclear strategy gained increased ethical if not religious legitimacy by being adopted by the US Catholic bishops in their much-discussed *The Challenge of Peace: God's Promise and Our Response*, which was published in 1983 at the peak of the anti-nuclear protest. A similar position was taken by some participants in the debate between 'philosophers' and 'strategists'. As explained by Shue, the position presumes that nuclear disarmament is impossible or that it must be rejected on other grounds. It also presumes that a threat of retaliation against civilian targets – MAD without plus – is morally unacceptable. Given these assumptions, a damage-limiting second strike against military targets is the least unacceptable position. The main thing is to make clear that the idea of a first strike is absolutely rejected: 'what is needed is a counterforce capability with a low ceiling on quantity'. Such deterrence is not based on a threat to kill civilians *en masse* and is therefore morally superior to MAD. It is also apt to inhibit crisis instability, which makes it preferable to the massive counterforce of MAD-plus (Shue 1986; the quote is from p. 71).

President Reagan's Strategic Defence Initiative, anathema not just to the bishops but to many of those who prided themselves on having taken a moral position on nuclear weapons, was in fact justified in similar terms. SDI was presented as an effort to reduce and ultimately to eliminate the threat to masses of innocents that MAD entailed. It was advocated as a way out of the ethical dilemmas of nuclear deterrence (Gray 1985: 286–7; Pfaltzgraff 1986: 82). Reagan characterized it as a 'moral obligation' (Gray 1985: 285).

A third effort to resolve the conflict between deontology and consequentialism, which is of particular interest for the Internationalists' Dilemma, is that of some authors to define a proper balance between the two. According to Hoffmann in *Duties Beyond Borders*:

> The criteria of moral politics are double: sound principles, and effectiveness. A morally bad design – say, naked aggression – does not become good because it succeeds. But a morally fine one – say, a rescue operation for the freeing of hostages – does not meet the conditions of the moral politician if the details are such that success is most unlikely, or that the cost of success would be prohibitive.
>
> (Hoffmann 1981: 29)

Hoffmann then suggests how deontology and consequentialism may be combined:

> One must . . . recognize that the calculation of effects, in international affairs, is always hazardous. Because of the huge political handicap of uncertainty, a statesman can never be sure that his means will deliver the results he expects. Therefore, even an ethics of consequences needs to be saved from the perils of unpredictability and from the temptations of Machiavellianism by a corset of firm principles guiding the choice of ends and means – by a dose of ethics of conviction covering both goals and instruments.
>
> (Hoffmann 1981: 33)

This is also the position taken by Nye in *Nuclear Ethics*. Nye rejects categorical principles; 'do what is right though the world should perish' is a thesis he considers even less reasonable in the nuclear age than in earlier times. Consequentialist reasoning, on the other hand, may become 'a morality of convenience'; if rules are abandoned we are soon 'on a slippery slope to rationalizing anything' (Nye 1986: 19). Both rules and consequences must be taken into account, but with an 'initial presumption in favor of rules and rights':

> [A]lways start with a strong presumption in favor of rules and place a substantial burden upon those who wish to turn too quickly to consequentialist arguments. That burden must include a test of proportionality, which weights the consequences of departure from normal rules – not only in the immediate case but also in terms of the probable long-run effects on the system of rules. For particularly

heinous practices such as torture or nuclear war, the presumption may be near absolute, and the burden of proof may require proof 'beyond reasonable doubt'.

(Nye 1986: 23)

He also writes:

Treat rules as prima facie obligations and calculate whether the consequences justify overriding that obligation, but if there is great uncertainty in the calculations and/or the expected values turn out to be roughly even, decide on the basis of rules.

(Nye 1986: 138)

Nye proposes a further rule to prevent easy consequentialism, and that is 'prudence in calculating consequences'. 'When an expected consequence depends upon a long chain of unexpected events', he writes, 'we must expect the unexpected' (Nye 1986: 24).

Nye does not argue against an ethics of consequences. He advocates a weighing of rules against consequences, where rules have priority and where the issue is whether the analysis of consequences leads to results sufficiently clear to justify a deviation from rules.

Lee proposes another way of weighing rules against consequences, namely, by departing from a theory of social institutions. When assessing individual actions, Lee argues, we generally give priority to non-consequentialist principles. We make exception only for situations in which 'a large amount of social benefits' is at stake. The same argument can be made about social institutions: they are morally justified if their social objectives are valuable and if they can be attained in a way that does not systematically violate non-consequentialist principles. According to this view, nuclear deterrence is unacceptable, since it implies such a systematic violation, Lee maintains.

Lee then goes on to suggest an alternative view: a social institution might be considered morally justified if it (a) leads to sufficient positive effects that (b) cannot be attained without a systematic violation of non-consequentialist principles while (c) no alternative institution exists that can realize at least an essential part of the positive effects with a lesser violation of non-consequentialist principles. Lee maintains that counterforce is a violation of condition (c), but not countercity. Counterforce, according to Lee, is more provocative than countercity and thus more apt to provoke a preventive or pre-emptive first strike; countercity therefore has more social utility. The application of limited counterforce, furthermore, is very likely to escalate and therefore it implies a larger rather than a smaller deviation from non-consequentialist principles than countercity (Lee 1985).

Nye and Lee are concerned with the weighing of principles against consequences, and there are similarities between their arguments. Lee appears inclined to give greater weight to consequences than Nye, however. He accordingly favours countercity, which can hardly be justified other than in a consequentialist way, rather than limited counterforce, which tends to be justified partly in deontological terms.

'There is no path other than one of continued wrestling with the ambiguities and contradictions inherent in any deterrent policy', the main political science advisor to the US Catholic bishops wrote in 1984 (Russett 1984: 54). It is difficult not to share his resignation.

The practicability of the alternatives

A further source of disagreement or uncertainty over nuclear ethics is the difficulty of determining whether specific courses of action are practicable. This is a problem with two courses of action that have tended to be justified in deontological terms: disarmament and strategic defence.

Thus, it may be difficult to avoid concluding from the principle of discrimination that total nuclear disarmament is a moral obligation – provided that this is a feasible option. If the continued existence of nuclear weapons must be assumed, the same principle may point in different directions. During the Cold War it led some to limited counterforce: if nuclear deterrence is inevitable, the principle of discrimination may oblige us to choose a strategy that discriminates in favour of the 'innocent'. It led others to advocate strategic defence.

Views have differed with regard to the practicability of proposals for total nuclear disarmament, just as they have differed about the practicability of SDI. There have been technological and political arguments on both sides of both issues. What is important in the present context is to point out that this is another problem with forming an ethically-based view about nuclear deterrence.

The consequences

There has been a tendency in the debate over deterrence to sweep the tension between deontology and consequentialism under the carpet. Those who have advocated counterforce or strategic defence on consequentialist grounds have made a deontological point of their providing an alternative to the mass killing of innocents; deontologists advocating disarmament or limited counterforce by reference to the principle of discrimination have been apt to add that consequentialist counter-arguments are false rather than irrelevant to deontologists. Wholehearted deontologists seem to have been as rare as wholehearted consequentialists, as pointed out previously. Thus few have escaped the third major problem with forming an ethically-based opinion on nuclear deterrence: uncertainty over consequences.

This uncertainty is unavoidable.[10] There has never been agreement over the consequences of the nuclear powers' adopting this or that strategy. There has been no way of testing the various hypotheses that have been put forward. We have not even been able to determine whether nuclear deterrence is 'easy' or 'difficult', as Buzan puts it (1987: 167–71). Very different conclusions have been drawn on the basis of so-called rational deterrence theory, a fact well-known to everybody familiar with the strategic debate. To this must be added the increasing evidence that rational deterrence theory is too simplified to be useful.[11] The basis for forecasts is weak indeed in this area. What does this imply for the ethics of nuclear deterrence?

One possibility is to consider the moral status of an action to be independent of the degree of certainty with which its consequences can be predicted. We are supposed to do what can be done to assess the extent to which each available course of action is likely to lead to a morally desirable outcome and to apply a model for rational decision-making under uncertainty; there is an obligation to choose the course of action that is best by this test. This obligation obtains regardless of whether the assessment of outcomes has a strong or a weak basis; we are obliged in any case to follow the course of action most likely to lead to a morally desirable result. This seems to have been the presumption of many of those, 'philosophers' as well as 'strategists', who have found a particular nuclear weapons policy to be morally compelling.

Goodin's possibilism represents an alternative. It presumes that an assessment is made of the outcomes that different courses of action will make possible or impossible; it does not presume the assessment of probabilities. The key argument against anything less than total nuclear disarmament then is that nuclear war will otherwise remain possible. It may be questioned, however, whether it is reasonable to make moral choices on complex issues on the basis of an analysis that lacks gradations – whether it is reasonable not to take into account, for example, if the likelihood of nuclear war will be large or small if nuclear weapons are retained (see Nye, 1986: 68–9, for a criticism of Goodin's view).

A third possibility is to take the position that rationalism is meaningless under great uncertainty and that intuition is a better guide in such circumstances. This view seems to have been uncommon in the nuclear

debate between 'philosophers' and 'strategists', however. Their debate
has been one between rationalists.

A fourth possibility is to maintain that if uncertainty is great, one
should stick to tradition. If probability assessments are necessarily of
low quality, and if a course of action has previously led to acceptable
results in similar situations, then this course should be retained. It can
be argued that conservatism in this sense – continued nuclear deterrence
in the present case – is an obligation when there is great uncertainty
over consequences (Tännsjö 1991).

All these solutions to the problem of uncertainty – probabilistic
rationalism, possibilistic rationalism, intuition, conservatism – may
appear unsatisfactory; they do to this author. A fifth view to be
considered is that when there is great uncertainty over consequences, it
is impossible to determine what is best from a moral point of view and
impossible to characterize any particular position as immoral.

This is not abandoning altogether the effort to consider nuclear
deterrence from a moral perspective. Even if it is impossible to arrive
at a morally compelling conclusion, there arguably remains an obligation to make the effort. To attempt to do what is right means, as a
minimum, doing what can reasonably be done to obtain as good
information as possible about consequences, to make an effort to
weigh the consequences of various courses of action against each
other, and, of course, to select the course of action that appears best
by this test, however weak.

An obligation to do one's best even when there is great uncertainty
over consequences, and not to rest content with intuition or tradition,
can be given a consequentialist justification. There is almost always
uncertainty over consequences. If we always do what we can to gain
knowledge of consequences, this is likely to make our choices better
from a moral point of view more often than if we do not. Furthermore,
the effort may increase our knowledge in such a way as to reduce the
degree of uncertainty in future situations.

A distinction is made in this argument between the moral evaluation
of opinions and actions and the moral evaluation of choice processes.
Even if it is impossible to determine whether a particular view of
nuclear deterrence is morally superior or inferior, the taking of a given
position may accord more or less with ethical standards. An analogy
may be drawn with the distinction between objective and subjective
rationality: even if objective consequentialism is impossible because of
uncertainty over consequences, there may remain an obligation to act on
a subjectively consequentialist basis.

There are two contingencies in which a political actor – an individual, a political party, a protest movement, a state – may be claimed to have acted immorally on this basis, in spite of the fact that no substantive position can be characterized as moral or immoral. One is negligence, spontaneity, improvisation – the taking of a position without having done what could have been done to analyse morally relevant consequences. The other contingency obtains when the considerations that have determined the choice have not been morally relevant: personal or national prestige, or personal or domestic-political advantage, rather than peace and security.

THE ETHICS OF INTERNATIONALISM

The insights gained from surveying the nuclear weapons debate will now be applied to a consideration of the ethics of internationalism. Is internationalism a moral obligation? Is there a solution in principle to the Internationalists' Dilemma?

The moral basis

The interpretation of deontological principles, a major problem in the ethics of nuclear deterrence, is not an issue so far as internationalism is concerned. The reason is obvious. Deontological argument pervades the debate about nuclear ethics; advocates of diverse deterrence postures strive to show that their view is compatible with established notions of *ius in bello* or similar principles; it seems uncommon to justify any posture other than countercity retaliation and maybe MAD-plus in purely consequentialist terms. To ascribe an inherent moral quality to the internationalist programme on deontological grounds is a less obvious thought. The moral case for internationalism may be taken to be consequentialist.

This would seem to be the case with all indirect approaches to the question of peace and security. A moral case for a direct approach may be made in both deontological and consequentialist terms; it may be derived from a categorical duty not to kill innocents as well as from an obligation to do whatever will have the best consequences from the point of view of human life. This leads on to uncertainty or controversy about the interpretation of deontological principles as well as about the relative merits of deontological and consequentialist arguments. The moral case for an indirect approach to peace and security cannot be but consequentialist, it would appear, whether it is a matter of reforming individuals, states, or the international system. This does not mean that the moral basis is unproblematic in such cases, as we shall now see.

Competing obligations

The existence of competing obligations may pose a problem in the moral assessment of proposals and actions, as argued previously. This problem seems to have played a remarkably small part in the debate about the ethics of nuclear weapons. 'Peace' appears to have been the only important criterion in the debate between 'philosophers' and 'strategists'. Judging from the texts considered in the previous section, there has not even been controversy over the meaning of 'peace' in this debate. The controversial concept of 'positive peace' (Galtung 1973) has been conspicuous by its absence; all of the contending standpoints have been justified in terms of the avoidance of mass killings, that is, in terms of what is peculiarly known as 'negative' peace. Thus there is little to suggest that contending viewpoints on nuclear weapons have reflected an inclination on the part of some to assign greater weight than others to values such as freedom, equality, or justice. The avoidance of nuclear war seems to have been given precedence over everything else by virtually all those intent on considering the issue of nuclear weapons from a moral point of view. It may be concluded on this basis that if we are concerned with the moral status of nuclear disarmament and deterrence, it is not necessary to take the possibility of competing obligations into account.

Matters are more complex so far as internationalism is concerned. National independence may be seen as a basic human value, a fundamental human right that we have an obligation to uphold. The object of internationalism, on the other hand, is to entangle states in a network of institutions and interdependencies. This may not be quite compatible with an obligation to help peoples attain and maintain their national independence. Internationalism, furthermore, is a programme for peace and security among states, and the avoidance of inter-state conflict may clash with an obligation to uphold individual rights.

There is no greater ambiguity in internationalism than its position with regard to national independence. The internationalist programme, as defined in this book, is an attempt to solve or reduce the security problem inherent in an anarchical political system without going so far as to replace anarchy with hierarchy. The issue here is why national independence and hence international anarchy are taken for granted in internationalist thinking. There are two possibilities: internationalists may accept the principle of national independence as a pragmatic necessity, or they may pursue it because of moral conviction. In the former case, they have resigned themselves to the fact that the principle of national independence has such a strong basis in the minds of people that it cannot be defeated; there is no clash between compelling principles so far as they themselves are concerned. In the latter case there is a clash: if it is considered compelling both to entangle states in a constraining network and to maintain their independence, the internationalist programme is inherently problematic.

Michael Walzer is an interesting author in this context because of his central position in the field of political philosophy and his concern with moral issues in international relations. In *Just and Unjust War*, Walzer advocates a quintessentially internationalist moral view of war on the basis of a view of national independence as positively good. Walzer appears to believe that there is an obligation to maintain rather than to undermine a system founded on the independence of states when he argues that every people has a right to its common existence as a nation, that it is therefore important for all states that every state defends its independence and integrity (Walzer 1977: 68–73), and that new nations in particular have a right to develop and strengthen their independence (Walzer 1986). On this assumption there is a moral tension – not an absolute incompatibility, but a tension – between preserving the structure of the international system and modifying it along internationalist lines.[12]

Internationalists thus may or may not be morally committed to the principle of national independence. They may regard the internationalist programme as a way of obtaining the essential benefits of hierarchy without relinquishing the essential benefits of anarchy, or they may find the benefits of anarchy to be illusory. They may find their obligation to be to define a proper balance between the demands of peace and security, on the one hand, and the necessity of retaining the essence of national independence, on the other, or they may set themselves the straightforward task of pursuing the internationalist programme to the limit. They may think that the supranational features of the European Community are taking internationalism too far and hope that developments toward a European Union will be arrested, or they may regard the avant-garde features of West European integration as a pleasant surprise and advocate the continued subversion of the European nation-state. The internationalist tradition 'remains profoundly ambivalent about nationalism and the idea of the nation-state', in the words of one analyst (Smith 1992: 212).[13]

In either case internationalists can hardly fail to be committed to the rights of individuals, however. The sanctity of individual human beings is what may make internationalism morally compelling, since this is what makes peace and security a moral issue. Thus the justification of internationalism hinges on concern with individuals.

Reforming the inter-state system is a means; the safeguarding of individuals is the goal.

That there may exist a tension between implementing the internationalist programme and upholding the rights of individuals is obvious, however. The internationalist programme is as state-centric as 'realist' theory. The essence of coercive internationalism is to prohibit war between states. The essence of accommodative internationalism is to bring states close to each other. Both are made more difficult if states are also considered obliged to concern themselves with each others' domestic affairs. It is difficult to oppose an oppressive regime while maintaining empathic and cooperative relations with it. It is sometimes impossible to liberate individuals from oppression without endangering or violating international peace and security.

That there is a normative tension between the level of the state and the level of the individual is a common theme in the literature. Bull conceives of the problem as one of a contradiction between order and justice (Bull 1977: 78–98). Buzan sees it as a matter of the different implications of security at different levels (Buzan 1983). The conflict between our obligations to individuals and to states is the main problem of international ethics (Reitberger 1993). The pursuit of the internationalist programme cannot always avoid colliding with obligations that internationalists must think that they have toward individuals.

Contradictory obligations may undermine each other. If there is an obligation both to constrain the independence of states and to maintain a system of independent states, this may reduce the compelling nature of both. If it is our duty both to empathize with foreign governments and to react forcefully when they violate the rights of their subjects, this may weaken both duties. When considering the plausibility of the claim that internationalism represents a moral obligation, we must take the existence of competing obligations into account.

Ostracism versus empathy

It remains to consider the Internationalists' Dilemma, that is, the tension between the obligation to ostracize aggressors and the obligation to empathize with every state – the normative tension between coercion and accommodation, in other words. What should internationalists do when they are faced with a state that is violating a rule which must be upheld for the sake of peace and security? Is coercion or accommodation the appropriate ambition of internationalists in this situation?

The Internationalists' Dilemma is twofold; see Figure 5.1. There is, first, a conflict between situation-orientated norms prescribing coercion and accommodation, respectively, with a view to long-term change in the international system. There is, second, a conflict between a situation-orientated norm to the effect that norm-breakers should be punished and an outcome-orientated norm to the effect that one should do whatever is most likely to limit the amount of killing in the immediate situation. Is there a solution in principle to this problem?

One possibility is to let the specific circumstances in each case decide the issue. The violation of a rule may be more or less evident: the factual circumstances may be more or less obvious, and the interpretation of the rule may be more or less controversial.[14] Punishing an offender is more important, the more obvious the violation, it may be argued. By the same token, the more likely accommodation is to succeed in the case at hand, and the more extensive the violence that may be avoided by accommodation, the stronger the reason to connive at the offence, it may appear. Internationalists pondering whether to take a stand against the violation of a rule might also take into account whether action by their own country is essential for bringing about an accommodative solution; there may be reason to conceive of a division of labour between countries that empathize and countries that ostracize (between Scandinavia and the USA, Scandinavians may feel).

The implication of such reasoning is that the choice between ostracism and empathy is made on the basis of the relative strength of the causal relationships indicated to the left in Figure 5.1 as they appear in the specific instance. This approach is problematic from an internationalist point of view, because the strengthening of inter-national institutions is inhibited if violations are dispensed with on occasion. Situation-orientated norms are weakened, if violations are assessed in an outcome-orientated perspective. Consistency in social control – equality before the rules – would seem to be essential for the maintenance of an institution. This condition is not met, if punishment varies with the circumstances.

Another way of managing the dilemma might be to follow the rule of always setting short-term peace and security before long-term con-siderations. The Internationalists' Dilemma may be said to comprise a collision between two rules of action: (1) it is wrong not to do everything in one's power to prevent or stop an imminent or ongoing war; (2) it is wrong not to do everything in one's power to prevent future wars. It is a reasonable argument that it is more important to prevent a war about to occur or to stop a war already in progress than to inhibit wars that may or may not occur in a distant future. This rule would resolve the dilemma by making it an obligation to set (1) before (2).

The opposite rule also appears reasonable, however – a rule to the effect that it is more important to make war in general less likely than to prevent or stop a single war. A way out may seem to be to give the long term priority over the short term unless there is an immediate threat of a particularly horrible war, such as one with nuclear weapons or one that would cause a major environmental catastrophe. But then we are back at the problem of inequality before the rules, in this case to the advantage of rule-breakers capable of unleashing nuclear war or greatly damaging the environment.

Let us turn, therefore, to the opposition between deontological and consequentialist arguments about nuclear deterrence. An analogy may be drawn between this opposition and the Internationalists' Dilemma: nuclear deontology is reminiscent of the principled coercion that internationalists think essential to uphold situation-orientated norms, and nuclear consequentialism is reminiscent of the outcome-orientated, pragmatic accommodation that they also believe is essential for the sake of peace. Two attempts to resolve the conflict between deontology and consequentialism were reviewed in the previous section. Can they be applied to the problem posed by the Internationalists' Dilemma?

First Lee's argument about social institutions. Lee, as we have seen, suggests that a social institution may be considered morally justified if it (a) leads to sufficient positive effects that (b) cannot be attained without a systematic violation of non-consequentialist principles, while (c) no alternative institution exists that can realise at least an essential part of the positive effects with less violation of non-consequentialist principles. Analogous reasoning about the Internationalists' Dilemma might be that an internationalist should connive at a violation of the rules if (a) this sufficiently increases the probability of an accommodative solution (b) which cannot be attained unless the violation is connived at, while (c) an accommodative solution is the only way of preventing or limiting a war. This obviously leads to the position of letting the specific circumstances in each case determine the issue, a solution that has already been found wanting.

Nye needs more than Lee to accept pragmatic deviations from the rules. Applying his nuclear ethics to the Internationalists' Dilemma means, roughly, that rules ought to be given priority except in certain extreme cases. It would seem to follow from the spirit of Nye's argument that an exception from a strict adherence to the rules would be justified if there were a significant probability of nuclear war. Otherwise the obligation would be to coerce rather than to accommodate. This may seem to be eminently reasonable: it is a prerequisite of long-term peace-building that international institutions are reinforced, but it is going too far to be prepared to unleash nuclear war for the sake of international law and organization. However, this is precisely the compromise solution rejected a moment ago; inequality before the law to the advantage of nuclear-armed Saddam Husseins can hardly avoid undermining the rules internationalists are out to reinforce. It does not solve the Internationalists' Dilemma to decide whether to apply or not to apply situation-orientated norms on the basis of the specific features of each case.

A solution in principle to the Internationalists' Dilemma seems difficult to find. You may choose to pursue coercive internationalism consistently, at the cost of sometimes doing the opposite of what is needed from the point of view of accommodative internationalism. Or you may pursue accommodative internationalism consistently, at the cost of working against what is required for coercive internationalism. Or you may try, as most internationalists probably do, to balance one against the other, thus following the paradoxical principle of deciding pragmatically whether to act in a principled fashion. This may be sound internationalist politics but weakens the moral persuasiveness of internationalism.

Practicability

Just as it is essential for nuclear ethics whether total nuclear disarmament is feasible, it is important for the question of the ethics of internationalism whether the internationalist programme is practicable. Is it possible to change the structure of the international system in the way internationalists suggest?

The assumption made throughout this book has been that the answer is yes. Attention has been devoted to the consequences rather than to the feasibility of internationalist change. A note about the practicability of the internationalist programme may be added, however.

The international system, to be sure, has often been conceived of in the same way as the weather: both are often unpleasant but since little can be done about either, rational adaptation is preferable to rituals in both cases. An example is provided by Waltz in his *Theory of International Politics* (1979): anarchy, the main feature of the international system in Waltz's theory, is presumed to be constant. It is obviously a waste of time to consider whether we have an obligation to change constants.

A different perspective on the international system is adopted by Gilpin in *War and Change in World Politics* (1981). The system is constantly changing in Gilpin's theory. This dynamic, however, is the result of a factor beyond the control of any single actor: a differential growth in power resulting from economic rather than political forces. Seen from this perspective, too, adaptation to systemic conditions, albeit variable rather than constant, is what is available to states.

It does seem necessary to assume world government to be out of the question for the foreseeable future and international anarchy to remain a constant. This is a decisive argument against regarding radical rather than moderate internationalism as a moral obligation. It seems necessary, furthermore, to assume some aspects of the international system to be variable without being manipulable; it is hardly a moral obligation to intervene in the kind of process Gilpin describes.

The internationalist programme is meant to do neither, however. The change internationalists have in mind is concerned neither with anarchy *à la* Waltz nor with shifts in the balance of power *à la* Gilpin. Factors such as these are taken for granted in the theory of internationalism. The very objective of the internationalist programme, in a way, is to set up controls and counterweights to check the disturbances following from international anarchy and shifts in the balance of international power.

It has been demonstrated in the twentieth century that large changes are possible in this regard. International organizations have multiplied. Interdependencies have increased. Communications have revolutionized. The extent to which developments such as these have been under deliberate control and direction may be debatable; they are similar in some degree to the power changes with which Gilpin is concerned. Parts of the internationalist programme are being deliberately and effectively pursued by many governments, however. Whether feasible change suffices to make international relations decisively less conflictive remains to be proven. Still there is insufficient reason to question the practicability of far-reaching, deliberate internationalist change.[15] The claim that the pursuit of the programme is a moral obligation can hardly be dismissed on the grounds of impracticability.

The consequences

The main thread of this book is that we do not know enough about the consequences of internationalist change. The conclusions that have been drawn about the potential of international opinion formation as well as about the consequences of cooperation are in essence that neither thought can be dismissed as unreasonable, that both appear to be valid only in specific circumstances, that there is insufficient evidence, and that more research is needed.

The problem of uncertainty is as serious with regard to internationalism as it is so far as nuclear armaments are concerned. It is arguably even more significant in the case of internationalism: whereas moral evaluation may be made in non-consequentialist terms when it is a matter of a direct approach to peace and security, this is essentially impossible in the case of an indirect approach such as internationalism. None of the solutions suggested in the nuclear weapons debate seem to offer a solution. Probabilistic rationalism is not applicable when there is absolutely no way of computing probabilities. Possibilism *à la* Goodin seems more appropriate to the case of proscriptions than with regard to prescriptions. Intuition and maybe traditionalism might be mobilized in support of internationalism, just as with regard to other matters, but perhaps not quite convincingly.

There remains the idea that there is an obligation to analyse consequences and let the result decide the issue, but no obligation to pursue a particular course of action. What does this thought imply for the moral status of the internationalist programme?

Every foreign policy action may have international-systemic effects. Countries cannot choose between influencing and not influencing the international system. There is no choice between activity and passivity in this regard. Just as with regard to nuclear deterrence, the choice is between more or less well-considered action. The obligation that may exist, according to the thought considered here, is to form a well-considered view of the long-term implications for international peace and security of each available course of action and to take this matter seriously into account, rather than to act blindly. It is not immoral not to be an internationalist, according to this line of thought, but it is immoral not to be seriously concerned with the problems raised by internationalists.

CONCLUSION

A claim to the effect that the internationalist programme is morally compelling rests on the assumption of an obligation to save human life. Peace and security will benefit from the implementation of the programme. Human lives will be saved in consequence. Therefore the pursuit of the programme is a moral obligation.

This claim is weakened, first of all, by the tension that obtains between the internationalist programme and other concerns for which an equal moral status may be claimed. Internationalism aims at prohibiting inter-state violence (the coercive dimension) and promoting inter-state harmonization (the accommodative dimension). This competes with an obligation that we may think that we have toward our fellow human beings as individuals, namely, the obligation to uphold their individual rights. It may also compete with the principle of upholding the essential independence of states rather than constraining their freedom of action and integrating them with each other. If it is true that competing obligations undermine one another, then this is apt to weaken the plausibility of the claim that the internationalist programme is obliging.

To this must be added the difficulty of finding a solution in principle to the Internationalists' Dilemma. It is impossible in some situations to determine whether the internationalist programme entails an obligation to escalate the conflict for the sake of coercion or an obligation to empathize with the rule-breaker for the sake of accommodation. That the objectives of a programme are difficult to reconcile with each other is a regular feature of politics. Internal inconsistency is more problematic, if the programme is claimed to be not just sensible but morally compelling.

A further problem has to do with the fact that the moral case for internationalism is consequentialist. Indirect approaches to the problem of peace and security have this in common. Our limited ability to predict consequences tends to make all moral claims debatable in such cases. This, of course, is the classical problem of utilitarianism: however obvious it may seem that utilitarianism is morally compelling, it is difficult to determine what this obligation entails in specific situations, very much including those in which peace and security is the issue.

A suggestion for how to deal with the problem of consequences in such instances has been outlined in this chapter. Even if no particular decision can be characterized as moral or immoral, I have suggested that there may remain an obligation to take long-term systemic consequences into serious account when the decision is made. The process of decision-making, even if not the final decision, may be assessed in moral terms.

This depreciated moral claim in fact may be strong rather than weak. It has been commonplace to debate nuclear weapons in ethical terms, as we have seen; to suggest that no particular nuclear posture can be characterized as moral or immoral and that our only obligation is to consider the consequences for peace and security may seem to be unduly restrained against this background. To maintain that there is such an obligation with regard to internationalism may appear moralistic, since we may be less accustomed to consider the matter of international-systemic change to be a moral issue. This much remains of the claim that the internationalist programme is morally compelling, however.

6 Internationalism: an assessment

The burden of proof is generally on the optimistic side so far as peace and security are concerned. Conflicts abound, and so do weapons. It is rarely difficult to show that we are living in perilous times and that there is reason to arm for the sake of deterrence or maybe to disarm for the sake of war-avoidance. Optimistic assumptions – that the adversary has no intention of attacking or that deterrence will lead to stability – generally seem audacious by comparison.

Internationalists find themselves in the standard situation of peace-and-security optimists when they argue that history can be prevented from repeating itself in its tragic way and that the old idea of peace by institution-building and cooperation is finally likely to work. 'Realistic' people in post-Cold War Europe emphasize the conflictive forces that have been let loose, the characteristic weakness of institutions like the CSCE, and the continuing unwillingness of countries to submit themselves to an effective system of collective security. Since all of this is obvious, the assertion that there is nevertheless an opportunity to build a lasting peace structure needs the support of good theory in order to be persuasive.

The solidity of the theoretical basis of the internationalist programme has been our preoccupation throughout the book. What has emerged is a theory of internationalism that may be characterized as neither implausible nor definitive. One purpose of this chapter is to recapitulate the assumptions of this theory as well as to summarize its limitations. The theory, such as it is, will then be used as a tool for assessing the international situation as it appears towards the end of the twentieth century. Finally the normative issue will be addressed: should we accept or reject the internationalist programme for peace and security?

INTERNATIONALISM AS THEORY OF INTERNATIONAL RELATIONS

The task of a theory of internationalism is to demonstrate that there are significant causal links between law, organization, exchange, and communication, on the one hand, and the strengthening of international peace and security, on the other. An argument to this effect was outlined in Chapter 2 in the form of a theory of coercive internationalism and one of accommodative internationalism (Figures 2.2 and 2.3). The objective in both cases was to explicate the chain of argument leading from each component of the internationalist programme to the avoidance of war as the final outcome. Two features of this reasoning were then considered in detail: the assumption that international opinions are significant in world politics (Chapter 3), and the assumption that there is a tendency for cooperative international relations to inhibit war (Chapter 4). This led on to a number of modifications of the original argument. The analysis, among other things, gave support to the insight that democracy, or at least political openness, is essential in order for internationalism to work.

The various parts of the argument may be combined into a single theory of international relations, whose main features are shown in Figure 6.1. In this figure, both coercion and accommodation are

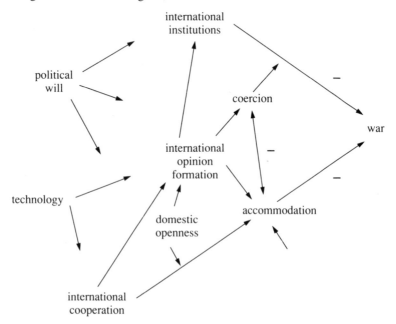

Figure 6.1 Internationalism as theory of international politics

variables. The four strategies of action in the internationalist programme, furthermore, are replaced by two variables called 'international institutions' and 'international cooperation'. 'Escalation' and
'incompatibility of interest', two variables that were introduced in
Chapter 2 to represent the dual causation of war and the twin objective
of internationalism (see Figure 2.1), are left out for the sake of lucidity.
The roles afforded to international opinion and domestic openness, on
the other hand, are given proper emphasis. These are crucial additions
to the original argument, since this is the basis of the assumption that
the internationalist programme may work in the future even if it did not
work in the past. The driving forces of the process are summarily
indicated as 'technology' and 'political will'; it may be considered part
of the theory of internationalism that technology provides new opportunities but that political will is necessary in order to exploit them. The
theory of internationalism is taken to be silent so far as the determinants
of 'technology' and 'political will' are concerned.

The coercive and accommodative dimensions of internationalism are
represented at the top and at the bottom of the figure, respectively. There
is at the top the assumption that international institutions will reduce the
incidence of war, provided that compliance is guaranteed by a credible
threat of coercive measures, which in turn is contingent on international
opinion formation. There is at the bottom the assumption that cooperation
of all kinds and at all levels will reduce the incidence of war by making
accommodation more likely. International opinion, furthermore, is presumed to encourage institution-building as well as accommodation.
Domestic openness is presumed to be essential in order for international
opinions to be formed and have an impact, and also in order for
cooperation to encourage accommodation. The tension between accommodation and coercion – the Internationalists' Dilemma – is represented
by the two-headed negative arrow from one to the other. That opinion-
formers may be cross-pressured in this fashion is clear from the figure.

This theory stands out as reasonably plausible so far as it goes. It
does not go very far, however. Several of its weaknesses have been
considered at various places in the book, including in particular its
problem-solving nature, its indeterminateness, and its lack of conclusive empirical support. The arguments pertaining to each of these
will now be summarized and rounded off.

The problem-solving approach

The theory outlined in Figure 6.1 is general in the sense of purporting to
be valid in a variety of contexts in the past as well as the future, and

structural in the sense of accounting for war and peace in terms of social arrangements. The term problem-solving has been used in the book to denote such theory and to contrast it with explanatory as well as critical theory. A theory of internationalism is necessarily of this kind, I have argued. Internationalism is a programme for social reform through structural change. Hence it presumes a theory to the effect that there is a law-like relationship between structure and action. So-called recipe causality, a common object of contempt among social scientists, is what the theory is out to demonstrate (Riker 1964). The aim is to explore the behavioural effects of structural change rather than to provide a full explanation, an insightful account, a deeper understanding, or a fundamental criticism of human action.

I have assumed throughout the book that the fact that the internationalist programme is necessarily based on general and structural reasoning does not suffice to invalidate it. A further comment is necessary on this point, however. The problem with a theory of peace and war such as this, it may be argued, remains that it ignores the fact that decisions about war and peace are highly context-dependent and strongly influenced by the autonomous thinking of individual decision-makers. Whether peace and war will result thus depends on the way in which each situation is defined by decision-makers, and this in turn is affected by cognitive phenomena such as research, learning, and information rather than by international institutions and cooperative structures. Is this view sufficiently well-founded to justify the conclusion that the theory of international relations outlined here is overly weak and that the internationalist programme for peace and security is untenable as a consequence?

It is important to note the similarity between the question raised here and the criticism levelled against what is virtually the opposite of internationalism, namely, 'neo-realism' *à la* Kenneth Waltz (see Keohane 1986 for a sample of the criticism). This is no accident. Methodologically, neo-realism and internationalism are siblings insofar as both assume the structure of the international system to be a powerful determinant of state action. The difference is substantive, not methodological: neo-realist theory presumes the essential features of the international system to be nearly constant, whereas internationalism presumes that some systemic features essential for war and peace are variable. They are equally vulnerable to the criticism that they are mistaken because of their neglect of context and autonomous thinking. This criticism gained ground as a result of the difficulty of reconciling the end of the Cold War with existing international relations theory (Allan and Goldmann 1992; Gaddis 1992/93).

If 'realism' is rejected on this basis, internationalism must be rejected too, as well as other programmes for rationalistic, large-scale reform of the international system. An alternative is to regard the significance of context and autonomous thinking, and hence the predictive power of general and structural theory, to be an empirical question, and to do what can be done to examine the matter empirically – in other words, to take it for granted that the predictive power of such a theory of international relations is limited by context and autonomous thinking but to insist that the degree to which this is the case can only be ascertained by empirical enquiry. The two views agree that the utility of a general and structural theory, such as the theory of internationalism, is limited. The difference concerns whether this weakness is very considerable and inherent in the method or whether the predictive power of a theory cannot be determined *a priori* but must be assessed by empirical study. I take the latter view in regarding the utility of the theory of internationalism to be essentially unknown rather than known to be small.

Indeterminateness

The theory of internationalism is not one from which precise propositions can be deduced about what will happen to variable Y, given particular values on variables $X_1, X_2, \ldots X_n$. The theory fails to specify necessary and sufficient conditions. It does not specify the strength of relationships between variables or even the predictive power of the theory as a whole. It says nothing about critical thresholds. Its propositions are about weakly specified trends and likelihoods, nothing more. This is a theory to the effect that more of X_1, or X_2, or X_n will reduce the amount or likelihood of Y to an unspecified degree and with an unspecified probability. The theory even permits contradictory conclusions about what will happen to Y as a result of a change in another variable; this is due to the built-in tension between coercion and accommodation.

A feature of weak theory about international relations is that it asserts that a particular phenomenon is likely to be taken into account by decision-makers but says little about the weight of this consideration as against other considerations that decision-makers are also likely to make. Much of international relations theory consists in the mere listing of factors presumed to affect foreign policy actions in this way. Propositions abound about concerns of governments, but there is little theory that can be used to predict the foreign policy actions following from the joint consideration of this variety of concerns.[1] The theory of internationalism is of this type. It predicts that institutions and patterns of cooperation will affect the calculations of governments. This is all.

And that is not enough, it may be argued, since the issue is not whether implementation of the internationalist programme will have some effect or no effect on international peace and security but whether the impact will be weak and superficial or strong and profound.

Another feature of weak theory about international relations is its lack of precision with regard to the time perspective. Internationalism is based on what I have elsewhere proposed to call sooner-or-later theory (Goldmann 1992). A sooner-or-later theory is one that predicts that something is likely to occur sooner or later, that it probably cannot be avoided indefinitely, that it is apt to be realized at some future time. Sooner or later an enslaved people will break its bonds. Sooner or later economic decline will lead to a foreign policy retreat. Sooner or later the build-up of international institutions and increases in international cooperation will make war unlikely.

Such propositions fail to offer more than marginal guidance when it is a matter of taking a stand on a specific issue, such as whether the nations of Europe may disarm now that the Cold War is over and European institutions are proliferating or whether there is reason to wait a generation or two.

Not that the theory of internationalism is uniquely weak in this regard. This is what theories of international relations are generally like. The lack of specificity in the theory of internationalism cannot but weaken the case for the internationalist programme – but also the case for its counter-programmes.

Empirical basis

It has been emphasized throughout that the empirical evidence that may be marshalled in support of the theory of internationalism is insufficient. Even those who reject the suggestion that a theory such as this is bound to have limited utility and who maintain that its utility is an empirical question must admit that the invariances assumed to obtain are less than well-confirmed by historical evidence. The theory of internationalism, as a matter of fact, is less a basis for political action than a programme for research.

Long-standing issues in international relations research, such as the role of international institutions and the relations between pacific and bellicose international relations, form part of this programme. Two further items on the research agenda have been emphasized in this book: the formation and effects of international opinions, and the interplay between international relations and domestic-political structures. Both are crucial for the question of the validity of internationalism, and both arguably represent increasingly significant phenomena.

The phenomenon of international opinion formation is largely unexplored. Here is a field of research that is topical at the present time and is at the same time related to enduring issues in the theory of international relations. The INF study summarized in Chapter 3 is but an explorative first step. There is a need for more ambitious efforts that will call for collaboration between scholars in three different fields: public opinion, mass communication, and international relations.

More effort has gone into the question of the relationship between democracy and war-avoidance, but this far from exhausts the issue of the way in which international relations of different kinds interact with domestic-political structures to produce policy outcomes. This, in contrast to the foregoing, is not a multidisciplinary undertaking but an intra-disciplinary task of political science, one cutting across traditional subdisciplinary borderlines, however.

The political science issue raised by internationalism, in its most general form, is whether politics among states is inherently different from politics within states. From the perspective of an internationalist, as pointed out previously, well-functioning societies are characterized by the rule of law as well as by social cohesion. The internationalist programme of institution-building and cooperation aims at promoting both at the international level. As cohesion increases at the international level – this is an argument internationalists may make – opinion formation on an international scale becomes increasingly likely, and compliance will be reinforced as a result. This will work best if states are democratic. Internationalism may be said to strive for an international system of independent democracies that manage their relations in a democratic way; the making of international politics should resemble the political process inside democracies, internationalists think. This presumes that international politics is not inherently different from politics at other levels. It presumes that interests may be accommodated by peaceful, rational discussion and with the general public as the ultimate arbitrator or sanctioner not just within states but also between them. The impact of internationality on political process is one of the more important issues in political theory; it is raised in a fundamental way by the internationalist vision.

A focus on opinion formation on an international scale, on the way in which domestic-political structures interact with international institutions and patterns of cooperation, and on the similarities and differences between politics between and politics inside countries is not unlike the research programme implicit in Immanuel Kant's *Zum ewigen Frieden*.

THE THEORY OF INTERNATIONALISM AND THE POST-COLD WAR CONDITION

It was widely thought in the aftermath of the Cold War that the fundamentals of international politics had been transformed. The 'realist' contention that international relations would basically remain as they had been before (e.g. Mearsheimer 1990) was not the prevailing view. Richard Ullman argued the case for optimism with particular completeness. It is illuminating to compare his analysis with the reasoning outlined in this book.

'[T]he era Europe has entered will be qualitatively different from those it has known before', Ullman wrote in *Securing Europe*, which was published in early 1991. Thus 'the international politics of the past are not a helpful guide for predicting the patterns of the future'. The decisive new factor was the absence of revisionist major powers in Europe: 'the revolutionary events of 1989–90 have left Germany and the Soviet Union with no vital interests in Eastern Europe except the negative one of seeking assurance that the region will not become a place where threats aimed at them originate'. There were subsidiary reasons for optimism, including the continuing integration, the fact that most European states were likely to be 'constitutional and democratic', and the revolution in communications and information. These factors were secondary in Ullman's view, however. Indeed, even if strong all-European security institutions could be useful, 'they may actually not be needed to prevent the gloomy future that the Realists expect'. Europe might not be free from violent conflict, but 'peace will nonetheless prevail among the major powers that define the European state system, including the two nuclear superpowers. Henceforward, Europe's peace is likely to be a divisible peace' (Ullman 1991: 138–45).

Ullman's analysis differs from internationalist reasoning as defined in this book in its rejection of the 'realist' assumption that features of the international system are of great importance for state action. Internationalism, no less than 'realism', questions the view that developments at the level of individual states suffice to safeguard international peace and security. From the point of internationalism as defined here, cooperation and institution-building are necessary in order to stabilize and render permanent a promising configuration of major power interests such as the one on which Ullman's argument rests; systemic change is a necessary condition for peace and security in the internationalists' view. Because of this, moreover, internationalists are disinclined to regard peace as divisible in Ullman's sense.

What I propose to do in the next few pages, therefore, is to examine whether there is ground for optimism also on internationalist assumptions, that is, to see what the post-Cold War condition may be like in the light of the theory of international relations outlined in the previous section. This theory suggests how structural change at the international level may reduce the likelihood of war. Since the internationalist vision is one of gradual change in the long term, setbacks like those in former Yugoslavia stand out as reminders of the need to modify the international system rather than as proof that this is an impossible task. Assuming that the theory of internationalism is reasonably plausible, is there ground for optimism or pessimism with regard to the long term?

Let us first do what Ullman does not in the book I have cited: adopt a global perspective. The visions of a new 'world order' put forward in the wake of the Cold War differed from each other. In Chapter 5 I quoted President Bush's thoughts about a 'world where the rule of law, not the law of the jungle, governs the conduct of nations' as well as a statement by the US National Council of Churches of Christ to the effect that there were present 'seeds . . . of a new era of international cooperation under the rule of international law' that might replace 'rule based on superior power' and 'the prospect of continuing dehumanizing chaos'. Both statements were made in November 1990 apropos of the Gulf Crisis. The former was concerned merely with the coercive aspect of internationalism whereas the latter emphasized the accommodative aspect, thus illustrating the Internationalists' Dilemma. It was probably common to expect both from the new world order at this time: both the strengthening of the UN and other international institutions and a more gradual but ultimately decisive increase in the ratio of cooperative to conflictive international relations, with worldwide peace and security as the final result.

The theory of international relations outlined in this book indicates at least four reasons for scepticism as regards this expectation.

First, there is reason to believe that increased cooperation has an impact on peace and security only if it is far-reaching and multidimensional; this is one of the conclusions drawn in Chapter 4. The relationship between cooperation and war, in other words, seems unlikely to be linear. There is no way of determining where the critical threshold is – the theory of internationalism is far from precise on this score – but there is reason to question whether the increases in international cooperation that can realistically be expected to be a feature of a 'new world order' will suffice to make international relations decisively less warprone than previously – generations ahead, perhaps, but not in the next few decades.

Second, widespread democracy or at least openness would seem to be essential in order for the implementation of the internationalist programme to do what it promises to do. Will this condition obtain in the 'new world order'? That, to say the least, is not certain by the mid-1990s.

A third reason for scepticism has to do with international opinion formation. Internationalists, who agree that the problematic of international peace and security is rooted in the fact that the international system is one of independent states, have reason to question an assumption to the effect that governments will keep working together to uphold international institutions unless compelled by world opinion. In particular, the problem of collective security has not been solved; a temporary constellation of national interests, such as the one with regard to Iraq in 1991, must not be taken for a decisive transformation of international politics. From an internationalist point of view, a 'new world order' presumes that international opinions at the non-official level will be formed when needed, and that they will prove to be effective, and that the result will be a decrease in the incidence of war. Enough has been said in Chapter 3 about questions in this regard.

Finally, however plausible the assumption that institution-building and cooperation reduce the likelihood that war will break out between states, it is an open question, to say the least, whether these same developments will reduce the likelihood of other wars. It was argued in Chapter 4 that the assumption that cooperation inhibits war is essentially invalid when it is a matter of war within states. It was pointed out, furthermore, that there is probably no general tendency for cooperation to inhibit external intervention in on-going wars, whether intra- or inter-state. International institutions, it may be added, have a long tradition of being based on the assumption of non-intervention in the internal affairs of others; indeed, the proscription of intervention arguably is essential from the point of view of inhibiting inter-state war. Hence international institution-building may have limited relevance for the task of inhibiting intra-state violence – a major function that a 'new world order' must be able to fulfil, as is obvious to everybody by the mid-1990s.

The bottom line is that, given the theory of international relations emerging from this book, global peace remains a distant possibility in spite of the fact that superpower confrontation has ceased to dominate world politics. A marginal increase in the effectiveness of the UN: yes. A major decrease in the propensity to wage war: not likely.

An optimist like Ullman does not deny this. His contention that decisive change has taken place is limited to major power relations in Europe.

Now, whereas the notion of a 'new world order' remained nebulous, the discussion of a new 'European architecture' was more specific. Furthermore, whereas fundamental change seemed unlikely at the global level, it was less farfetched to expect peaceful integration to be substituted for conflictive chaos so far as Europe was concerned. In Europe, even if not globally, it seemed a realistic possibility that the invariances of history could be broken and the conflictive features of a system of competing nations be kept in check by a network of international institutions and cooperative ties. The problem of how to twin the network accordingly moved to the top of the agenda in European politics. Europe by 1990 seemed to carry the possibility of extreme conflictfulness in the short term but also the promise of uncommon peacefulness in the long term. There was no question that the former represented a serious possibility, as demonstrated in the Balkans, the Caucasus, and elsewhere. The issue was whether the latter – long-term peace and security by institution-building and cooperation – was also a plausible scenario.

That the answer is unknown has been sufficiently emphasized in this book. The theory of internationalism is too weak to decide the issue. However, the theoretical argument has indicated some reasons for considering the conditions for successful internationalism to be more promising in Europe than globally.

So far as institution-building is concerned, Europe has been a source of innovation. The compliance problem as conventionally conceived relates to inter-governmental institutions such as the UN. The only organization broad enough to encompass Europe from Vancouver to Vladivostok, the CSCE, is of this traditional type. However, the European Community is a radical departure from the traditional pattern with its supranational features and semi-federal institutions. NATO with its integrated military structure and the European Council with its body of parliamentarians also represent new departures. The problem of inhibiting war by law and organization remains a matter of ensuring compliance, and this in turn remains a matter of credibly overcoming everybody's 'reluctance to get involved in the quarrels and squabbles of others' (Freedman 1992). This classical problem of collective security may prove to be less intractable in organizations departing from the traditional inter-state model, however. It seems worthwhile by the mid-1990s to entertain the idea of European institutions stronger than the CSCE and yet encompassing most of Europe, and hence capable of inhibiting or managing conflicts more successfully than has been the case with regard to former Yugoslavia.

Conditions also seem to be more promising in Europe than elsewhere so far as the development of a strong and multidimensional structure of cooperation is concerned. Even if there is no way of specifying where the threshold is, the cooperative network in Western Europe had probably become sufficiently complex and tightly meshed for peace and security to have ceased to be a problem long before the Cold War ended. The remaining task from an internationalist point of view is twofold: to make the countries of non-EC Europe, and especially Russia, partners in intense cooperation of all kinds with the EC countries, and to see to it that adversary relations between non-EC countries become equally embedded in intense, multi-dimensional cooperation, including relations between newly independent countries now at war with each other. This may fail but is not utopian.

If societal openness is essential in order for the internationalist programme to be effective, as I have suggested, then the situation in Europe seems reasonably reassuring by the mid-1990s also on this account. The democratic form of government has never before had such strong standing in Europe; even Russia is characterized by a reasonable degree of openness. In this regard, as in the other two, there are clouds on the horizon but the conditions for favourable developments are clearly more pronounced regionally in Europe than they are globally.

At the time of writing, two factors in particular seem to stand in the way of successful regional internationalism. One is specific to the 1990s, whereas the other may be more profound. The specific obstacle is the economic situation, which could not have been less favourable to developments along internationalist lines. The more profound obstacle is the widespread assumption of national independence as a fundamental value. Internationalism presumes that concern with national independence is compatible with the implementation of the internationalist programme (see Chapter 2). There are indications to the opposite effect in post-Cold War Europe, both in a self-assertive, East and Southeast European form and in the form of popular West European opposition to the further integration of the EC.[2] Furthermore, relatively weak popular concern with war and persecution in the Balkans suggests the vision of a broad international opinion in support of internationalist objectives to be distant even in Europe of the 1990s, where conditions for the formation of such opinions are more favourable than they have ever been anywhere.

In spite of this, the optimistic scenario is less implausible in the case of Europe than globally. The argument in this book has been that the internationalist programme is relevant only with regard to some of the world's violence, lacks a basis in strong theory, and suffers from a built-in tension between its main dimensions but that some of the objections that can be levelled against it are less compelling in the special case of Europe. The pessimistic scenario for Europe – traditional international politics with its attending tensions and power-struggles – remains a very serious possibility by the mid-1990s. Invariance-breaking cannot be ruled out, however. Holsti may exaggerate when he argues that whereas the conditions for peace and security remain as they have been in the third world, radical change has already taken place among the industrial countries (Holsti 1991). However, if we permit ourselves to be guided by the theory of internationalism as it emerges from this book, we are led to the conclusion that what is unlikely to happen globally may not be out of the question in Europe.

INTERNATIONALISM AS OBLIGATION

The perspective on international relations adopted in the previous section was that of a passive observer asking himself whether matters are likely to change in the way preferred by internationalists, and whether the consequences are likely to be those indicated in the theory of internationalism. The main question raised in this book concerns internationalism as a programme of action, however. What is the validity of this programme? Is this something that we ought to support? Do we have an obligation to be internationalists?

To act in accordance with the internationalist programme means, first of all, to advocate and support institution-building and cooperation at the international level with a view to peace and security, and to set this consideration before others when the objective of peace-building collides with other objectives. It also means, as we have seen, a concern with promoting political openness everywhere. Furthermore, since opinion formation about violations of international norms is essential in order for the internationalist programme to succeed, each individual internationalist arguably is committed to monitor developments and to take a stand when needed.

It is debatable what a commitment to internationalism entails in two respects. One results from the tension between upholding rules and promoting accommodation – the Internationalists' Dilemma, as it has been called in this book. When a rule is violated, the internationalist programme prescribes both ostracism and empathy, and it is difficult to see what a priority-creating norm would be like. The other is the tension that may obtain between the global and regional levels. Radical internationalist change is unlikely at the global level but a less distant possibility in a region like Europe, and it is difficult to exclude the possibility that the strengthening of regional cohesion will prove to be negative from the point of view of global peace and security. These are problems with which committed internationalists must wrestle.

There are three positions in principle one could take with regard to the internationalist programme, with its recommendations and its unresolved questions of priority: that it should be rejected, that it should be taken into account as a matter of prudence, and that it should be pursued as a moral obligation in spite of its internal tensions.

No straightforward conclusion can be drawn about this matter on the basis of the present study: there are too many ambiguities and un-answered questions for this to be possible. I would suggest, however, that there is sufficient basis for regarding the internationalist pro-gramme as plausible, albeit with very considerable qualifications. If there are 'realists' arguing that the internationalist programme has been proved to be fundamentally flawed, this study has demonstrated that their position is difficult to sustain. The theory of internationalism is not well substantiated, but it can hardly be dismissed as obviously un-tenable. There is reason to believe that the effect of pursuing the internationalist programme may become significant in Europe and perhaps other regions, whereas it seems likely to be marginal at the global level; a 'new world order' is not in sight. Marginal effects are also worthwhile, however.

The more interesting question is whether there is reason to take the further step of arguing that the internationalist programme comprises not just guidelines for prudent action but represents a moral obligation. Such a claim would rest on an assumption to the effect that we have an obligation to protect human life. A distinction has been proposed in this book between direct and indirect approaches to the question of peace and security (between, for example, deterrence and disarmament, on the one hand, and peace education and internationalism, on the other). So far as direct approaches are concerned, moral justification may be made in deontological as well as consequentialist terms; it is common to do both. A moral claim for an indirect approach, on the other hand, is necessarily consequentialist. The moral case for internationalism thus hinges on whether the implementation of the internationalist pro-gramme will in fact produce peace and security.

The bottom line of the argument pursued in the book is that we do not know. Some may want to go so far as to argue that the internationalist programme is flawed because it is based on defective epistemology. From a less sceptical point of view, the consequences of implementing the internationalist programme need not be unknowable in principle but remain uncertain in practice. What is offered by the theory of inter-nationalism is a research programme in the first instance.

What does uncertainty over consequences imply for a moral claim based on consequentialist reasoning? Various answers to this question were surveyed in Chapter 5, including probabilistic rationalism, possibilistic rationalism, intuition, and conservatism. A further alternative was outlined and is more appealing to this author: it is difficult to sustain the claim that there is an obligation to pursue the internationalist programme, but there may still be an obligation to take international-systemic implications into account in the consideration of issues of foreign policy. There is arguably an obligation to afford the international system priority with regard to the allocation of political attention – a moral obligation to attempt to pursue prudent internationalism, as it were. The idea of such an obligation is worth further consideration, as suggested in Chapter 5. To do this is one more item on the internationalists' research agenda.

What would it mean in practice for an internationalist to be obliged to take systemic implications into account? The answer has a short-term and a long-term aspect.

The short-term obligation is obvious: to see to it that when an issue is being debated, the international-systemic implications of various courses of action are taken into consideration. In the autumn of 1990 this entailed, for example, an obligation to consider how international law and the UN would be affected if Iraq were to keep Kuwait indefinitely and how they would be affected if the Iraqis were thrown out by force, and to make this a decisive consideration when the final decision was made. In 1991 it entailed an obligation to assess what various courses of action with regard to the war in the Balkans might imply for the development of a new international order. In 1992, by the same token, Europeans had an obligation to consider the international-systemic consequences of saying 'yes' or 'no' to the Maastricht agreement of the EC countries. Even if the particular action chosen cannot be construed as moral or immoral because of the uncertainty that obtains about consequences, the process of choice can be characterized in such terms; it would be morally questionable to take a stand merely on the basis of, say, the national interest, as well as to take a stand emotionally and without an effort at analysis.

So much for the short term. The long-term obligation is one of improving our knowledge of these matters. It is satisfying for an academic to find himself concluding at the end of a study that the pursuit of his research has been a moral obligation.

Notes

1 INTRODUCTION

1 It has been common among peace researchers to distinguish between peace on the one hand and security on the other and even to maintain that there is an opposition between the two. No such distinction is made in this book. It is here assumed that the objective of internationalism is validly represented by the expression 'international peace and security' which, of course, is taken from the preamble and Article 1 of the UN Charter. Expressions like 'peace and security', 'peace', and 'international security' will be used interchangeably for stylistic reasons.

2 It is important to note what 'anarchy' means and does not mean in this context. The term anarchy has a dual sense: its literal meaning is absence of government but it also carries overtones of disorder, violence, and lawlessness. It is a truism in the theoretical literature of international politics that the two do not necessarily go together. 'Anarchy' in this literature generally means merely the former (absence of government) and does not include the latter (disorder etc.). As pointed out by Rosenau (1992: 7), it is a characteristic feature of world politics that 'centralized authority is conspicuously absent from this domain of human affairs even though it is equally obvious that a modicum of order, or routinized arrangements, is normally present in the conduct of global life'.

The concept of international order is not altogether clear, however. Hedley Bull has devoted particular attention to this concept (1977: 3–22). By his definition, an international order is a 'pattern or disposition of international activity' that sustains certain 'goals of the society of states'. There are three such goals in particular: (1) the 'preservation of the system and society of states itself'; (2) 'maintaining the independence or external sovereignty of individual states'; and (3) peace. There is a priority between these goals, according to Bull: (1) takes precedence over (2), and (2) takes precedence over (3). However, the very point of internationalism is to set up a system in which there is no need for priorities, since (1) and (2) can be attained without any sacrifice with regard to (3). 'International order' in this book refers to a system in which this has been achieved; the book is concerned with the question of whether international order in this sense is attainable.

3 This also seems to be compatible with ordinary language. 'Internationalism'

is defined in *The Concise Oxford Dictionary* (1990) as 'the advocacy of a community of interests among nations' and in *Webster's New World Dictionary of the American Language* (1982) as the principle or policy of 'international cooperation for the common good'.

4 It is debatable whether this is a valid characterization of the difference between Kant and Grotius. Kant's *Zum ewigen Frieden* may just as well be seen as one of the classics of internationalism in the Grotian sense, as it will in this book. Kant may not have been quite Kantian in Bull's sense. For a comment on Kant's ambiguity on this score see Mapel (1992: 190).

5 Suganami (1989: 165–96) has constructed a typology of world order proposals in terms of their use of what he terms the domestic analogy. What Suganami calls the 'legal school' comprises mainstream ideas of what is here called internationalism. 'Welfare internationalism' is critical of the limited objective of international order and advocates international co-operation for broader purposes; still it may be seen as part of internationalism as defined in this book, since internationalism must be taken to include the assumption that cooperation for broader purposes may reinforce peace and security as a by-product. 'Democratic confederalism' and 'federalism', on the other hand, represent radical rather than mild internationalism since the purpose in these cases is to replace the system of independent states with a world federation.

6 If the object had been to account for the historical emergence of internationalist ideas, this approach would have been inadequate. It would then have been necessary to consult a vast literature in the field of political philosophy and to go back to the original texts of authors such as Rousseau, Bentham, and Kant. The thrust of this book is not historical, however; the object of the present chapter is merely to remind the reader of the fact that the ideas with which the book is concerned have a history.

7 See de Wilde (1991) for a study of Mitrany's views and those of other twentieth-century thinkers with an internationalist inclination (Norman Angell, Ramsay Muir, Francis Delasi, and Charles Merriam).

8 This idea was put forward with especial persistence on the Soviet side. See Nygren (1984).

9 Zacher (1992: 61) argues that the ongoing 'decay' of the 'Westphalian temple' depends on a single development: the reluctance of great powers to wage war with each other because of the costs of nuclear war.

2 A THEORY OF INTERNATIONALISM

1 Beer (1981) has published what he calls an ecological model of peace and war that may be regarded as an explication of some of the thoughts called internationalist in the present study. It is superior to the present effort in so far as it is systematically related to empirical findings. What makes Beer's theoretical effort unsuitable as a point of departure for the present analysis, however, is that it conceives of international change as the result of developments of a technical and socioeconomic nature rather than of deliberate policy. What is needed here is something else: a theory about the relation between means and goals – between the pursuit of certain policies, on the one hand, and the maintenance of international peace and security, on the other.

A thoughtful study of relevance to this chapter is Kacowicz (1992).

2 Modern authors seeing the Anarchy Model of international relations as ideological myth rather than empirical theory include Ashley (1981) and Lifton and Falk (1982: 234–43).

3 See Chapter 1, for a comment on the concept of international order.

4 It is debatable whether internationalists should be assumed to favour national independence rather than merely to take it for granted. This is traditionally an ambiguous point in internationalist writings (Smith 1992: 212). More about this in Chapter 5.

5 For a brief but perceptive summary of the difference between classical realism and the view here called internationalism see Forde (1992: 80–2).

6 Much unnecessary effort has gone into arguing the silliness of social scientists claiming 'general' validity for their theories. True, many of us have expressed ourselves as if we meant to suggest our generalizations to be valid everywhere and anywhere from Creation to Armageddon. It has mostly been obvious that this has not been the author's intention, however. What the claim for 'general' applicability mostly means is that one's theory is not merely an account of a single case or a descriptive generalization but that it is general enough to apply to cases that have not yet been studied or even occurred.

7 Determinism in a strong sense is ascribed to some structural theories of international relations by their critics but tends to be denied by their authors. A case in point is Waltz's much-discussed *Theory of International Politics* (1979). One of the criticisms levelled against Waltz's theory is in essence that the theory claims to be deterministic while disregarding a variety of factors that affect international-political action. Waltz's reply is in effect to maintain that he has deliberately limited his theory to systemic factors while choosing not to consider potentially significant variables at other levels of analysis (Waltz 1986).

8 International lawyers have argued that the Helsinki Act is not legally binding (Kühne 1977: 138; McWhinney 1978: 164–6; Schütz 1977: 158–9) but they have also maintained that it is more than a non-binding declaration of intentions. One commentator has characterized the Act as 'not irrelevant' from the point of view of international law (Schütz 1977: 165) and another as *rechtsähnlich* (Kühne 1977: 138).

9 This is similar to Kenneth Waltz's argument about the virtues of anarchy: there is, according to this thought, much to be gained for peace and security if states are free to leave each other alone (Waltz 1979: 114–17).

10 This expression is from a talk given by Johan P. Olsen, University of Bergen, at the University of Stockholm, 19 April 1993.

11 An additional way in which international norms may have an impact on international politics is as a means for coordinating the expectations of bargainers. This idea comes from Schelling's *The Strategy of Conflict* (1960) and in essence is that when two actors attempt to come to agreement, they need to coordinate their expectations of what the other party will consider to be a reasonable settlement. Schelling argues that coordination requires 'focal points'. One function of international norms may be to provide focal points – to define an outcome that both sides can perceive as obvious.

The thought may be elaborated in the following way. There often exists a 'bargaining range' in which both parties would prefer agreement to no agreement (Snyder and Diesing 1977: 36–7); this is a condition for agreement. The problem of two bargainers bent on making a deal is to specify precisely where in this range the final settlement should be located. International norms may be capable of offering a solution by defining a position characterized by uniqueness, distinctiveness, and legitimacy.

This notion may help to explain the role of international law in day-to-day international politics. Its relevance, however, is limited to those instances in which the zone of agreement is large and bargaining is mainly a matter of coordinating the expectations of the parties. This is unlikely to be the case when it is a matter of peace and war. Therefore, the idea that international law is effective by coordinating expectations in bargaining is probably marginal to a theory of internationalism.

3 INTERNATIONAL OPINION AND WORLD POLITICS

1 These words were used by the British Foreign Minister about the League of Nations in the House of Commons in 1919 (Parkinson 1977: 157).
2 This section and the next draw on research conducted jointly with Alexa Robertson. See Goldmann and Robertson (1990) for an early version of some of the text.
3 Thus the so-called mood theory of foreign policy opinions has come under increasing criticism on the basis of survey studies. This theory dates back to Almond, who wrote in 1950 that the 'reaction of the general [American] population to foreign policy' could be described as 'one of mood' in the sense that 'foreign policy attitudes among most Americans lack intellectual structure and factual content' and hence were 'bound to be unstable' (Almond 1950: 69). More recent survey studies purport to show that individuals are as capable of taking a considered and well-founded position on issues of foreign policy as they are on domestic issues (Everts and Faber 1990).
4 This view of the concept of the 'exercise' of power and its relationship to the concepts of the 'possession' of power and power 'base' is explained in Goldmann (1979).
5 This contrasts with the finding that it is more common for references to 'world opinion' in the *International Herald Tribune* and the *Frankfurter Allgemeine Zeitung* to have a 'moral component' than a 'pragmatic component' (Rusciano and Fiske-Rusciano 1990).
6 Alexis de Tocqueville and Walter Lippmann are among those who have argued along these lines. (See Goldmann *et al.* 1986, ch. 1.)
7 The very label INF was controversial during the conflictive process leading to the INF Treaty. Synonyms included 'long-range theatre nuclear weapons' (LRTNF), 'medium-range nuclear weapons', and 'Eurostrategic weapons'. The Stockholm International Peace Research Institute (SIPRI), for example, declared INF to be an American concept and insisted on using LRTNF until the mid-1980s (SIPRI 1982: xviii–xxi).
8 Works consulted include Carter (1989), Dean (1987), Garthoff (1985, 1990), Haslam (1990), MccGwire (1987, 1991), Talbott (1985), and several issues of the *SIPRI Yearbook*. Talbott's account, even though journalistic rather than scholarly, is considered by such a well-informed specialist as

Garthoff to be 'the most complete review of the INF negotiations' (Garthoff 1985: 1024).

9 END was European in its aims and contacts, and its annual conventions took place in a different country every year. At the same time, however, it was an integral part of the British peace movement: it was founded by the Bertrand Russell Peace Foundation; it was part of the National Peace Council of Britain; it was identified in the *END Journal* as part of the British movement; Britons were over–represented among its leaders, and this included some of the more influential figures in the British peace movement. (See Coates *et al.* 1981.)

10 Much of this section is based on research carried out by Alexa Robertson in cooperation with the present author and reported primarily in Robertson (1992).

11 Leading members of the British peace movement, including its more prominent ideologues, were often to be found in European Nuclear Disarmament (END) rather than in CND. END was a transnational organization but was also part of the British peace movement; see note 9 above.

12 In October 1984, the number of Britons perceiving international relations to be 'troubled' still exceeded those seeing them as 'peaceful' by 29 percentage points, whereas in Germany the difference had dropped to 9 percentage points. Similarly, whereas in May 1984 32 per cent of the British still thought nuclear weapons to be among the greatest concerns, the figure had dropped to 25 per cent in West Germany (Robertson 1991: 14; Den Oudsten 1988: 11).

13 For a further discussion of the impact of foreign policy orientation and domestic-political factors see Roberton (1992: 265–8).

14 It is interesting to note that *The Guardian* and *The Times* devoted far more space to the German peace movement than *Frankfurter Rundschau* and *Frankfurter Allgemeine Zeitung* did to British protests (Robertson 1992: 177).

15 According to Garthoff, 'decoupling' was never a Soviet objective; the deployment of the SS-20s merely represented an effort to deter NATO from limited war (Garthoff 1990: 73).

16 See Talbott (1985: 56–84) for an account of the debate within the Reagan administration.

17 Garthoff suggests that the prime Soviet interest had been to prevent a US deployment long before the zero proposal was accepted (1990: 73). However, in an earlier work Garthoff maintains that the zero proposal was so disadvantageous to the Soviet Union that the only realistic result of making it was to preclude agreement; in Europe, the proposal was seen as 'the nonnegotiable propaganda platform it was' (1985: 1023–4, 1031). The extreme and unrealistic if not absurd nature of the US position is also stressed by MccGwire (1987: 250–1).

18 A particularly ambiguous stand was taken by those citizens of NATO countries who protested against Western rather than Soviet missiles on the basis that it was their task to turn to their own government rather than to a foreign one (see, for example, an address by West German Social Democrat Erhart Eppler, quoted in Deile *et al.* 1981: 113). This may be seen as a variant of what is here called spurious asymmetry.

19 Kvitsinsky is reported to have said in December 1981 that the negotiations

remained in the 'political phase', by which he apparently meant that both sides were still jockeying for position before their main audience, which was the West Europeans. They could not move into the 'technical phase' before an agreement had been reached at the top, he thought (Talbott 1985: 97).

20 See *World Politics*, Vol. 41, No. 2 (January 1989), which is a special issue about deterrence theory.

21 The available evidence does not suggest that the Reagan administration was equally influenced in its arms control policy by the freeze movement in the US. It appears as if the Reagan administration felt strong enough to resist a domestic anti-nuclear pressure and that it was more worried about the weakness of some of the allied governments in Europe.

4 COOPERATION AND WAR

1 An early exception is Karl Deutsch's theory of integration in the sense of the formation of security communities (Deutsch *et al.* 1957).

2 For a survey of the uses of the single-case method see Eckstein (1975).

3 Quantitative data about Soviet–Western relations suggest that 'conflict-solving' interaction has tended to precede 'cooperation-creating' interaction (Nygren 1980). This fuels the suspicion that lack of conflict is a cause of cooperation rather than the reverse.

4 For an attempt to solve a similar problem see Weede (1983).

5 The 1989 edition of the *SIPRI Yearbook* included a list of thirty-three 'major conflicts in the world' in the year 1988 (pp. 342–55). The vast majority were essentially intra-state, or intra-state with foreign intervention; it will be shown in this chapter that the proposition under review does not apply to such instances. Only four of the cases on SIPRI's list (China–Vietnam, Ethiopia–Somalia, India–Pakistan, and Iran–Iraq) were clearly inter-state. In addition to China–Vietnam, Iran–Iraq may be interpreted as a 'co-operation failure', albeit not a serious one since the cooperative nature of the relationship did not become nearly as pronounced as in the case of Vietnam and China. Saddam Hussein and the Shah made an agreement in March 1975 that claimed to settle all outstanding issues and to eliminate 'completely . . . the conflict between the two brotherly countries' (*Keesing's Contemporary Archives* 1975: 27054). A treaty was signed in June, in which the parties expressed their desire to establish a 'new era of friendly relations', to 'consolidate the ties of friendship and good neighbourliness between them', and to 'deepen their economic and cultural relations' (p. 27285). The main implication was that Iran withdrew its support for Kurdish rebels inside Iraq in return for an equitable division of the Shatt-al-Arab river (Halliday 1979: 272–7; Ramazani 1988: 58; Vatikiotis 1984: 108–10). Relations improved 'dramatically', and friendly gestures continued to be made even after the fall of the Shah. The turning-point did not come until the spring of 1979, when Iranian support of the Shias in Iraq triggered a war of words as well as a series of border skirmishes. Iraq subsequently abrogated the pact that had been made and finally launched the attack that would lead to one of the longest and most murderous wars in recent times (Ramazani 1988: 58–60).

6 Game theory has had its ups and downs in the fashion cycles of international relations research. Major works such as Schelling (1960) Snyder and Diesing (1977), and Axelrod (1984) have seemed to demostrate the utility of this tool for thinking systematically about international relations, only to be followed by a literature denouncing game theory for being simplistic and static. It is worth noting in passing that a recent issue of such a leading professional journal as *International Studies Quarterly* opens with two major game-theoretical papers (Zagare and Kilgour 1993; McGinnis and Williams 1993). My own view is that game-theoretical concepts have indeed proven useful for explicating common assumptions about international relations and for discovering some of their implications but that the explanatory power of propositions put in game-theoretical terms is an altogether different matter. In this book elementary game-theoretical notions are used accordingly to explicate an idea that is essential for internationalism; I take it for granted that the validity of the idea cannot be determined on this basis alone.

7 It is not unthinkable that both DC and CD are preferred to both CC and DD. This is the central feature of the game of Hero (Hamburger 1979: 89). Hero, however, models a conflict about how to organize cooperation – rather than one in which the issue is war or escalation. That is why the impact of preferences of the Hero type are not considered here.

8 Indifference is here seen as an aspect of the degree of clarity of a decision situation. See the end of the present section.

9 It goes without saying that there is a large literature about bargaining, not to mention *détente* and interdependence. Since the object of the next few pages is limited to outlining the specific contribution of each of these familiar approaches to explaining why cooperation may inhibit war, it has seemed unnecessary if not confusing to include large numbers of references to works dealing with them in ways unrelated to the argument pursued here.

10 For this concept of *détente* see Goldmann (1988, ch. 4). For a major work about *détente* see Frei and Ruloff (1983).

11 This is considered in more detail in Goldmann (1988: 31–3).

12 The problem of making these distinctions is discussed in detail in Goldmann 1971: 280–92.

13 This is based on the lists of 'major conflicts in the world' included in the 1989 and 1990 editions of the *SIPRI Yearbook*.

14 See Goldmann (1988: 209–10) for the point that Axelrod's theory of cooperation presumes a degree of flexibility that is unrealistic in many cases because policies tend to become stabilized. See also Oye (1985: 16).

15 This insight grew out of an analysis of the problem of combining deterrence with détente (Goldmann 1988: 206–10).

16 A contrary finding is reported in Rummel (1983).

17 Maoz and Russett make an institutional argument that applies specifically to relations between democracies and in which the rate of mobilization is the key variable. The complexity of the democratic process and the requirement of securing a broad base of support for risky policies make their leaders

reluctant to wage wars, they contend, 'except in cases wherein war becomes a necessity'. The time required to prepare for war thus is far longer than for non-democracies. In a conflict between a democracy and a non-democracy, the latter 'determines . . . the timing of the mobilization process, thereby imposing on the democratic political system emergency conditions during which the government can rally support rather rapidly. . . . The democratic state finds itself in a no-choice situation and leaders are forced to find ways to circumvent the due political process' (Maoz and Russett 1992). This is a peculiar description of some of the instances in which democracies have gone to war in the twentieth century. However, for a powerful counter-instance see Gelb and Betts (1979).

18 Russett argues that the democratic form of government has proven sufficient to inhibit war and points out that no war has occurred between democracies outside the community of prosperous integration, such as those in Latin America (Russett 1990: 121). The non-occurrence of war in the absence of close cooperative relations cannot suffice to establish the irrelevance of the latter, however.

19 A possibility worth looking into is that this interaction differs between democracies. Democratic systems differ from each other in respects that would seem to be relevant to the proposition that cooperation inhibits conflict. There is a difference between the pluralism and weak political structures of the United States and the democracies of Western Europe, which tend to have the opposite features. Foreign policy-making in Washington is characterized by a degree of institutional pluralism that is probably not rivalled elsewhere and this, on the argument pursued in the text, should contribute to increasing the influence of previous cooperation on choices between cooperative and conflictive action. On the other hand, the US political parties are weaker and the individual political leaders probably stronger than is generally the case in Western Europe; the organizational forgetfulness of the US is therefore likely to be stronger, which should tend to make some of the effects of cooperation less lasting in the USA than elsewhere.

5 THE ETHICS OF INTERNATIONALISM

1 Much of this chapter is based on a paper written with the assistance of Kristina Boréus (Goldmann and Boréus 1990).

2 I take it for granted that the view that moral argument is irrelevant at the international level is untenable. A much-cited argument against this view can be found in Beitz (1979: 13–66). See Hoffmann (1981: 10–27) for a less extreme position.

3 This is further discussed in Goldmann and Robertson (1988: 2–7). The last-mentioned trichotomy comes from Waltz's classical *Man, the State, and War* (1959).

4 Cf. Walzer's reasoning to the effect that those who defend themselves against aggression defend everybody (Walzer 1977: 70–3).

5 Cf. Hedley Bull's discussion of the tension between sanctions and balance-of-power politics (Bull 1977: 144).

6 It is even common to use the term consequentialism only with respect to views that reckon the value of consequences in terms of the well-being of humanity at large (Mapel and Nardin 1992: 298).

7   The distinction between problems of precision and problems of information is discussed in detail in Goldmann (1971), which also includes an empirical study of problems that have arisen in the application of international norms to fifty-nine cases of participation in war.

8   General works in which the nuclear issue is considered include Hare and Joynt (1982), Phillips (1984), and Fotion and Elfstrom (1986). Deterrence is considered from a Christian point of view in Davis (1986), Fisher (1985) and Paskins (1986).

9   See Dworkin (1985) on the question of whether there is a moral difference between the possession of nuclear weapons and their deployment for deterrence.

10 See Lackey (1982) for a contrary view.

11 For an exchange of views about rational deterrence theory see the articles by Achen and Snidal, George and Smoke, Jervis, Lebow and Stein, and Downs in *World Politics*, Vol. 41, No. 2 (January 1989).

12 Walzer may not accept this, since he thinks that 'given the uneven development of the state system, and the uneven distribution of power among existing states, we need a set of proposals and programmes adapted to different stages of state-building and self-determination and to different levels of "greatness"' (Walzer 1986: 238). – For critical considerations of the principle of national independence, autonomy, or self-determination see Beitz (1979: 67–123) and Østerud (1991).

13 Smith is concerned with what he calls the liberal tradition of international ethics, but this is similar to what is called internationalism in the present book.

14 Both types of problem with applying international norms to specific situations are richly exemplified in Goldmann 1971, Part II.

15 Works keep being published in which it is argued that 'realist theory' rejects the feasibility of cooperation and in which this allegedly 'realist' assumption is proven to be untenable. A seminal demonstration of the feasibility of cooperation under anarchy is Axelrod (1984). A more recent paper is that by Powell (1991).

6 INTERNATIONALISM: AN ASSESSMENT

1   See Goldmann (1992) for a more detailed argument.

2   Current developments in Europe amount to a natural-scale test of the 'realist' assumption that man's concern with national independence renders the internationalist programme ineffective. I have suggested elsewhere that what is being tested is what, precisely, man stands up for when he stands up for his national independence. The internationalization of issues, societies, and political processes has complicated the issue, I have argued, thus making the limits of internationalism even more obscure than previously. This is why developments in contemporary Europe are apt to provide new insights into fundamental issues in political philosophy (Goldmann 1993).

References

Achen, C. H, and Snidal, D. (1989) 'Rational deterrence theory and comparative case studies', *World Politics* 41, 2: 143–69.

Allan, P., and Goldmann, K. (eds) (1992) *The End of the Cold War: Evaluating Theories of International Relations*, Dordrecht: Martinus Nijhoff Publishers.

Allison, G. T. (1971) *Essence of Decision: Explaining the Cuban Missile Crisis*, Boston: Little, Brown.

Almond, G. A. (1950) *The American People and Foreign Policy*, New York: Praeger.

Ambrosius, L. E. (1987) *Woodrow Wilson and the American Tradition: The Treaty Fight In Perspective*, Cambridge: Cambridge University Press.

Art, R. J. (1985) 'Between assured destruction and nuclear victory: the case for the "Mad-Plus" posture', in J. Hardin, J. J. Mearsheimer, G. Dworkin and R. E. Goodin (eds), *Nuclear Deterrence: Ethics and Strategy*, Chicago / London: University of Chicago Press.

Ashley, R. K. (1981) 'Political realism and human interests', *International Studies Quarterly* 25, 2: 204–36.

——, and Walker, R. B. J. (1990) 'Speaking the language of exile: dissidence in international studies', *International Studies Quarterly* (special issue) 34, 3: 257–416.

Axelrod, R. (1984) *The Evolution of Cooperation*, New York: Basic Books.

Bachrach, P. and Baratz, M. S. (1963) 'Decisions and non-decisions: an analytical framework', *American Political Science Review* 57: 632–42.

Bäck, H. (1979) *Den utrikespolitiska dagordningen. Makt, protest och internationella frågor i svensk politik 1965–1973*, Stockholm: Dept. of Political Science, University of Stockholm.

Baldwin, D. A. (1985) *Economic Statecraft*, Princeton, NJ: Princeton University Press.

Bartelson, J. (1993) *A Genealogy of Sovereignty*, Stockholm: Dept. of Political Science, University of Stockholm.

Beer, F. (1981) *Peace against War: The Ecology of International Violence*, San Francisco: W. H. Freeman and Company.

Beitz, C. R. (1979) *Political Theory and International Relations*, Princeton, NJ: Princeton University Press.

Beloff, M. (1955) *Foreign Policy and the Democratic Process*, Baltimore: Johns Hopkins University Press.

Blainey, G. (1973) *The Causes of War*, New York: Macmillan.

Bresheeth, H., and Yuval-Davis, N. (eds) (1991) *The Gulf War and the New World Order*, London / New Jersey: Zed Books.

Bull, H. (1977) *The Anarchical Society: A Study of Order in World Politics*, London: Macmillan.

Buzan, B. (1983) *People, States, and Fear: The National Security Problem in International Relations*, Brighton: Wheatsheaf Books.

—— (1984) 'Economic structure and international security: the limits of the liberal case', *International Organization* 38, 4: 597–624.

—— (1987) *An Introduction to Strategic Studies: Military Technology and International Relations*, London: Macmillan.

Carlsnaes, W. (1993) 'On analyzing the dynamics of foreign policy change: a critique and reconceptualization', *Cooperation and Conflict* 28, 1: 5–30.

Carter, A. (1989) *Success and Failure in Arms Control Negotiations*, Oxford: Oxford University Press.

Clemens, C. (1985) 'The antinuclear movement in West Germany: angst and isms, old and new', in J. E. Dougherty and R. L. Pfaltzgraff, Jr (eds), *Shattering Europe's Defense Consensus: The Antinuclear Protest Movement and the Future of NATO*, Oxford: Pergamon-Brassey's.

Coates, K., Duff, P., Smith, D., Kaldor, M., Thompson, E.P., and Medvedev, R. (1981) *Eleventh Hour for Europe*, Nottingham: Spokesman.

Cohen, R. (1992) 'Premature celebration: a reappraisal of the democracy-peace theory', Annual Convention of the International Studies Association, Atlanta, GA, 31 March–4 April 1992.

Davis, H. (ed.) (1986) *Ethics and Defence*, Oxford: Blackwell.

Dean, J. (1987) *Watershed in Europe: Dismantling the East-West Military Confrontation*, Lexington, MA / Toronto: D. C. Heath and Company.

Deile, V., Freü, U., Hartmann, T., Meier, A., and Zumach, A. (eds) (1981) *Bonn 10.10.1981*, Berlin: Lamuv Verlag.

Den Oudsten, E. (1988) 'Public opinion on international security: a comparative study of the Federal Republic of Germany, the Netherlands, the United Kingdom and the United States, 1979–1987', unpublished Master's Thesis , Dept. of Sociology, Groningen University.

Deutsch, K. W., Burrell, S.A., Kann, R.A., Lee, M. Jr, Lichterman, M., Lindgren, R.E., Lowenheim, F.L. and Van Wagenen, R. W. (1957) *Political Community and the North Atlantic Area*, Princeton, NJ: Princeton University Press.

de Wilde, J. (1991) *Saved from Oblivion: Interdependence Theory in the First Half of the 20th Century*, Aldershot: Dartmouth.

Domke, W. K. (1988) *War and the Changing Global System*, New Haven / London: Yale University Press.

Donaldson, T. (1985) 'Nuclear deterrence and self-defense', in J. Hardin, J. J. Mearsheimer, G. Dworkin, and R. E. Goodin (eds), *Nuclear Deterrence: Ethics and Strategy*, Chicago / London: University of Chicago Press.

Downs, G. W. (1989) 'The rational deterrence debate', *World Politics* 41, 2: 225–38.

——, Rocke, D. M, and Siverson, R. M. (1985) 'Arms races and cooperation', *World Politics* 38, 1: 118–46.

Doyle, M. W. (1986) 'Liberalism and world politics', *American Political Science Review* 80, 4: 1115–70.

Dworkin, G. (1985) 'Nuclear intentions', in J. Hardin, J. J. Mearsheimer, G.

Dworkin, and R. Goodin (eds), *Nuclear Deterrence: Ethics and Strategy*, Chicago / London: University of Chicago Press.

Eckstein, H. (1975) 'Case study and theory in Political Science', in F. I. Greenstein and N. W. Polsby (eds), *Handbook of Political Science. Vol. 7: Strategies of Inquiry*, Reading, MA: Addison-Wesley.

Eduards, M. (1985) *Samarbete i Maghreb. Om regionalt samarbete mellan Marocko, Algeriet, Tunisien och Libyen*, Stockholm: Dept. of Political Science, University of Stockholm.

Ember, C. R., Ember, M., and Russett, B. M. (1992) 'Peace between participatory polities: a cross-cultural test of the "Democracies Rarely Fight Each Other" hypothesis', *World Politics* 44, 4: 573–99.

Everts, P. P. (1990) 'The peace movement and public opinion', unpublished ms, Leiden: Institute for International Studies.

——, and Faber, A. (1990) 'Public opinion, foreign policy and democracy', ECPR Joint Sessions of Workshops, Bochum, 2–7 April.

Fisher, D. (1985) *Morality and the Bomb: An Ethical Assessment of Nuclear Deterrence*, London / Sydney: Croom Helm.

Flynn, G. and Rattinger, H. (eds) (1985) *The Public and Atlantic Defense*, London: Rowman and Allanheld.

Forde, S. (1992) 'Classical Realism', in T. Nardin and D. R. Mapel (eds) *Traditions of International Ethics*, Cambridge: Cambridge University Press.

Fotion, N. and Elfstrom, G. (1986) *Military Ethics: Guidelines for Peace and War*, Boston, London: Routledge & Kegan Paul.

Fraser, N. M. and Kilgour, M. (1986) 'Non-strict ordinal 2 x 2 games: a comprehensive computer-assisted analysis of the 726 possibilities', *Theory and Decision* 20, 2: 99–121.

Freedman, L. (1992) 'Control and order in the new international system', Conference organized by the Swedish International Development Agency and the Swedish Institute of International Affairs, Saltsjöbaden, Sweden, 18–20 May.

Frei, D. (1980) *Evolving a Conceptual Framework of Inter-Systems Relations*, New York: UNITAR.

—— and Ruloff, D. (1983) *East-West Relations*, Cambridge, MA: Oelge-schlager, Gunn & Hein.

Friedman, G. and Lebard, M. (1991) *The Coming War with Japan*, New York: St Martin's Press.

Gaddis, J. L. (1992/93) 'International relations theory and the end of the Cold War', *International Security* 17, 3: 5–58.

Gaisorowski, M. J. (1986) 'Economic interdependence and international conflict: some cross-national evidence', *International Studies Quarterly* 30, 1: 23–38.

Gallie, W. B. (1978) *Philosophers of Peace and War*, Cambridge: Cambridge University Press.

Galtung, J. (1973) 'Våld, fred och fredsforskning', in L. Dencik (ed.), *Fred, våld, konflikt*, Lund: Studentlitteratur.

Garthoff, R. L. (1985) *Détente and Confrontation: American-Soviet Relations from Nixon to Reagan*, Washington, DC: The Brookings Institution.

—— (1990) *Deterrence and the Revolution in Soviet Military Doctrine*, Washington, DC: The Brookings Institution.

Gauthier, D. (1985) 'Deterrence, maximization, and rationality', in J. Hardin,

J. J. Mearsheimer, G. Dworkin, and R. E. Goodin (eds), *Nuclear Deterrence: Ethics and Strategy*, Chicago / London: University of Chicago Press.

Gelb, L. H. and Betts, R. K. (1979) *The Irony of Vietnam: The System Worked*, Washington, DC: The Brookings Institution.

George, A. L. (1983) *Managing U.S.-Soviet Rivalry: Problems of Crisis Prevention*, Boulder, CO: Westview.

——, and Smoke, R. (1989) 'Deterrence and foreign policy', *World Politics* 41, 2: 170–82.

Gilpin, R. (1981) *War and Change in World Politics*, Cambridge: Cambridge University Press.

Glasgow University Media Group (1985) *War and Peace News*, Milton Keynes: Open University Press.

Gleditsch, N. P. (1992) 'Democracy and peace', *Journal of Peace Research* 29, 3: 369–76.

Goldmann, K. (1971) *International Norms and War between States: Three Studies in International Politics*, Stockholm: Esselte Studium .

—— (1979) 'The international power structure: traditional theory and new reality', in K. Goldmann and G. Sjöstedt (eds), *Power, Capabilities, Interdependence: Problems in the Study of International Influence*, London / Beverly Hills: Sage Publications.

—— (1988) *Change and Stability in Foreign Policy: The Problems and Possibilities of Détente*, Princeton, NJ: Princeton University Press.

—— (1988a) 'The concept of "Realism" as a source of confusion', *Cooperation and Conflict* 23, 1: 1–14.

—— (1991) 'The Swedish model of security policy', *West European Politics* 14, 3: 122–43.

—— (1992) 'Bargaining, power, domestic politics, and security dilemmas: Soviet "new thinking" as evidence', in P. Allan and K. Goldmann (eds), *The End of the Cold War: Evaluating Theories of International Relations*, Dordrecht: Martinus Nijhoff Publishers.

—— (1993) 'Internationalisering, internationalism och nationell självständighet', in B. von Sydow, G. Wallin and B. Wittrock, *Politikens väsen Idéer och institutioner i den moderna staten*, Stockholm: Tiden.

——, Berglund, S. and Sjöstedt, G. (1986) *Democracy and Foreign Policy: The Case of Sweden*, Aldershot, Hants: Gower Publications.

——, and Boréus, K. (1990) 'Etik och politik: kärnvapen och internationalism,' *Statsvetenskaplig tidskrift* 93, 2: 113–35.

——, and Robertson, A. (1988) *Strategies for Peace: The Political Parties, Churches, and Activists in West Germany, Great Britain and Sweden*, Stockholm: Dept. of Political Science, University of Stockholm.

——, and Robertson, A. (1990) *International Opinion, International Politics, and Democracy: A Framework of Analysis*, Stockholm: Dept. of Political Science, University of Stockholm.

Goodin, R. E. (1985) 'Nuclear disarmament as a moral certainty', in J. Hardin, J. J. Mearsheimer, G. Dworkin, and R. E. Goodin (eds), *Nuclear Deterrence: Ethics and Strategy*, Chicago / London: University of Chicago Press.

Gorbachev, M. (1987) *Perestroika: New Thinking for Our Country and the World*, London: Collins.

Grass, G. (1987) On *Writing and Politics*, Middlesex: Penguin.

Gray, C. (1985) 'Strategic defense, deterrence, and the prospects for peace', in

J. Hardin, J. J. Mearsheimer, G. Dworkin and R. E. Goodin (eds), *Nuclear Deterrence: Ethics and Strategy*, Chicago / London: University of Chicago Press.

Haas, P. M. (ed.) (1992) *Knowledge, Power, and International Policy Co-ordination, International Organization* 46, 1 (special issue).

Haggard, S. and Simmons, B. A. (1987) 'Theories of International Regimes', *International Organization* 41, 3: 491–517.

Halliday, F. (1979) *Iran: Dictatorship and Development*, Harmondsworth: Penguin.

Hamburger, H. (1979) *Games as Models of Social Phenomena*, San Francisco: W. H. Freeman and Company.

Harary, F., Norman, R. Z. and Cartwright, D. (1965) *Structural Models: An Introduction to the Theory of Directed Graphs*, New York: John Wiley.

Hardin, R., Mearsheimer, J. J., Dworkin, G. and Goodin, R. E. (eds) (1985) *Nuclear Deterrence: Ethics and Strategy*, Chicago / London: University of Chicago Press.

Hare, J. E. and Joynt, C. B. (1982) *Ethics and International Affairs*, London: Macmillan.

Harsanyi, J. C. (1977) *Rational Behavior and Bargaining Equilibrium in Games and Social Situations*, Cambridge: Cambridge University Press.

Haslam, J. (1990) *The Soviet Union and the Politics of Nuclear Weapons in Europe, 1969–87*, Ithaca, NY: Cornell University Press.

Hemleben, S. J. (1943) *Plans for World Peace through Six Centuries*, Chicago: University of Chicago Press.

Herz, J. H. (1968) 'International relations: ideological aspects', in *International Encyclopedia of the Social Sciences*, London: Macmillan, and New York: The Free Press.

Hinsley, F. H. (1963) *Power and the Pursuit of Peace: Theory and Practice in the History of Relations between States*, Cambridge: Cambridge University Press.

Hoekema, D. A. (1986) 'The moral status of nuclear deterrent threats', in E. Paul, F. D. Miller Jr, J. Paul and J. Ahrens (eds), *Nuclear Rights / Nuclear Wrongs*, London: Basil Blackwell.

Hoffmann, S. (1981) *Duties beyond Borders*, Syracuse, NY: Syracuse University Press.

—— (1992) 'Bush abroad', *The New York Review of Books* 39, 18: 54–9.

Holsti, K. J. (1991) *Peace and War: Armed Conflicts and International Order 1648–1989*, Cambridge: Cambridge University Press.

—— (1992) 'Governance without government: polyarchy in nineteenth-century European international politics', in J. N. Rosenau and E.-O. Czempiel (eds) *Government without Governance: Order and Change in World Politics*, Cambridge: Cambridge University Press.

Holsti, O. and Sullivan, J. D. (1969) 'National-international linkages: France and China as non-conforming alliance members', in J. N. Rosenau (ed.) *Linkage Politics*, New York: The Free Press.

Homans, G. C. (1950) *The Human Group*, New York: Harcourt, Brace and Company.

Hung, N. M. (1979) 'The Sino-Vietnamese conflict: power play among Communist neighbors', *Asian Survey* 19, 11: 1037–52.

Iyengar, S. and Kinder, D. R. (1987) *News That Matters*, London: University of Chicago Press.

Jacobson, H. K. (1984) *Networks of Interdependence: International Organizations and the Global Political System*, 2nd edn, New York: Alfred A. Knopf.

Jervis, R. (1976) *Perception and Misperception in International Politics*, Princeton, NJ: Princeton University Press.

—— (1988) 'Realism, game theory, and cooperation', *World Politics* 40, 3: 317–49.

—— (1989) 'Rational deterrence: theory and evidence', *World Politics* 41, 2: 183–207.

——, Lebow, R. N. and Stein, J. G. (1985) *Psychology and Deterrence*, Baltimore / London: Johns Hopkins University Press.

Jones, D. V. (1992) 'The declaratory tradition in modern international law', in T. Nardin and D. R. Mapel (eds) *Traditions of International Ethics*, Cambridge: Cambridge University Press.

Kacowicz, A. M. (1992) 'Peaceful territorial change', unpublished Ph.D. thesis, Dept. of Politics, Princeton University.

Karns, M. P. and Mingst, K. A. (1987) 'International organizations and foreign policy: influence and instrumentality', in C. F. Hermann, C. W. Kegley Jr and J. N. Rosenau (eds), *New Directions in the Study of Foreign Policy*, Boston: Allen & Unwin.

Karvonen, L. (1981) *'Med vårt västra grannland som förebild'. En undersökning av policydiffusion från Sverige till Finland*, Åbo: Åbo Akademi.

Kelman, H. C. (1958) 'Compliance, identification, and internalization: three processes of attitude change', *Journal of Conflict Resolution* 2, 1: 51–60.

Keohane, R. O. (1984) *After Hegemony*, Princeton: Princeton University Press.

—— (ed.) (1986) *Neorealism and its Critics*, New York: Columbia University Press.

—— (1989) *International Institutions and State Power: Essays in International Relations Theory*, Boulder, CO: Westview Press.

—— and Nye, J. S. Jr., (1977) *Power and Interdependence: World Politics in Transition*, Boston: Little, Brown.

Kitschelt, H. (1986) 'Political opportunity structures and political protest: antinuclear movements in four democracies', *British Journal of Political Science* 16, 1: 57–85.

Köcher, R. (1986) 'Bloodhounds or missionaries: role definitions of German and British journalists,' *European Journal of Communication* 7, 2: 43–64.

Krasner, S. (1982) 'Structural causes and regime consequences: regimes as intervening variables', *International Organization* 36, 2: 185–205.

—— (ed.) (1983) *International Regimes*, Ithaca, NY: Cornell University Press.

Kühne, W. (1977) 'Die Schlussakte der KSZE: zur Bedeutung, Auslegung und Anwendung von Verhaltensregeln in den Ost-West-Beziehungen', in J. Delbrück, N. Ropers and G. Zellentin (eds) *Grünbuch zu den Volgewirkungen der KSZE*, Cologne: Verlag Wissenschaft und Politik.

Lackey, D. P. (1982) 'Missiles and morals: a utilitarian look at nuclear deterrence', *Philosophy & Public Affairs* 11: 189–231.

—— (1986) 'Immoral risks: a deontological critique of nuclear deterrence', in E. Paul, F. D. Miller Jr, J. Paul and J. Ahrens (eds), *Nuclear Rights / Nuclear Wrongs*, London: Basil Blackwell.

Lange, C. L. (1919) *Histoire de l'internationalisme*, Kristiania: H. Aschehoug.

Lapid, Y. (1989) 'The third debate: on the prospects of international theory in a post-positivist era', *International Studies Quarterly* 33, 3: 235–54.

Lebow, R. N. and Stein, J. G. (1987) 'Beyond deterrence', *Journal of Social Issues* 43, 4: 5–71.

—— and Stein, J. G.(1989) 'Rational deterrence theory: I think, therefore I deter', *World Politics* 41, 2: 208–24.

Lee, S. (1985) 'The morality of nuclear deterrence: hostage holding and consequences', in J. Hardin, J. J. Mearsheimer, G. Dworkin and R. E. Goodin (eds), *Nuclear Deterrence: Ethics and Strategy*, Chicago / London: University of Chicago Press.

—— (1986) 'Morality and paradoxical deterrence', in E. Paul, F. D. Miller Jr, J. Paul and J. Ahrens (eds), *Nuclear Rights / Nuclear Wrongs*, London: Basil Blackwell.

Levy, J. S. (1989) 'The causes of war: a review of theories and evidence', in P. E. Tetlock *et al.*, *Behavior, Society, and Nuclear War*, Vol. 1, New York: Oxford University Press.

Lifton, R. J. and Falk, R. (1982) *Indefensible Weapons*, New York: Basic Books.

Liliehöök, C. (1992) 'Aktören och observatören', unpublished seminar paper, Dept. of Political Science, University of Stockholm.

McGinnis, M. D. and Williams, J. T. (1993) 'Policy uncertainty in two-level games: examples of correlated equilibria', *International Studies Quarterly* 37, 1: 29–54.

MccGwire, M. (1987) *Military Objectives in Soviet Foreign Policy*, Washington, DC: The Brookings Institution.

—— (1991) *Perestroika and National Security*, Washington, DC: The Brookings Institution.

Mack, E. (1986) 'Three ways to kill innocent bystanders: some conundrums concerning the morality of war', in E. Paul, F. D. Miller Jr, J. Paul and J. Ahrens (eds), *Nuclear Rights / Nuclear Wrongs*, London: Basil Blackwell.

McKinlay, R. D. and Little, R. (1986) *Global Problems and World Order*, London: Frances Pinter.

McMahan, J. (1985) 'Deterrence and deontology', in J. Hardin, J. J. Mearsheimer, G. Dworkin and R. E. Goodin (eds), *Nuclear Deterrence: Ethics and Strategy*, Chicago / London: University of Chicago Press.

McWhinney, E. (1978) *The International Law of Détente: Arms Control, European Security, and East-West Cooperation*, Aalphen aan den Rijn: Sijthoff and Noordhoff.

Madsen, M. H. (1985) 'The image and impact of world opinion: foreign policy making and opinion abroad', unpublished Ph.D. thesis, Dept. of Government, Harvard University.

Maoz, Z. and Russett, B. M. (1991) 'Alliances, wealth, contiguity and political stability: is the lack of conflict between democracies a statistical artifact?', *International Interactions* 17: 3.

—— (1992) 'Normative and structural causes of democratic peace, 1946–1986', Annual Convention of the International Studies Association, Atlanta, GA, 31 March–4 April 1992.

Mapel, D. R. (1992) 'The contractarian tradition and international ethics', in T. Nardin and D. R. Mapel (eds) *Traditions of International Ethics*, Cambridge: Cambridge University Press.

——, and Nardin, T. (1992) 'Convergence and dissonance in international ethics', in T. Nardin and D. R. Mapel (eds) *Traditions of International Ethics*, Cambridge: Cambridge University Press.

Mearsheimer, J. (1990) 'Back to the future: instability in Europe after the Cold War', *International Security* 15, 1: 5–56.

Miller, J. D. B. (1986) *Norman Angell and the Futility of War*, London: Macmillan.

Morgenthau, H. J. (1961) *Politics Among Nations: The Struggle for Power and Peace*, 3rd edn, New York: Alfred A. Knopf.

Morris, C. W. (1985) 'A contractarian defense of nuclear deterrence', in J. Hardin, J. J. Mearsheimer, G. Dworkin, and R. E. Goodin (eds), *Nuclear Deterrence: Ethics and Strategy*, Chicago / London: University of Chicago Press.

Nardin, T. and Mapel, D. R. (eds) (1992) *Traditions of International Ethics*, Cambridge: Cambridge University Press.

Noelle-Neumann, E. (1983) 'The missile gap: the German press and public opinion', *Public Opinion* Oct.-Nov.: 45–9.

Nye, J. S. Jr (1971) *Peace in Parts*, Boston: Little, Brown.

—— (1986) *Nuclear Ethics*, New York: The Free Press.

Nygren, B. (1980) 'The development of cooperation between the Soviet Union and three Western Great Powers, 1950–75', *Cooperation and Conflict* 15, 3: 117–40.

—— (1984) *Fredlig samexistens: klasskamp, fred och samarbete. Sovjetunionens detente-doktrin*, Stockholm: Dept of Political Science, University of Stockholm.

Ornauer, H., Wiberg, H., Sicínski, A. and Galtung, J. (eds) (1976) *Images of the World in the Year 2000: A Comparative Ten Nation Study*, Mouton: Humanities Press.

Oye, K. A. (1985) 'Explaining cooperation under anarchy: hypotheses and strategies', *World Politics* 38, 1: 1–24.

Østerud, Ø. (1991) *Nasjonenes selvbestemmelsesrett: Søkely på en politisk doktrine*, Oslo: Universitetsforlaget.

Parkinson, F. (1977) *The Philosophy of International Relations*, Beverly Hills / London: Sage.

Paskins, B. (ed.) (1986) *Ethics and European Security*, London: Croom Helm.

Paul, E. F., Miller, F. D. Jr, Paul, J. and Ahrens, J. (eds) (1986) *Nuclear Rights / Nuclear Wrongs*, Oxford: Basil Blackwell.

Pfaltzgraff, R. L. Jr (1986) 'Nuclear deterrence and arms control: ethical issues for the 1980s', in E. Paul, F. D. Miller Jr, J. Paul and J. Ahrens (eds), *Nuclear Rights / Nuclear Wrongs*, London: Basil Blackwell.

Phillips, R. L. (1984) *War and Justice*, Norman: University of Oklahoma Press.

Ponsonby, A. (1915) *Democracy and Diplomacy*, London: Methuen.

Powell, R. (1987) 'Crisis bargaining, escalation, and MAD', *American Political Science Review* 81, 3: 717–36.

—— (1991) 'Absolute and relative gains in international relations theory', *American Political Science Review* 85, 4: 1303–20.

Putnam, R. D. (1988) 'Diplomacy and domestic politics: the logic of two-level games', *International Organization* 42, 427–60.

Ramazani, R. K. (1988) *Revolutionary Iran: Challenge and Response in the Middle East*, Baltimore/London: Johns Hopkins University Press.

Reitberger, M. (1993) 'Intervention för mänskliga rättigheter: tre perspektiv på internationell etik', unpublished seminar paper, Dept. of Political Science, University of Stockholm.

Riegert, K. (1991) 'The Lebanon crisis: the influence of foreign policy orientation in international reporting', unpublished fil.lic. thesis, Dept. of Political Science, University of Stockholm.

Riker, W. H. (1964) 'Some ambiguities in the notion of power', *American Political Science Review* 58: 341–49.

Risse-Kappen, T. (1991) 'Did "peace through strength" end the Cold War? Lessons from INF', *International Security* 16: 162–88.

Robertson, A. (1990) 'Misguided dangerous subversives? An analysis of the international protests against nuclear arms of 1980–83', Annual Meeting of the Swedish Political Science Association.

—— (1991) 'Lies, damned lies, and opinion polls: the Western European publics and the Nato consensus', unpublished paper.

—— (1992) *National Prisms and Perceptions of Dissent: The Euromissile Controversy Reflected in Opinion and the News in the UK and FRG 1980–83*, Stockholm: Dept. of Political Science, University of Stockholm.

Rochon, T. R. (1988) *Mobilizing for Peace: The Antinuclear Movements in Western Europe*, London: Adamantine Press.

Rosenau, J. N. (1990) *Turbulence in World Politics: A Theory of Change and Continuity*, London: Harvester, Wheatsheaf.

—— (1992) 'Governance, order, and change in World Politics', in J. N. Rosenau and E.-O. Czempiel (eds) *Governance without Government: Order and Change in World Politics*, Cambridge: Cambridge University Press.

——, and Czempiel, E. O. (eds) (1992) *Governance without Government: Order and Change in World Politics*, Cambridge: Cambridge University Press.

——, and Holsti, O. R. (1983) 'U.S. leadership in a shrinking world: the breakdown of consensus and the emergence of conflicting belief systems', *World Politics* 35, 3: 368–92.

Roszak, T. (1985) 'A just war analysis of two types of deterrence', in J. Hardin, J. J. Mearsheimer, G. Dworkin and R. E. Goodin (eds), *Nuclear Deterrence: Ethics and Strategy*, Chicago / London: University of Chicago Press.

Rummel, R. J. (1983) 'Libertarianism and international violence', *Journal of Conflict Resolution* 27, 1: 27–71.

Rusciano, F. L. and Fiske-Rusciano, R. (1990) 'Towards a notion of world opinion', *International Journal of Public Opinion Research* 2, 4: 305–22.

Russett, B. M. (1984) 'Ethical dilemmas of nuclear deterrence', *International Security* 8, 4: 36–54.

—— (1990) *Controlling the Sword: The Democratic Governance of National Security*, Cambridge, MA: Harvard University Press.

Sabin, P. A. G. (1986) *The Third World War Scare in Britain*, London: Macmillan.

Salisbury, H. E. (1967) *Behind the Lines – Hanoi*, London: Secker & Warburg.

Schell, J. (1982) *The Fate of the Earth*, New York: Avon Books.

Schelling, T. C. (1960) *The Strategy of Conflict*, Cambridge, MA: Harvard University Press.

Schlesinger, A. M. Jr (1965) *A Thousand Days: John F. Kennedy in the White House*, London: André Deutsch.

Schütz, H.-J. (1977) 'Probleme der Anwendung der KSZE-Schlussakte aus völkerrechtlicher Sicht', in J. Delbrück, N. Ropers and G. Zellentin (eds) *Grünbuch zu den Volgewirkungen der KSZE*, Cologne: Verlag Wissenschaft und Politik.

Shepsle, K. A. (1989) 'Studying institutions: some lessons from the rational choice approach', *Journal of Theoretical Politics* 2, 1: 131–47.

Shubik, M. (1970) 'Game theory, behavior, and the paradox of the Prisoner's Dilemma: three solutions', *Journal of Conflict Resolution* 14: 181–93.

Shue, H. (1986) 'Conflicting concepts of deterrence', in E. Paul, F. D. Miller Jr, J. Paul and J. Ahrens (eds), *Nuclear Rights / Nuclear Wrongs*, London: Basil Blackwell.

Sifry, M. L. and Cerf, C. (eds) (1991) *The Gulf War Reader: History, Documents, Opinions*, New York: Times Books.

Silberner, E. (1946) *The Problem of War in Nineteenth Century Economic Thought*, Princeton, NJ: Princeton University Press.

Simon, H. (1957) *Models of Man: Social and Rational*, New York: John Wiley & Sons.

SIPRI (1982) *World Armaments and Disarmament: SIPRI Yearbook 1982*, London: Taylor & Francis.

—— (1983) *World Armaments and Disarmament: SIPRI Yearbook 1983*, London: Taylor & Francis.

—— (1985) *Policies for Common Security*, London and Philadelphia: Taylor & Francis.

—— (1987) *SIPRI Yearbook 1987: World Armaments and Disarmament*, Oxford: Oxford University Press.

—— (1989) *SIPRI Yearbook 1989: World Armaments and Disarmament*, Oxford: Oxford University Press.

—— (1990) *SIPRI Yearbook 1990: World Armaments and Disarmament*, Oxford: Oxford University Press.

Sjöstedt, G. (1986) 'Participation and information', in K. Goldmann, S. Berglund and G. Sjöstedt, *Democracy and Foreign Policy*, Aldershot, Hants: Gower.

Smith, M. J. (1992) 'Liberalism and international reform', in T. Nardin and D. R. Mapel (eds) *Traditions of International Ethics*, Cambridge: Cambridge University Press.

Snyder, G. H. and Diesing, P. (1977) *Conflict among Nations: Bargaining, Decision Making, and System Structure in International Crisis*, Princeton, NJ: Princeton University Press.

Snyder, J. (1990) 'Averting anarchy in the new Europe', *International Security*, 14, 1: 5–41.

Stenelo, L. G. (1984) *The International Critic*, Lund: Studentlitteratur.

Suganami, H. (1989) *The Domestic Analogy and World Order Proposals*, Cambridge: Cambridge University Press.

Talbott, S. (1985) *Deadly Gambits: The Reagan Administration and the Stalemate in Nuclear Arms Control*, New York: Alfred A. Knopf.

Tännsjö, T. (1991) *Conservatism for Our Time*, London: Routledge.

Teichman, J. (1986) *Pacifism and the Just War: A Study in Applied Philosophy*, Oxford: Basil Blackwell.

Turner, R. F. (1975) *Vietnamese Communism: Its Origin and Development*, Stanford: Hoover Institution Press.

Ullman, R. H. (1991) *Securing Europe*, Twickenham: Adamantine Press.

Van Dijk, T. A. (1988) *News Analysis: Case Studies of International and National News in the Press*, London: Lawrence Erlbaum Associates.

Vatikiotis, P. J. (1984) *Arab and Regional Politics in the Middle East*, London: Croom Helm.

Vedung, E. (1977) *Det rationella politiska samtalet. Hur politiska budskap tolkas, ordnas och prövas*, Stockholm: Aldus/Bonniers.

Waltz, K. N. (1959) *Man, the State, and War: A Theoretical Analysis*, New York: Columbia University Press.

—— (1979) *Theory of International Politics*, Reading, MA: Addison-Wesley.

—— (1986) 'A reply to my critics', in R. O. Keohane (ed.) *Neorealism and Its Critics*, New York: Columbia University Press.

Walzer, M. (1977) *Just and Unjust Wars*, New York: Basic Books.

—— (1986) 'The reform of the international system', in Ø. Østerud (ed.) *Studies of War and Peace*, Oslo: Norwegian University Press.

Weede, E. (1983) 'Extended deterrence by superpower alliance', *Journal of Conflict Resolution*, 27, 2: 231–54.

Wiberg, H. (1989) *Konfliktteori och fredsforskning*, 2nd edn, Stockholm: Almqvist & Wiksell Läromedel.

Wittner, L. S. (1988) 'The transnational movement against nuclear weapons, 1945–1986: a preliminary survey', in C. Chatfield and P. van den Dungen (eds) *Peace Movements and Political Culture*, Knoxville: University of Tennessee Press.

Young, O. R. (1979) *Compliance and Public Authority: A Theory with International Applications*, Baltimore and London: Johns Hopkins University Press.

—— (1989) *International Cooperation: Building Regimes for Natural Resources and the Environment*, Ithaca, NY: Cornell University Press.

—— (1992) 'The effectiveness of international institutions: hard cases and critical variables,' in J. N. Rosenau and E.-O. Czempiel (eds) *Governance without Government: Order and Change in World Politics*, Cambridge: Cambridge University Press.

Zacher, M. W. (1992) 'The decaying pillars of the Westphalian temple: implications for international order and governance', in J. N. Rosenau and E.-O. Czempiel (eds) *Governance without Government: Order and Change in World Politics*, Cambridge: Cambridge University Press.

Zagare, F. C. (1987) *The Dynamics of Deterrence*, Chicago/London: University of Chicago Press.

——, and Kilgour, D. M. (1993) 'Asymmetrical deterrence', *International Studies Quarterly* 37, 1: 1–27.

Index